Bratich, Jack Z.

Conspiracy panics

CONSPIRACY PANICS
Political Rationality and Popular Culture

Jack Z. Bratich

STATE UNIVERSITY OF NEW YORK PRESS

Cover photo: Copyright Anna Pustoyava, iStockphoto. Turbulence image in viewfinder courtesy of Isaac Held, http://www.gfdl.noaa.gov/~ih/images/turbulence.gif, originally published in: Surface quasi-geostrophic dynamics, *Journal of Fluid Mechanics* 282(1995), 1–20. Cover concept by Jack Z. Bratich.

Published by
State University of New York Press, Albany

© 2008 State University of New York

For information, contact State University of New York Press, Albany, NY
www.sunypress.edu

Production by Dana Foote
Marketing by Michael Campochiaro

Library of Congress Cataloging-in-Publication Data

Bratich, Jack Z., 1969–
    Conspiracy panics : political rationality and popular culture / Jack Z. Bratich.
        p. cm.
    Includes bibliographical references and index.
    ISBN 978-0-7914-7333-7 (hardcover : alk. paper)
    ISBN 978-0-7914-7334-4 (pbk. : alk. paper)
    1. Radicalism—United States.   2. Right and left (Political science) 3. Popular culture—United States.   4. Public opinion—United States.   I. Title.

HN90.R3B725 2008
306.0973'090511—dc22   2007016960

                        10 9 8 7 6 5 4 3 2 1

CONTENTS

Acknowledgments

Any work on conspiracies, conspiracy theories, or conspiracy panics must confront the ur-claim that "everything is connected." This is no more evident than in writing acknowledgments, as it seems that everyone I've met over the course of this project has some link to, or impact on, the result. This ranges from those who've had a direct influence on it to those whose brief encounter augmented some aspect. They appear in many guises—a turn of phrase, a borrowed metaphor, a sequence of questions, a synthesis of ideas, a tone.

The seeds of this project began at the Institute of Communications Research, a hotbed of cultural studies and a warm home for friendship and collegiality. So thanks first and foremost goes to my mentors, who have each provided an intellectual space for this work in addition to making a mark on it. Paula Treichler's tireless efforts to hone my ideas and clarify the political stakes were vital. She continually urged me to remember why this project was important, furnishing me with a necessary grounding in concrete practices. I am truly fortunate to have had her mentorship.

James Hay provided consistent encouragement and support; in fact, the idea for this project emerged out of one of his seminars. James taught me how to appreciate the material and institutional contexts of ideas, and as a collaborator and friend he continues to shape my thinking on this and other topics. Cameron McCarthy's inexhaustible enthusiasm gave me the strength and confidence to persevere. He persistently reminded me of my work's political and intellectual tradition and challenged me to find my place in that tradition. Lawrence Grossberg provided me with invaluable ways of translating philosophy into theory, and his mark is on virtually every page here.

Other teachers have made invaluable impressions on me throughout my career. Norman Denzin was an immeasurable resource. Our daily interactions over the course of four years prepared me to be a professional, an intellectual, and a person. Biswarup Sen opened the door for me to cultural studies and to the Institute of Communications Research. His intellectual clarity and provocative humor are the standards for pedagogy, mentoring, and friendship. Even before this project took shape, many teachers sowed the seeds of my thinking that would eventually blossom in this book. Among them I count Stephen David Ross, John Tagg, Ladelle McWhorter, and David Gruber. They introduced me to and nurtured my interest in continental philosophy and critical theory, especially the work of Michel Foucault. I have never recovered. Collectively, these mentors have formed a powerful intellectual constellation around me that I continue to call upon (whether they know it or not).

The friends, colleagues, classmates, and peops from Champaign-Urbana in the 1990s have been priceless. Jeremy Packer and I traveled similar paths, riding many rollercoasters late into the night and holding a decade-long conversation about Foucault's work. Brian Michael Goss and I shared innumerable after-hours discussions—his sharp intellect and political commitments became a constant reference point. He also provided me with a model for disciplined research. It is difficult to imagine my writing and thinking without these fellow travelers. Others in this network of support and joy include Theodore Bailey, Richard Bradley, Mary Coffey, Greg Dimitriadis, Michael Elavsky, Kelly Gates, Lisa King, Sammi King, Marie Leger, Dan McGee, Jen Mercieca, Shawn Miklaucic, Radhika Mongia, Mark Nimkoff, Liz Perea, Carrie Rentschler, Craig Robertson, Gil Rodman, Milla Rosenberg, Gretchen Soderlund, Jonathan Sterne, Dan Vukovich, and many others. Their importance cannot be contained in a list of their proper names. Special thanks here goes to Cheryl Cambras, Natasha Ritsma, and Heidi Brush, each of whom provided patience, support, and love during different moments of this project. Each in their own way also taught me that there's more to life than writing.

Since moving to New York City and getting involved in a number of activist projects, I have met people who have provided clarity regarding the political relevance of conspiracy research, especially regarding 9/11 skeptics. The last chapter of this book grew out of this milieu, and so credit goes to Brooke Lehman, Spencer Sunshine, Stevphen Shukaitis, Seth Weiss, and Kevin Van Meter.

Much gratitude goes out to my family as well. Milovan Bratic and Vasilija Bratic, my parents, labored with great hardship in a land foreign to them so as to provide a better future for their children. This book is a result of their ceaseless encouragement, sustenance, and sacrifice. My sister Olivera gave me confidence that the future generation will be intelligent, politically active, and life affirming.

Much editorial help and thought clarification has come my way over the years. Peter Knight, Toby Miller, Alisdair Spark, Laura Marks, and the anonymous reviewers for this book have been invaluable in this regard. At State University of New York Press, Michael Rinella's initial faith in the project, his patience, and his shepherding all made the process a smooth and pleasurable one. Dana Foote kept the project and me on a timely production schedule, with her enthusiasm and gentle persistence. And thanks go to copyeditor Kay Butler for shaping up my writing style with her keen eye and to cover designer Amy Stirnkorb for the wonderful final look.

The students in my conspiracy culture courses (from UC–Berkeley to Rutgers University) reminded me of the significance and stakes of the topic, especially for the younger generation. A shout-out goes to the Lotus Café, Alt Coffee, and Drink Me, the spaces that tolerated my many hours of squatting with laptop and beverages. The staff members at these establishments as well as the fellow writers/squatters comprised a vital social network that alleviated the solitude of the book writer. A special note of thanks goes to Diana Good, whose presence at the Lotus was a true gift. She made the space live up to its name—a zone of transformation and becoming.

Finally, acknowledgment must be given to the unnameable. From the murmurings of ancestors whose names are forgotten to the future guests whose proper names are yet to be formed, these unknown figures haunt these pages. They make it clear that saying "everything is connected" must make room for a community without identity and a people to come.

Portions of this work have been published elsewhere:

Portions of chapter 1 appeared in Bratich, Jack Z. (2003). Making politics reasonable: Conspiracism, subjectification, and governing through styles of thought. In J. Z. Bratich, J. Packer, & C. McCarthy (Eds.), *Foucault, cultural studies, and governmentality* (pp. 67–100) Albany: State University of New York Press.

Portions of chapter 3 appeared in Bratich, Jack Z. (2004). Trust no-one (on the Internet): The CIA-Crack-Contra conspiracy theory and professional journalism. *Television & New Media* 5(2), 109–139.

Portions of chapter 4 appeared in Bratich, Jack Z. (2002). Injections and truth serums: AIDS conspiracy theories and the politics of articulation. In P. Knight (Ed.), *Conspiracy nation: The politics of paranoia in postwar America* (pp. 133–156). New York: New York University Press.

INTRODUCTION
Grassy Knolledges

The scenario is familiar: On a clear morning at approximately 9 a.m. a building on U.S. soil is destroyed, causing numerous fatalities and a shock wave of horror. The U.S. media and government officials determine that the mastermind is one man, operating with sleeper cells in a network fueled by fanaticism and extremist ideology. Soon afterward, the U.S. president uses this terrorist event to pass sweeping antiterrorism legislation.

Another recounting of 9/11? Yes, but it also applies to the bombing of the Alfred P. Murrah Federal Building in Oklahoma City in 1995. While public discourse has been replete with the phrase "9/11 changed everything," it is obvious that that fateful day also mimicked and accelerated already existing events.

Beyond the details of the events, one other similarity emerges. In each case, the official account of responsibility for the attack resembles a *conspiracy theory*. One figure (McVeigh, Bin Laden) is placed at the head of a shadowy network (armed Patriot movement, Al Qaeda) responsible for the terrorist act. Obviously there are some differences in the accounts: One was a domestic conspiracy, the other global; McVeigh planned, funded, and actually carried out the act while Bin Laden only planned, funded, and inspired his version. In both instances, however, the official account assigned a simple solution to a complex set of events. This led underground "conspiracy theorist" David Ray Griffin to claim that there are two competing explanatory accounts for 9/11, both conspiracy theories—official (Bin Laden) and alternative (the U.S. government did it). Surely categorizing these official accounts as conspiracy theories is audacious and unfounded, but it performatively brings us to a seemingly simple question, What is a conspiracy theory?

What Is "Conspiracy Theory"?

On the face of it, defining it seems obvious. We can easily list a set of examples (the various agents behind the assassinations of JFK, RFK, MLK, Malcolm X, Princess Diana, Tupac Shakur; U.S. foreknowledge of Pearl

1

Harbor, the Oklahoma City bombing, and 9/11; we never went to the moon, we went to the moon but covered up alien presence there, U.S./extraterrestrial collaboration, downing of TWA Flight 800, CIA importation of crack into the United States, and AIDS as a bioweapon). Sometimes the very mention of certain terms, like New World Order, Freemasonry, Illuminati, or black helicopters, automatically places an account into the conspiracy theory slot.

But argument from example gets us very little, as the inductive reasoning obviously does not account for why other theories that share narrative characteristics (like Bin Laden and 9/11) do not get called a conspiracy theory. What we are often left with is a cultural version of Justice Potter Stewart's 1964 legal argument about pornography: when it comes to conspiracy theory we "know it when we see it." This rationale did not hold up as precedent for long, and it pertained to visual representations—materials more concrete than a "theory"!

To further our investigation, I pose another question: Is a conspiracy theory defined primarily by its internal narrative characteristics or by its external discursive position? In other words is it something inherent in the theory itself or is it more about the forums it appears in, its relation to other theories, and the legitimation accorded it? To start exploring this, we can turn to an accepted textual authority on definitions. We look to a dictionary reference work not to discover the term's true meaning, but to locate its appearance as *meaningful*.

A conspiracy theory is different from a conspiracy. A conspiracy exists when two or more persons agree privately to commit a reprehensible, illegal, or criminal act, especially in relation to sedition, treason, or murder, hence especially against the state (*Oxford English Dictionary*, 1971; paraphrased, not quoted). It is traced by the OED back to Chaucer in 1386. By contrast, Alisdair Spark (1998) remarks that "in July 1997 the supplement to the *Oxford English Dictionary* included the term 'conspiracy theory' for the first time. This was a recognition that in recent years conspiracy has become increasingly popular as an explanation for unfolding events, most overtly in the United States" (*Conspiracy Thinking and Conspiracy Studying*, http://www.wkac.ac.uk/research/ccc/index2.htm). Here I want to make the first attempt at defining this book's project by adding this: it is not primarily the rise of conspiracy theories as such that makes them appear in the dictionary, but rather the increased *degree of scrutiny paid to* conspiracy theories that pushes the term into the official lexicon.

The question, What is a conspiracy theory? presupposes a stable object and assumes our term is merely descriptive. For some reason, when it comes to conspiracy theory, many semiotically savvy analysts adhere to a reflectionist model of language. While other terms are afforded a deconstructive analysis, this one somehow escapes the linguistic turn, circulating in a world where language simply refers to already existing objects. But let us not deceive ourselves in thinking that calling something a conspiracy theory is simply a neutral description of a type of account. We know it is also a term of derision, disqualification, and dismissal. To elucidate, let's take a quick look at the Warren Commission's findings regarding that grandfather of U.S. conspiracy theories, the JFK assassination.

Technically, a conspiracy theory would be any theory that posits multiple shooters acting in concert to assassinate Kennedy. In this case, the Warren Commission itself *could have* promoted a conspiracy theory if it had found more than one assassin involved, regardless of the sinister intentions or nefarious organizations behind the assassination. Under this legal definition of conspiracy, it becomes clear that federal prosecutors have often promoted conspiracy theories: examples include the actions of the Chicago Seven at the 1968 Democratic Convention, the bombing of the World Trade Center in 1993, the Murrah Federal Building bombing in 1995, and some cases associated with the post–9/11 terror/war. Defendants in these cases were often charged with precisely that—conspiracy. At the denotative level, conspiracy theories (as accounts that posit a co-ordination of multiple agents as the cause of criminal or violent acts) are mundane and pervasive.

But defining conspiracy theories in this legalistic manner is both semiotically dissonant and highly selective. Conspiracy theories *could have* this meaning in a neutral marketplace of ideas; they *could be* one kind of descriptive narrative among many. But this is not the case. Conspiracy theories exist as a category not just of description but of disqualification.

For example, when Oliver Stone's film *JFK* entered the sphere of Kennedy assassinology, it was rarely dismissed at the level of evidence. The film was, however, often called a "conspiracy theory" (Stone & Sklar, 1992). This did not eliminate it as false but disqualified it from the JFK assassination's "sphere of legitimate controversy" (Hallin, 1986). In Michel Foucault's terminology, *JFK* does not engage in the "game of truth" appropriate to JFK assassination accounts. The game of truth is "a set of rules by which truth is produced. It is not a game in the sense of amusement; it is a set of procedures that lead to a certain result, which, on the basis of its principles and rules of procedure, may be considered valid or invalid, winning or losing" (p. 297).

Conspiracy theories are not just false; they are what Christopher Hitchens (drawing from science's procedures) calls "not even wrong" (2004). That is, they do not reach the threshold of acceptability to even be tested, to be falsifiable. If the mind is that sphere that can distinguish between truth and falsity, then conspiracy theories are beyond that sphere. They are *para* (beyond or beside) the *nous* (mind). They are *paranoid*.

Conspiracy theories are defined not merely by their strictly denotative, inherent properties, but by their discursive position in relation to a "regime of truth." As Foucault (1980a) defines it:

> Each society has its regime of truth, its "general politics" of truth: that is, the types of discourse which it accepts and makes function as true; the mechanisms

and instances which enable one to distinguish true and false statements, the
means by which each is sanctioned; the techniques and procedures accorded
value in the acquisition of truth; the status of those who are charged with
saying what counts as true. (p. 131)

Once we recognize that conspiracy theories are simultaneously a type
of narrative and a sign of narrative disqualification, we can say that this book
is "about" conspiracy theories. But unlike the vast majority of analyses, I
examine the latter: its discursive position. In other words, the question is no
longer What is a conspiracy theory? but What counts as a conspiracy theory?
To make this clearer, it is helpful to lay out some synonyms that get linked
to conspiracy theories. This constellation of concepts should give some sense
of the slipperiness and the political stakes in defining conspiracy theories as
an object of study.

The Synonyms

The paranoid style. Coined by Richard Hofstadter (1967) in his germinal
essay "The Paranoid Style in American Politics," this term transformed a
multiplicity of beliefs in conspiracy into a *style* of thought. Transposing a
clinical psychology term onto the field of politics, Hofstadter not only
pathologized conspiracy theories, he gave them formal coherence, historical
persistence, and intelligibility as a genre of political knowledge. Hofstadter's
essay also marks a moment when conspiracy theories were articulated to
political extremism. Most serious contemporary analysts of conspiracy theories (on various points of the political spectrum) cite Hofstadter. In so doing,
they use conspiracy theories as paradigmatic instances of "the paranoid style."

Political paranoia. Often used synonymously with the paranoid style,
this more recent term gives conspiracy theories a dangerous edge. Perhaps
most thoroughly elaborated by Robert Robins and Jerrold Post in *Political
Paranoia and the Psychopolitics of Hatred* (1997), "political paranoia" is closer
to a clinical diagnosis than is the paranoid style. The label is so intertwined
with political beliefs that "extremism" becomes not so much a point on the
political spectrum as a category of social psychology. Conspiracy theories
designate the bodies of knowledge produced by these politically pathological
individuals and groups.

Conspiracism. Also a recent invention, this term drops some of the
psychological baggage. It gathers conspiracy theories together under the unity
of an "ism" to describe a body of thought that regards conspiracies as a
driving force in history. The term preserves a dangerous quality by linking
conspiracy theories to other isms: racism, extremism, Stalinism, Nazism.
Commentators from a variety of political positions employ this term. Chip
Berlet, a progressive researcher, calls the militia movement's ideology
"conspiracism." In Berlet's case, conspiracism is akin to supremacism—a broad
ideological vision of how things are—and a militia member would be defined

as a "conspiracist." Daniel Pipes (1997) and Christopher Buckley (1997) also wield the term, aiming it both at militias and at "leftism." For Buckley, "conspiracism" leads to the spread of "hate crimes" and ultimately to "democide" (the wholesale annihilation of a people) (p. 44).

The above terms are in essence more sophisticated ways of calling someone a crackpot. In these three cases, conspiracy theories are understood as false, irrational, even pathologically dangerous. In these formulations, conspiracy theorizing is not the harmless pastime of a few obsessive loners; it is a social threat that reflects profound political malaise. At best, conspiracy theories are a distraction from real politics and real social problems. At worst, conspiracy theories represent dangerous knowledges, potentially fostering domestic terrorism. "The paranoid style," "political paranoia," and "conspiracism" are used by debunkers, or "theorists of conspiracy theories." I will primarily refer to these debunkers in this book as "problematizers," "conspiracy theory experts" (not experts *in*, but *on* conspiracy theories), or part of the conspiracy panic discourse.

But these are not the only meanings at play. Most often employed by those considered "conspiracy theorists," other terms not only avoid the disqualifying articulations but also deliberately refuse them.

Conspiracy research. This term attempts to authorize and legitimize the knowledge claims of the enterprise. Calling it "research" obviously tries to give the accounts intellectual grounding in social science or journalism. It is often used interchangeably with *political research* and *investigative research*. In a sense, it takes the existence of conspiracies to be true, and studies their occurrence and effects much as one would study policy and political institutions.

Conspiratology. Moving one step closer toward legitimacy, this term attempts to consolidate *conspiracy research* into a body of work that asks to be considered scientific. Conspiratologists are those researchers who study conspiracies.

Conspiracy narratives or *conspiracy accounts.* Used by analysts who are neither quick to disqualify nor to valorize conspiracy theories, these terms try to accentuate the descriptive component. In this view, a conspiracy narrative is simply any narrative that accounts for an event by positing a collusion of agents who seek to determine the course of the event according to the agents' agenda, and at the expense of others' agendas. In addition, the collusion, the agenda, and/or the determination are shrouded in secrecy. I would also add here that a conspiracy narrative often (but not always) suspects the agendas embedded in other accounts.

Besides its synonyms, conspiracy theory is a contested term within the conspiracy research community. While some do not mind calling their work a conspiracy theory, others reject it as a media buzzword that derides, ridicules, and even demonizes its referent (see Alan Cantwell, 1995, "Paranoid/ Paranoia: Media Buzzwords to Silence the Politically Incorrect"; Michael Parenti, 1995, "Conspiracy Phobia"). As Barry Zwicker puts it, "conspiracy

theory is a thought stopper" (2004, p. 7). Finally, some conspiracy researchers use the label ironically; recognizing it as a category of subjugation, they
nevertheless reclaim it as a strategy of conceptual counterattack (see Vankin
and Whalen (2001), pseudonymous book from the National Insecurity Council
1992, and zines like *Paranoia!*).

Conspiracy theory is thus a *bridge* term—it links subjugating conceptual
strategies (paranoid style, political paranoia, conspiracism) to narratives that
investigate conspiracies (conspiratology, conspiracy research, conspiracy account). *Conspiracy theory* is a condensation of all of the above, a metaconcept
signifying the struggles over the meaning of the category. We need to recognize where we are on the bridge when we use the term.

In addition to being a bridge, I argue that conspiracy theory is a *portal*
concept. Conspiracy theories are like doorways into the major social and
political issues defining U.S. (and global) political culture since the end of
the cold war. Among these issues are the rise of new technologies; the social
function of journalism; U.S. race relations; the parameters of dissent; globalization, biowarfare, and biomedicine; and the shifting position within the
Left. It is difficult to separate the public consideration of these pivotal social
issues from their intertwinement with conspiracy theories. In a number of
cases (especially the rise of the Internet and the limits of dissent), conspiracy
theories were a *defining* trope through which social phenomena were discussed. Bringing conspiracy theories into the deliberation over these social
concerns meant bringing *rationality* into the discussion.

The definition of conspiracy theory, which inaugurates this book "on"
conspiracy theories, is precisely part of the clash of interpretive forces. Rather
than assuming we know what one is, I am arguing for the need to examine
the very conditions of recognition, the contexts that make this object visible
and intelligible. Conspiracy theories are portals to specific issues, but more
importantly they collectively function as doorways to a broader *context*. It is
this context that is at the heart of this project, and that can be reached via
what I call "conspiracy panics."

CONSPIRACY PANICS

While conspiracies have engrossed political analysts for centuries, conspiracy
theories have only recently become a significant object of concern in political discourse. Throughout the 1990s, books and articles on conspiracy theories multiplied, for both academic and popular audiences. After the Oklahoma
City bombing in the spring of 1995, published commentaries rose significantly.
A Lexis-Nexis search for the term *conspiracy theory* in the *New York Times*
and the *Washington Post* found a combined total of 685 hits in the ten years
from 1985 to 1994. From 1995 to 2004 this number jumped to 1625. A scan
of *Time* magazine found no citations in the first half of the decade, but 21

in the second half. In the first five years of the 1990s, the *Reader's Guide to Periodical Literature* cites a total of 20 articles on the topic of "conspiracy" or "paranoia," with a total of 88 listings for the years 1995–1999. In 1995 alone this number jumped to 22 articles.

The *fact* of increased attention doesn't tell us much about the *form* of attention. Instead of belaboring the obvious by proving that conspiracy theories were disparaged by mainstream sources, I will begin with the assumption that commonsense constructions (not necessarily the commonly held beliefs of a population, but the hegemonic meanings) positioned conspiracy theories as illegitimate knowledges. One is hard pressed to find mainstream sources that are anywhere but on the side of the bridge that equates conspiracy theories to paranoia and conspiracism.

To understand this form of attention, I borrow a line from Dick Hebdige on youth culture and say that conspiracy theory emerges as a category only when it is a *problem*. Put another way, conspiracy theories are "subjugated knowledges." In the first of his "Two Lectures," Foucault (1980b) distinguishes "official knowledges" from subjugated knowledges. Subjugated knowledges are "blocs of historical knowledge which were present but disguised within the body of functionalist and systematic theory" (p. 80). They "have been disqualified as inadequate to their task or insufficiently elaborated: naïve knowledges, located low down on the hierarchy, beneath the required level of cognition or scientificity" (p. 83). In other words, "not even wrong."

These buried and popular knowledges can, through research and analysis, emerge to reveal the "ruptural effects of conflict and struggle that the order imposed by functionalist or systematizing thought is designed to mask" (p. 80). Studying conspiracy theories as subjugated knowledges would demonstrate how some accounts become dominant only through struggle. An official account comes to *be* official only through a victory over, and erasure of conflict with, conspiracy accounts. Among the competing accounts for any event, the official version is not merely the winner in a game of truth—it determines who the players can be.

These constitutive and disqualifying practices are my main topic. Certainly this project will discuss particular conspiracy narratives or case studies. Yet I will focus primarily on *strategies of subjugation*, for they succinctly foreground the relations between power and knowledge. Despite the value of analyzing conspiracy theories as unified narratives (elaborating their characteristics, delineating their rhetorical tropes), I am more interested in assessing the forms of rationality and politics that lead us to be *concerned with* interpreting these narratives. In John Fiske's (1994) terms, I evaluate "the strategies by which . . . disbelief is validated and . . . counterknowledge is discredited" (p. 192). Rather than positing the conceptual unity of conspiracy theories in order to identify their deep meaning, I analyze the discursive practices that channel, shape, incite, and deploy conspiracy theories as meaningful.[1]

But here I want to stress that this method is more than labeling theory. A strategy of subjugation is not just a repressive practice (though it can be that, too). Conspiracy accounts are not just excluded with sheer conceptual power by official knowledges from the public sphere. For one thing, power often incites us to discuss these subjugated knowledges (in popular culture, in journalism, in legislative bodies, in courts). These conceptual practices have a *productive* power for official apparatuses. Rather than being suppressed, conspiracy theories are, if anything, useful.

We can begin to see this usefulness in the kinds of metaphors often employed in making sense of conspiracy theories. Numerous articles described the 1990s as an "age of paranoia" or a "culture of paranoia" (Alter, 1997; Mishra, 1995; Fukuyama, 1995; Gardner, 1997).[2] "Paranoia—not the clinical but the cultural kind—may well be our national religion," says Richard Leiby (1995) in the Style section of the *Washington Post*. Especially in the Oklahoma City bombing aftermath, pundits had a habit of turning "the paranoid style" (already a synthetic and abstract concept) into a sign of the historical conjuncture. The ineluctable Zeitgeist was invoked through repeated environmental tropes, as in an "atmosphere" or "climate" of paranoia. This naturalized imprecision gives the conspiracy theory "problem" the status of a mood, a tone, and an indeterminate quality.

Even in scholarly analyses, meteorological metaphors abound. Elaine Showalter (1997) goes one step further, linking the weather with epidemiology:

> Cultural hysteria and its paranoid accelerators have caused much harm: the hysterical epidemics of the 1990s have already gone on too long, and they continue to do damage: in distracting us from the real problems and crises of modern society, in undermining a respect for evidence and truth, and in helping support an atmosphere of conspiracy and suspicion. (p. 206)

Here we see a prime example of what I'm calling "conspiracy panic." The term *panic* is borrowed from a sociological framework, best known in the work of Stanley Cohen. The theory essentially argues that Western society maintains its identity via the management and expulsion of deviance. A moral panic defines a minority group as folk devils, "a condition, episode, person or group of persons [who] become defined as a threat to societal values and interests" (Cohen, 1972, p. 9).

Cohen studied mod and rocker subcultures and the means by which they were depicted as antisocial. While most of the time the cultural target is a definable group, at times it can inform phenomena like the introduction of new technologies (e.g., the early 20th-century condemnations of film and radio by religious leaders, see Bratich, 2005). Now the term applies to moral outrages over the violent effects of media on youth, video games, pornography, drug use, AIDS, cyberculture, satanic ritual abuse, pedophilia, immigration, cults. They often involve protecting some dominant group (children, white women, heterosexuals) from perceived pernicious influences.

Jeffrey Weeks, in his famous work on the historical regulation of sexuality, says that a panic "crystallizes widespread fears and anxieties, and often deals with them by not seeking the real causes of problems and conditions which they demonstrate but by displacing them onto . . . an identified social group (1981, p. 14; quoted in Soderlund, 2002). For Cohen these panics spread through informal channels (rumor, gossip, and urban legends) but to become a broader public discourse they circulate through mass mediated news outlets. They are "amplified" by journalism (Young, 1971). As Hall, Critcher, Jefferson, Clarke, & Roberts argue in their groundbreaking cultural studies work, *Policing the Crisis* (1978), panics over "mugging" were promoted by mainstream news outlets and fed into a greater public outcry for more law and order. They expanded the sociological studies to place a greater emphasis on journalism's ideological role, making moral panics a matter of hegemonic maintenance and paradigm repair (Soderlund, 2002).

The moral panics framework has undergone numerous modifications. Its explanatory power has been challenged, especially in light of sociological analyses based on a notion of risk society (Ungar, 2001). Others have responded that trumping the moral panic framework with risk society presumes a rational basis for social anxieties in "real" risks while neglecting the construction and mobilization of crises (Hier, 2003; Packer, 2008). As Jeremy Packer argues with regard to the governing of/through automobility,

> The question then is not "*how risky is* motorcycling or hitchhiking," but "*why* have these forms of mobility come to be thought of in terms of risk and safety *at certain moments,* while at other times they have been largely understood in economic or phenomenological terms?" (p. 9)

Packer also notes that the moral panics/cultural constructionist approach offers a political analysis difficult to find in risk society frameworks, since the former "examines the cultural production of risk and its use as a tool in political struggles" (p. 11). In a similar way, I would argue that rather than accept conspiracy theories as a real danger to the health of the body politic, we need to ask how the risky thought encapsulated in the conspiracy theory problem is generated discursively, under what conditions, and to what ends.

Kenneth Thompson (1998) argues that the number and types of moral panics are increasing, and thus need to become more central to social analyses (see also Peter Jenkins, 1998; 1999). For Angela McRobbie and Sarah Thornton (1995), moral panics are now such common strategies by various groups in cultural public discourse that they do not represent isolated instances, but a normal mode of operation (especially on the part of the Right). They are the "the norm of journalistic practice, the way in which daily events are brought to the attention of the public" (McRobbie, 1994, p. 202), no longer an "unintended outcome of journalistic practice, [but] a goal" (McRobbie & Thornton, p. 560). In addition, a moral panic can constitute a "priceless PR campaign'" as with the case of youth rave culture (p. 565). In other words, not all panics are hegemonic—some can be contested.

For McRobbie and Thornton, classic moral panic theory needs updating. Its own traditional reliance on a notion of reality to arbitrate "exaggerated" or "spectacular" panic representations blocked its ability to understand the ideological power of the panics (p. 564). A postmodern moral panic involves recognizing the constructed nature of the panic discourse, as well as refusing an appeal to some nondiscursive reality to combat it. Moral panics, according to McRobbie and Thornton, have also changed insofar as they circulate in a multimedia environment, not just through mainstream journalism. They appear in a broader public sphere (including pundits and experts who appear both in print and in person). Finally, it should be noted that moral panics are not just labeling rhetoric. As conceptual devices they provide the underpinning for material practices such as legislation, social policy, and policing techniques. In addition, they can inform the very constitution of some institutions, including professional journalism (Soderlund, 2002).

While moral panic sociologists have tended to focus on subcultures, panics have a longer history. Mary Douglas's anthropological classic *Purity and Danger* (1966) examines social boundary maintenance where a social order seeks to cleanse pollutants from itself, and has been updated around the question of risk (Douglas, 1992). This social hygiene is a function of many kinds of societies in many eras. Anthropologists have been discussing the social function of these exile rituals for at least a century. In *The Golden Bough*, James Frazer examines the social ritual of scapegoating (Frazer, 1922, p. 629). In his examples, the scapegoated target is not an external threat. It is an internal instability, a slackening of hygienic practices and a weakening of the immune system in the political body. The threat is not an invasion, but subversion. A sluggish regime (or a new one) needs revitalizing, or, as Frazer puts it, the "main object of the ceremony is a total clearance of all the ills infecting a people."

One can update this anthropological ritual with recent social theory. In contrast to an analysis of society based on contradiction (the classic Marxist framework), Gilles Deleuze posits that "what is primary in a society are the lines, the movements of flights," "its points of deterritorialization" (Deleuze, 1990a, p. 171; 1977, p. 135; Patton, 1985, p. 65). Examining the integrity of a regime entails giving methodological primacy to those elements that cannot be contained within the regime, and thus need to be expelled. The scapegoat, according to Deleuze and Guattari in *A Thousand Plateaus*, "incarnates that line of flight the signifying regime cannot tolerate" (1987, pp. 116-117). The condemned scapegoat is the vehicle that "carries away" the ills of the social before it "carries off" the mainstream and ruptures the social fabric.

Laclau and Mouffe's *Hegemony and Socialist Strategy* (1985), especially chapter 3, also discusses the antagonisms and expulsion practices infusing social identity. In their deconstructive analysis, society is defined by the effort to constitute itself as identity by erasing antagonism. Antagonism must be sent to flee: "every 'society' constitutes its own forms of rationality and intelligibility by *dividing* itself; that is, by expelling outside itself any surplus of meaning subverting it" (pp. 136–137, italics added). And "it is only through this cutting out that the totality constitutes itself as such . . . only through negativity, division, and antagonism that a formation can constitute itself as a totalizing horizon" (pp. 143–144). Fusing these theories and interdisciplinary studies together, we can say that moral panics are profoundly linked to the constitution and health of a homeostatic society.

My argument is that "conspiracy theory" functions as an intolerable line and an antagonism. While occasionally linked to particular groups (militias, African Americans, political extremists) the panic here is over a particular *form of thought* (and its potential links to action). The scapegoating of conspiracy theories provides the conditions for social integration and political rationality. Conspiracy panics help to define the normal modes of dissent. Politically it is predicated on a consensus "us" over against a subversive and threatening "them" (Fowler, 1991; Dean, 2000).

We can update the panic model also via noting changing political contexts. The panic model, when tied to labeling theory or deviance studies, tended to focus on threats that could be clearly defined as a social group. As borne out by the climatological metaphors, the conspiracy theory threat is different. It is nonspecific, a vague menace. I will discuss this further in the chapter on dissent and extremism, but for now I'll just note that framing conspiracy theories as a symptom of a culture or climate of paranoia makes for a diffuse threat. This mirrors the nascent reorganization of U.S. political culture in a post–cold war landscape. As Brian Massumi, Paul Virilio, and others note, the nineties classification of 'otherness" changed from the Soviet Bloc to the "unspecified enemy."

For Peter Knight, this context of diffuse enemies is expressed in the changing nature of conspiracy theories *themselves*. Conspiracy culture expresses not a fear of a secure enemy like communists, but an anxiety over a network like terrorism or a viral outbreak. The history of political demonology (as Michael Rogin [1987] calls it) as a construction of enemies thus changes over time.

For my purposes, the unspecified enemy is less significant regarding how conspiracy theories have changed *their* enemies (from clear to diffuse). Rather than look at how conspiracy theories construct their "others," I examine how conspiracy theories are taken to *be* enemies, to be a pervasive and nonspecific threat against democracy. Conspiracy panic is directed against a mood, style, mindset, tendency, or climate.

Perhaps the best cultural example here is the film *Arlington Road*. This film's villains comprise a shadowy network of domestic dissenters, whose cunning lies in their ability to disguise themselves as "good neighbors." While the threat is embodied in a few characters (e.g., Oliver Lang), they are merely foot soldiers in the real menace: "millions of us" as Tim Robbins's character puts it, a ubiquitous and occasionally violent populism dressed up as friendly suburban homeowners. In some ways, this free-floating version is closer to the true meaning of panic. It is more pervasive—a diffuse anxiety over a pandemic that could emerge in many places and many forms. A panic is not a fear-induced condition (which has a specific object) but an anxiety-induced one (whose very nonspecificity is an instigator) (see Massumi, 2005).

And this is where the moral panics research can expand. As Sheldon Ungar (2001) notes, Stanley Cohen's own original analysis did not presume the moral panics necessarily led to the construction of a folk devil or target a specific social group. The diffuse and unspecified enemy thus makes the folk devil model less specific. Threat detection in a conspiracy panic is not focused on the visible (as in behavioral conduct), but on the *virtual* (signs of danger). Not from a specific threat, but an omnipossible menace. Nikolas Rose (1999) notes this shift as similar to the biomedical one from normalization of deviance to preventive behavioral modifications. Robert Castel, in an early essay connecting risk to governance, notes this diffusion when he states that the governance of risk is designed "not to confront a dangerous situation, but to anticipate all the possible forms of eruption of danger" (1991, p. 288). Placing moral panics within a series of prevention strategies for dissent avoids some of the more mechanical applications of the framework. This shift also demonstrates that moral panics are themselves strategies in a combative context, not simply tools for the maintenance of a social order, or a stabilizing technique. Unlike a notion of risk society, there is no need to totalize a panic into the social field—there is no "conspiracy panic society."

Returning to the inaugural question, What is a conspiracy theory? then, we can say that the inability to define conspiracy theory is no failure or flaw. It is precisely the motor that allows a conspiracy panic to operate. By never having final criteria for what counts as a conspiracy theory, the term can be wielded in a free-floating way to apply to a variety of accounts. It is no wonder then, that the genealogy of *conspiracy theory* so closely approximates that of the *terrorist* (as a "whatever enemy"). Here, in this twinning of conspiracy theories with terrorism, is where we can glimpse a core claim of this book: that what we see in conspiracy panics is a consequential linkage of thought to action.

IRRATIONAL THOUGHT/EXTREMIST ACTION: ITINERARY OF AN ARTICULATION

In July 2005, the White House announced a change in the name of its post–9/11 mission. No longer was the United States fighting a "war on terror"; it was now a "global struggle against extremism." This corresponded to the newly emerging commonsense that the real U.S. enemy was not an entire people (Muslims) nor simply a tactic (terrorism) but an *ideology* (at various points called fanaticism, fundamentalism, hateful ideology, or extremism).

The phrases "struggle against extremism" and hateful ideology are sensible partially as a result of a decade-long process of linking irrational thought to extremist action. Hateful ideology does not emerge suddenly into public discourse; it is an outgrowth of a conceptual context that took time to forge. It is this context, formed in part via conspiracy panics, that needs to be studied.

Rewind a decade: It is no accident that the spike in attention to conspiracy theories comes after the Oklahoma City bombing in April 1995. Beliefs about a New World Order replete with black helicopters and concentration camps were seen as providing tinder for domestic terrorism. During Timothy McVeigh's trial, his alleged obsessive viewing of a Waco conspiracy videotape was brought in as evidence of the mindset that leads to violent action. The militias, culturally (though never juridically) blamed for the bombing, were consistently associated with a "conspiratorial worldview." This armed populist movement was considered the concrete embodiment of conspiracy theories. In the militias, one could find the figure of extremism par excellence: the dangerous hybrid of hate speech and violent action.

This fusion of thought and action, irrationality and extremism, has obviously changed in a decade. We have moved from domestic terror to a foreign network, from a national problem to a global concern. But at a conceptual level we have inherited a context where forms of thought, styles of thinking, have become an "unspecified enemy." A material consequence of this has been the determination by the U.S. State Department that "subcultures of conspiracy and misinformation" are one of the sources that terrorism "springs from" (*National Strategy for Combating Terrorism*).

Conspiracy panics, with a diffuse anxiety over a diffuse menace, "problematize" conspiracy theories as a relation between power and thought. Foucault (1988c) defines "problematization" in the following manner: it is

> not the representation of a pre-existing object, nor the creation by discourse of an object that does not exist. It is the totality of discursive and nondiscursive practices that introduces something into the play of true and false and constitutes it as an object for thought. (p. 257)

Thinking of conspiracy panics this way, as part of a conceptual context, forces us to update the conspiracy panics model in one more methodological

way: by considering thought as part of what Foucault calls "political rationality," specifically its liberal and neoliberal forms of governance.

LIBERALISM, POLITICAL RATIONALITY, THOUGHT

To study conspiracy theories as a zone where politics and reason meet
means taking *thought* seriously as it is folded into strategies of governing.
Part of this book's agenda is to bolster links between philosophy and cultural studies. Philosophy, as a set of analytic tools, gives primacy to what
Paul Patton (1996) calls "conceptual politics." While thought has often
been relegated to the anemic status of idealism (in the more materialist
strains of cultural studies), I wish to argue here that conceptual practices—
not the same as ideas—are constitutive of cultural practices. As we'll see
in the chapter on liberalism and dissent, some problematizers certainly
believe that conspiracy theories have such a constitutive power and thus
deserve scrutiny. While that chapter will examine conspiracy panics and
U.S. liberalism in greater detail, here I will sketch as background the relation between thought and governing.

For Foucault, studying what he calls liberal "governmentality" means
assessing the specific "political rationality" that composes liberal arts of governance. Essentially, liberalism's political rationality requires governing at a
distance, respecting the immanent dynamics of society, and seeking to incorporate freedom as a formula of rule. An autonomized and responsibilized
citizenry is the goal, and can be accomplished via the use of reason. Liberal
political rationality thus signifies both a form of governing (at a distance,
indirect regulation) and its content (a subject that relies on the exercise of
reason and thought). A political rationality is not an ideal type or univer-
salizing logos: "It's not 'reason in general' that is implemented, but always a
very specific type of rationality" (Foucault, 1988a, p. 73). But while it is not
universalized, political rationality does seem to act as a generalizing or coor-
dinating force. That is to say, a rationality cannot be located within any
particular institution as *its* logic, or in a specific program as *its* means and
ends. Political rationality exists prior to the specific programs and institutions being formulated and implemented, since programs "either articulate or
presuppose a *knowledge* of the field of reality upon which it is to intervene
and/or which it is calculated to bring into being" (Gordon, 1980, p. 248).[3]

What is the political rationality that produces conspiracy panics? To
investigate this context, this project employs the method of discourse analysis, but one that could also be called a "symptomatology." As we'll see,
symptomatology is a typical conspiracy panic approach to conspiracy theories. Conspiracy theories are usually taken as a sign of something else (individual mental condition, collective delusional state of mind, a cultural/political
slackening). The conspiracy accounts take on the status of being a kind of

cultural folklore, whose claims have no truth-value other than expressing the truth of their storytellers.

Alisdair Spark (1998) has named this desire to seek external explanations for phenomena "dietrology." It is "taken from an Italian term for conspiracy theory which translates roughly as 'behind-ology' " (http://www2.winchester.ac.uk/ccc/resources/essays/thinkstudy.htm). For him, conspiracy theories are dietrological (they seek behind-the-scenes explanations of world events) but so are analyses of conspiracy theories.

In chapter 4, for instance, I note the shift in panics over African American conspiracy theories from a psychologically based approach to a sociocultural one, where conspiracy theories are no longer a product of collective irrationality, but are rendered understandable due to oppressive historical circumstances. The sociocultural approach is still dietrological, insofar as it seeks to explain the phenomena with an appeal to a plane behind the claims themselves. Conspiracy accounts have no explanatory power to tell others about their objects; they can only explain themselves as objects-for-us.

Here I wish to reverse this perspective, by turning the norm into a set of symptoms. Why is it acceptable and popular for rationality to study, classify, and understand its other, but not vice versa? A Nietzschean diagnosis, this assumes that the history of a thing (in this case, conspiracy theories) is a succession of the forces that take possession of it, and the coexistence of forces that struggle over it (Foucault, 1977). A genealogical approach thus analyzes these skirmishes and the "hazardous play of dominations" (1977, p. 148). One of those forces, the conspiracy panic discourse, is the target of this diagnosis.

Given this diagnostic approach to conspiracy panics or the anti-conspiracy theory discourse, one might justly ask what the difference is between my analysis and the conspiracy panics themselves. Isn't this simply a reversal of perspective, turning the tables on the conspiracy panics by performing a dietrology on them? Yes and no. Conspiracy panics do become an object of scrutiny; they become problematized. This temporary reversal indicates that dietrology itself is not inherently something to be avoided. My analysis is not antidietrology as such, but does situate it as a technique of knowledge/power. When and where is this form of analysis employed? By whom, and with what effects?

Even given this similarity, I would argue that other elements are significantly different. My diagnosis is designed, as Nikolas Rose (1999) puts it, "not to locate an essence, but to establish a singularity or individuation within a whole set of relations by means of a work on symptoms" (p. 57). Unlike the conspiracy panics, my analysis does not presume a separation between object and subject of study. Conspiracy panic diagnosis is primarily performed on an other; it is a way of situating subject/object via distance. Especially in the case of the Left, I do not consider myself removed from the milieu; it is an analysis from within. More succinctly, my analysis does not study "strange or aberrant phenomenon": It doesn't ask why conspiracy panickers believe what they do; it doesn't inquire into the "state of mind of leftists" or into their social underpinnings that they do not have access to.

It could be said that while conspiracy panics operate with a transcendent critique (appeal to a plane of settlement that only the analysts have access to), mine is an immanent diagnosis: statements remain within the discourse that produces them. A discourse analysis primarily works by locating layers of rules, protocols, and assumptions that are in large measure *unenunciated*. In other words, contextual and discourse analysis needs to draw the connections that are operational but not articulated within the discourse (Grossberg, 1992; 1995). To do otherwise would mean subscribing to a thin notion of context and of human conduct, namely that which is manifested in explicitly reported self-description.

Instead of uncovering a hidden plane that explains conspiracy panics, the panics are assessed for their presuppositions. It is a "symptomatic reading" in the sense Jason Read gives: "attentiveness to the unstated presuppositions and problematics" of a discourse (p. 12). The statements often articulate their own presuppositions: announcing a need for rationality, explicitly deploying techniques of dismissal (e.g., calling conspiracy theories "dangerous"). Also, I examine the framing techniques performed in conspiracy panics, an immanent discourse analysis.

There is, however, an appeal to a context for conspiracy panics. Whether it is called neoliberal political rationality, the Left's conflicted relationship to that mode of governance, or the professional history of journalism, context is used as an explanatory device. But this contextual analysis does not presume a context separate from the conspiracy panics that can be appealed to. Furthermore, unlike the dietrological approach of conspiracy panics, there is no judgment on the panics' relation to that context, as in the claim that conspiracy theories are a misrecognition of conditions or a poor person's cognitive mapping.

This symptomatology asks the following questions: What commitment to rationality exists when a narrative is identified as a conspiracy theory? Whose authority is affirmed? In other words, this book asks, "how is reason exercised?" (Rabinow, 1997, p. xxiv). In which rationality are we investing our faith? Rather than asking conspiracy theories to act as symptoms that tell us about their roots, we can investigate what forms of thought surround and produce the categories. Ultimately, conspiracy theory (CT) *is* a symptom, but in the reversed perspective I'm proposing, a symptom of the discourse that *positions* it. This discourse of conspiracy panics does not offer itself easily as an object of study. It is penumbral, latent, elusive, and scattered across various domains and institutions. The project is to map this context.

Who is interested in defining, problematizing, and subjugating conspiracy theories? At what moments do these conceptualizations arise, and how do they define their context? And what effects do these problematizations have? Throughout this book, I argue that a *will-to-moderation* permeates our political rationality, and that conspiracy panics have been a significant symptom of this will in action.

CULTURAL ANALYSES OF CONSPIRACY THEORIES

Around the turn of the millennium, a number of scholars produced book-length analyses of conspiracy theories (among them Mark Fenster's *Conspiracy Theories* [Minnesota, 1999], Elaine Showalter's *Hystories* [Columbia, 1997], Timothy Melley's *Empire of Conspiracy* [Cornell, 1999], Robert Goldberg's *Enemies Within* [Yale, 2001], Peter Knight's *Conspiracy Culture* [Routledge, 2001], and Michael Barkun's *Culture of Conspiracy* [University of California, 2003]). Collections on the subject were also published (*Paranoia Within Reason: A Casebook of Conspiracy as Explanation*, edited by George Marcus, 1999, and *Conspiracy Nation* [New York University 2002], edited by Peter Knight). It is de rigueur for a book on conspiracy theory to survey and summarize these works, and I would recommend to the reader that they go to them to discover this. For an excellent discussion of the stakes and intertwining of conspiracy theorizing and cultural studies' modes of interpretation, see Clare Birchall (2004; 2006). Since this book is not on conspiracy theories but on conspiracy panics, I will sketch out these works with a narrow focus on their place in conspiracy panic discourse.

Almost exclusively, these works have performed a symptomatology on conspiracy theories. Many focus on the inherent properties of theories themselves (elaborating their characteristics, rhetorical tropes, and narrative forms). These works are often concerned with describing conspiracy theories as sociological curiosities (if not outright social problems). They ask questions like Why do people believe? Why did they arise? And what problems do they pose? Some find conspiracy theories to be a danger to the health of the political and cultural body (Showalter, Melley, Goldberg, Barkun). The significantly more nuanced analysis of Mark Fenster takes conspiracy theories seriously as an expression of populist sentiment that emerges out of conditions of state secrecy and malfeasance. Ultimately, however, he reifies the conspiracy theories, fixating on their inherent properties. Employing a version of Frederic Jameson's definition of conspiracy theories as a "poor person's cognitive mapping," Fenster finds them to be a disfigured expression of critical populism (1988, p. 356). Others who are more generous (like Peter Knight and George Marcus) find that conspiracy theories convey new forms of pervasive suspicion. Revelations of scandals and cover-ups have created a scenario where conspiratorial skepticism is a sensible initial perspective. These authors expand conspiracy theories to a broader concept of "conspiracy culture" or "reasonable paranoia," undermining our comfort at the stable object "conspiracy theory." Yet they too remain focused on conspiracy theories (even with expanded definitions).

Whether perceived as a direct menace, a misfired expression, or an appropriate cultural narrative mode, the object of study remains conspiracy theory. In each of these cases, a symptomatology is employed on a cultural phenomenon we seemingly *already know*. Despite the value of describing and interpreting conspiracy theories in this manner, my project centers on what the *concern* over conspiracy theories tells us about the current context. What's missing in this literature is an analysis of the institutions and discourses that come to be obsessed with conspiracy narratives, or what Keith Goshorn (2000) in a review essay calls "anti-conspiracy discourse" (http://muse.jhu.edu/ journals/ theory_and_event/v 004/4.3r_goshorn.html). Goshorn even goes so far as to describe some of the above books as *part* of this discourse.

To put it simply, while many analysts begin with the question, Why do otherwise normal people believe in weird things? my opening gambit is Why do weird people believe in normal things? This crude reversal signals a simple shift in perspective. Furthermore, my interest is not so much in why people do or believe anything, but in the broader discursive cultural contexts that constrain and enable thought/action. Studying the composition and effectiveness of the norm (in this case, a political rationality functioning via the management of extreme thought/action) entails a shift away from studying a particular problem.

Not all works in cultural studies are as monolithic as the ones I've just described. While no book-length treatments of conspiracy panics/problematizations have been published, the sentiments have peeked through in shorter writings. Keith Goshorn's review, where he discusses the anticonspiracy discourse is perhaps the most explicit. Clare Birchall's "Cultural Studies on/as Conspiracy Theory" (2004) develops the stakes in cultural studies' problematizations of conspiracy theories (see also 2006). John Fiske has an important chapter in *Media Matters* where he discusses African American AIDS conspiracy narratives as "counterknowledges" and calls for a study of the strategies of disqualification against them. Finally, some of Jodi Dean's work also is relevant here. While many would include her *Aliens in America* within the pantheon of conspiracy analysis literature, only parts of it deal with conspiratology—it is mostly about Ufology (which doesn't necessarily include a conspiracy element). Her later writing on the role of conspiracy theories in American political thought ("Declarations of Independence") clearly begins to address the discourses that problematize conspiracy theories, and does so in sophisticated ways.

What these works open up, and what this book elaborates, is the sense that the context of conspiracy theories matters as much as the theories themselves. Moreover, what a context *is* also matters. For most analysts, the context of a conspiracy theory is made up of its conditions of emergence, the soil that nourished its growth. The panic discourse often uses "root" metaphors in this way. "Root analysis" seeks to address its object by unearthing its origins. The root, a hidden yet necessary source of an object, arrests and grounds conspiracy theories into a stable substance whose "sprouting" can now be accounted for. This type of context (e.g., post–cold war need for enemies, backlash against the 1960s, history of oppression) works to explain a narrative's emergence but not its disqualified status. It assumes the narrative's lack of truth effects, and goes on to perform a diagnosis upon a pathological body. The most generous book-length analyses (e.g., by Fenster [1999] and Knight [2001]) acknowledge that the context includes the National Security State and governmental secrecy. But even here the context invoked only demonstrates the *intelligibility* of conspiracy theories. They offer explanations of the account's existence but not of its status as CT. In other words, the conspiracy theories cannot speak to or about this context; they can only be spoken by it.

In this book, context is not the source for the emergence of a particular knowledge/account but the source of its *status*. Context gives CT a name, identity, weight, and places for circulation. The context is not responsible for the rise of a conspiracy account but does generate conspiracy theory (as a discursive position). For example, let's take the suspicion that the UN is implementing a New World Order, complete with concentration camps and black helicopters. We can just treat it as a false claim. We can also treat it as a collective psychological delusion. In addition, we can sociologically trace it back to white working-class resentment following a growing disempowerment at the hands of globalization (codified in NAFTA). All these are attempts to define a context for the account. But none are contextual explanations of this theory as "conspiracy theory." We need to examine where and when it appears, who speaks it, what else it is linked to, and what it opposes. In other words, the context is the regime of truth and the broader political rationality. The context is not separate from conspiracy theories; it is constitutive of them.

I argue that what we are witnessing is a new fusion of culture and rationality, one that is increasingly shared across the political spectrum. Conspiracy theories tell us less about the people who believe in them or the cultural milieu that produces them than they do about the dominant forms of rationality that are so enraptured with them as problems. They are portals into the contexts that problematize them. The panics surrounding conspiracy theories demonstrate that trust, truth, and rationality are at the heart of the current political context. In their prominence as objects of public concern, conspiracy theories provide insights into the current configuration of political rationality.

CHAPTER SUMMARIES

Chapter 1 briefly summarizes the history of problematizations of conspiracy theories via the link between rationality and dissent. I begin by evaluating the writings of Harold Lasswell, Richard Hofstadter, Seymour Lipset, and others as the groundwork for more contemporary problematizations. I then survey more recent interpreters of the phenomenon of the "paranoid style," "political paranoia," or "conspiracism." These texts frame conspiracy theories in terms of domestic political extremism, improper forms of dissent, and styles of thought. I argue that the concern over conspiracy theories (old and new) is closely linked to panics over extremist political activity and populism. From the scares over communists and Birchites in the 1960s to the alarm over militias and domestic terrorists in the last decade, public discussions have intertwined a form of thought (irrational conspiracy theories) to a form of political activity (extremism). In doing so, knowledges are presented as inherently dangerous, certain styles of dissent are disqualified, and new forms of consent are forged. I examine the effects of these mainstream problematizations on contemporary possibilities of dissent.

The cultural discourse of conspiracy panics relies on institutional supports. The next two chapters deal with one of the more prominent of these institutions: professional journalism. In both chapters, I examine how professional power was being renewed in relation to popular culture. In chapter 2, I look specifically at how this was done via a turn to public or civic journalism. A professional renewal took place amid sociological claims about a waning of civic participation. Public journalism was part of a broader effort to reintegrate citizens into civil processes. The public being hailed was considerably moderate, counterposed to an extremist populism emerging at the same time. At times these distinctions were made according to medium: the participatory and civil debate of print versus the hate-filled, irrational, and uncivilized medium of talk radio. In addition, professional journalism's notion of a public was distinguished from the phenomenon of popular culture, an issue finding acute expression in the controversy over Oliver Stone's film *JFK* earlier in the decade, but one that hearkens back to the founding of the profession. Constructing a public, then, depended on a particular version of rationality, one contrasted to popular knowledge's excesses.

In chapter 3 I continue examining journalism, but in this case concentrate on how the Internet was problematized through its association with conspiracy theories. Conspiracy theories function as a portal to major social and political issues, and here that issue is the emergence of new information technologies. I assess how professional journalism handled a conspiracy theory in its own midst. Gary Webb's 1996 investigative journalism series "Dark Alliance" on the CIA/Contra/crack cocaine links was taken as an object of concern—a problem—at a moment when the profession of journalism was figuring out its relationship to "going online." Webb's story caused little stir until it took off on the Net. Only then was it deemed to violate journalistic protocols and discredited as a conspiracy theory. Along with a number of other conspiracy theories, Webb's story was defined as a "sign of the times" in which new technologies created a swarm of unreliable information. In turn, the Internet was coded as a chaotic space, the "medium of choice for conspiracy theorists," and thus intrinsically untrustworthy. New technologies do not simply make their appearance on the scene with already encoded meanings, and I argue that professional discourses (like journalism) are crucial to how we think of trust, reason, and truth vis-à-vis new media.

Chapter 4 begins a two-chapter analysis of alternative conspiracy panic discourses, namely the Left. In this chapter, I examine the political stakes involved in the production and problematization of AIDS conspiracy theories. AIDS conspiracy accounts, with their ability to provoke heated responses around life-and-death issues, crystallize the political stakes involved in the overall problematization of conspiracy theories. With this in mind, I examine a progressive critique of AIDS conspiracy theories, David Gilbert's "Tracking the *Real* Genocide: AIDS—Conspiracy or Unnatural Disaster?" I analyze this essay in detail in order to foreground the way an explicitly leftist analysis deals with AIDS conspiracy accounts. I also provide a chart that demonstrates the variety of origin stories, historical contexts, prescriptions, and political accents that make up nonofficial AIDS accounts. Operating via a "sociocultural approach" to conspiracy theories, the Left conspiracy panic does not dismiss conspiracy research for its adherents' mental states or for its threat to consensus politics. Instead, Left analyses attempt to explain conspiracy research via assessing their origins (even sympathetically). Conspiratology is distinguished from proper politics and research in this discourse, which names it a diversion, distraction, and manipulative oversimplification. The effects of this Left conspiracy panic on a politics of articulation are examined.

The fifth chapter continues a discussion of the Left's relationship to conspiracy theories by discussing their uneasy relationship with 9/11 conspiracy accounts. While in the 1990s New World Order conspiracy narratives were seen as a misfired attempt at understanding globalization, the U.S. conspiracy research around 9/11 has complicated the relationship of critical work to conspiracy accounts. The Left has simultaneously been the target of the problematizations as well as participating vociferously in conspiracy panics over 9/11 conspiracy accounts. I focus on the work of the 9/11 Truth Movement, in its internal composition as well as the ways it has been problematized by what they call the "gatekeeper Left." Who is authorized to provide compelling accounts but more importantly to call for investigations? I examine in this case what I call the "sphere of legitimate dissensus," and how various elements of the Left over the years come in and out of it. Finally I ask, Is a politics of articulation possible across different projects of counterglobalization?

Methodological Note

A methodological note is warranted here regarding the examples chosen, as well as those omitted. One might ask why, for instance, conspiracy accounts of the John F. Kennedy assassination have not been treated at length. It is true that the conspiracy research surrounding that event is fundamental to understanding the place of conspiracy theories in U.S. culture (as has been well analyzed in the works of Knight, Fenster, and Barkun). As I have been noting in this introduction, this book is about conspiracy panics, which were less prominent when the Kennedy assassination theories were circulating. The research was marginalized without a major public discourse comprised of experts, journalists, and politicians. The theories themselves did not circulate in such a way that would make them "popular" and thus a threat that needed curtailing. As chapter 1 notes, there *were* some serious reflections during the 1960s on the link between types of dissent and extremist politics. However, these rarely addressed JFK assassination theories directly. I discuss that time period in order to set the conceptual conditions for conspiracy panics of the post–cold war era.

Even if we grant the methodological centrality of the post–cold war era, some might question the exclusion of something as pervasive as extraterrestrial conspiracy theories. Alien abduction narratives and Ufology certainly comprised much of the popular cultural imagination in the mid- to late 1990s. As Jodi Dean's book *Aliens in America* so thoroughly argues, these marginalized yet popular beliefs became a site where numerous political and cultural issues were negotiated (e.g., public sphere, knowledge production, cybercultural community making). However, Ufology did not have a necessary conspiratorial element: alien abduction narratives and the search for extraterrestrials did at times overlap with conspiratological research (in the belief that the U.S. government was covering up its knowledge of and relationship with the aliens), but not always. Moreover, extraterrestrial conspiracy theories were rarely a *central* concern within conspiracy panics. Rather, they functioned more as a guilt-by-association device to disqualify conspiracy research that often had nothing to do with Ufology (even research that *refused* to associate).

Beyond the methodological exclusions, there is the question of why select and highlight particular components of the conspiracy panics. The chapters dealing with post–cold war panics (2–5) can be divided into two main problematizing discourses: professional journalism and the U.S. Left. Conspiracy panics do not just have effects on the particular social groups targeted nor on a more amorphous "social order": They are symptoms of transformations going on in the specific discourses that problematize conspiracy theories. In the case of the Left, the two chapters here focus on changes in the post–cold war U.S. Left, one that had to come to terms with the Clinton regime, with a mid 1990s panic over right-wing domestic dissent, with competing globalization narratives, and with their own marginalized status during the George W. Bush/war on terror era. The Left's complicated relationship with political rationality, conspiracy panics, and advanced liberalism underpins chapters 4 and 5 (on AIDS and 9/11 globalization accounts).

Two earlier chapters focus on professional journalism. On a basic level, any discussion of conspiracy panics, following the moral panics framework, would need to examine the way that the news media articulates these problems and the proposed solutions (as with the classic work *Policing the Crisis*). But more than looking at journalism as an institutional support for conspiracy panics, this book examines what conspiracy panics do to the support discourse itself. Journalism has increasingly become a subject of concern regarding its public role and its relationship to governance. Understanding professional journalism as a discourse that governs at a distance through rationality gives a glimpse into the broader political rationality. It also allows us to make sense of the profession's own history and development. So, a subtext to this book is the recent professional history of journalism, especially as it has attempted to reestablish its social function via the harnessing of digital technologies and via a revival of one of its founding dynamics, namely the profession's relationship to popular culture.

The specific case of public or civic journalism also needs some explanation: What is the value of studying, as some would note, a marginal and failed movement within professional journalism? Even more, isn't it a bit gratuitous to harp on public journalism in an age where sensationalist and propagandistic forms of news are pervasive? To be sure, public journalism was an attempt at obviating the more sensationalist elements of journalism that we now see so baldly exhibited as routine news. However, it's important to examine this experiment because: (1) it exemplifies well a governing strategy that, during the mid- to late 1990s, sought to ground itself in a civil society or communitarian discourse. Moreover, (2) it can serve as an example of how rejecting popular culture in the name of rationality is an ineffectual and undesirable strategy. In other words, in shaping our strategies of combating information warfare and news spectacle today we can learn from the public journalism gambit.

The limited choices of examples in this book, then, indicate the impossibility of a totalizing notion of conspiracy panics. Conspiracy panics do not define our age (even while these panics themselves often invoke a "paranoid age"), nor is there a single political rationality that organizes the totality of the social. Instead, the problematizations of conspiracy theories are forces at work in the ongoing political composition of U.S. governance, contributing to a milieu that is neither unitary nor stable. In this piecemeal manner we can contribute to what Foucault calls an "ontology of the present."

1

POLITICAL SCIENCE FICTION

Expert Monitors, Excessive Skepticism, and Preventive Rationality

A few days after September 11th, 2001, George W. Bush declared a national Day of Reflection. This moment of contemplation, while infused with sentiments of mourning and grief, also coincided with another kind of national reflection. On September 26, then-White House spokesperson Ari Fleischer announced that Americans should "watch what they say." This self-monitoring of thought, especially around the limits of dissent, took on a spectacular prominence at that conjuncture, but it has a longer history. And in many cases recently these limits have been articulated to conspiracy thinking.

This chapter traces some of the foundational texts that made rationality a crucial factor for conspiracy panics in defining proper forms of consent and dissent. I begin with a brief summary of the writings of Harold Lasswell, Richard Hofstadter, and others in the mid- to late 1960s as the groundwork for contemporary conspiracy panics. I then survey more recent interpreters of the "paranoid style," "political paranoia," or "conspiracism." Explored here are the conceptual contexts that produce, and ultimately get reinforced by, conspiracy panics.

The chapter will be a close reading of these expert texts, focusing on the following conspiracy panic issues: domestic political extremism, forms of dissent, and dominant styles of thought. I argue that the concern over conspiracy theories (old and new) is closely linked to panics over extremist political activity. From the scares over communists and Birchites in the 1960s to the alarm over militias and terrorists since the mid 1990s, public discussions have intertwined a form of thought (irrational conspiracy theories) with a form of political activity (extremism). In doing so, knowledges are presented as inherently dangerous, certain styles of dissent are disqualified, and new forms of consent are forged. I examine the effects of these mainstream problematizations on contemporary parameters of dissent.

How do liberal political rationalities attempt to organize thought? Examining these conspiracy panics illuminates current efforts to produce "reasonable politics."

Harold Lasswell and Preventive Political Rationality

Harold D. Lasswell's pioneering work in the field of political psychology in the 1930s and 1940s, especially his construction of political personality types, sets the conceptual stage for later conspiracy panics. While certainly not the first to use psychological methods and concepts to define political phenomena, Lasswell is perhaps the most systematic, sophisticated, and influential thinker to advance political psychology. As Lasswell himself indicates, the field of social psychology had already begun in piecemeal fashion to expand into the domain of politics. In addition, it had only been a decade since World War I, a war in which propaganda and psychological warfare were key components (and out of which Lasswell himself emerged). This spurred whole new fields of study, including political psychology. Here I examine *Psychopathology and Politics* (1930) and *Power and Personality* (1948), major works that span two decades of Lasswell's research into the psychologization of politics.

The preface to *Psychopathology and Politics* announces Lasswell's departure from his previous attention to propaganda techniques. He now seeks to "discover what developmental experiences are significant for the political traits and interests of the mature. This means that we want to see what lies *behind* agitators, administrators, theorists, and other types who play on the public stage" (p. 8). Through the method of life history, Lasswell seeks to isolate the personality traits and contextual determinants of different political types.

Lasswell makes no claims to scientific neutrality. His research is explicitly defined as practical and interventionist. The chapter "A New Technique of Thinking" expresses Lasswell's concern with his social and political context. According to him, we are witnessing a deterioration of reason: "In spite of our best efforts to disseminate logicality, people are always 'letting their prejudices run away with them,' even when they have a baggage of good intentions" (p. 31). But a response to the decline of reason does not simply entail giving a logic antidote. He contends, "our faith in logic is misplaced. . . . The supposition that emotional aberrations are to be conquered by heroic doses of logical thinking is a mistake. The absence of effective logic is a symptom of a disease which logic itself cannot cure" (p. 31).

Rather than responding to these conditions with "more and better logic," Lasswell argues for psychoanalysis and the construction of Freudian case studies. A kind of reason does prevail, however, as the analyst interprets and sorts subjects' stories, desires, and images into categorical types with personality traits. We see this recoding of free fantasy a little later in the book. While discussing the prominence of "hate" in politics, Lasswell finds that it emanates from a "private motive": "a repressed and powerful hatred of authority . . . in relation to the father" (p. 75).¹ Displaced from "family objects to public objects," private motives are rationalized by the agitator as "public interests" (p. 75).

Marking his particular fixation on political agitators, Lasswell devotes two chapters to the subject (the latter called simply "Political Agitators—Continued"). These case studies, reported in lyrical detail, produce a typological profile of the agitator's essential traits: high value on public emotional response, narcissism, and suspicion. Excessive suspicion is a key characteristic. Lasswell states that "ever on the alert for pernicious intrusions of private interest into public affairs, the agitator sees 'unworthy' motives where others see the just claims of friendship" (p. 79). This exaggerated mistrust will reappear in later problematizations of the paranoid style as "hypersuspicion," which signals a kind of extremism.

Important here is the fact that Lasswell accuses agitators of engaging in a type of what we examined in the introduction as *dietrology* (seeking causes behind events). At the same time, he himself performs dietrology in classifying personality types/motivations. I say this not simply to turn the tables on Lasswell, but to pinpoint a moment where different kinds of dietrology are being demarcated. Reasonable forms of "behind-ology" trump unreasonable ones. Even more, reasonable forms *apply their form of dietrology* to the unreasonable ones, thus determining the field of engagement between them.

Lasswell's commitment to interventionist research is especially evident in "The Politics of Prevention," a chapter devoted to reorienting politics and knowledge production toward the prevention of conflict. As Lasswell puts it:

> The time has come to abandon the assumption that the problem of politics is the problem of promoting discussion among all the interests concerned in a given problem. . . . The problem of politics is less to solve conflicts than to prevent them; less to serve as a safety valve for social protest than to apply social energy to the abolition of recurrent sources of strain in society. . . . The politics of prevention draws attention squarely to the central problem of reducing the level of strain and maladaption in society. (pp. 196–197)

Conceptually and practically, Lasswell's fusion of psychology with politics is designed to prevent conflict and dissent, and therefore to normalize politics: "Some of these human results will be deplored as 'pathological,' while others will be welcomed as 'healthy' " (p. 200).² An obvious effect of psychopolitics is the labeling of some political knowledge as maladjusted or deviant. But equally important is Lasswell's call to identify and head off trends *before* they coalesce into movements.

Lasswell's reliance on the discipline of psychology signals another main point: he does not seek direct State intervention into political activities. Preventive politics does not depend on a series of changes in the organization of government. It depends upon a reorientation in the minds of those who think about society around the central problems: What are the principal factors which modify the tension level of the community? What is the specific relevance of a proposed line of action to the temporary and permanent modification of that tension level? (p. 198)

The fostering of preventive politics falls to society's problematizers, those experts who can produce authoritative visions and diagnoses of society. Changing the nature of the problems they construct is paramount, for "achieving the ideal of preventative politics depends . . . upon improving the methods and education of social administrators and social scientists" (p. 203). Special training of professionals is needed: A "different type of education will become necessary for those who administer society or think about it," Lasswell writes, "thorough curricular reconstructions will be indispensable" (pp. 201–202).

Preventive Rationality

Lasswell's prescriptions are historically consonant with liberalism's strategy of governing through the figure of the "expert." According to Foucauldian scholars Andrew Barry, Thomas Osborne, and Nikolas Rose (1996) experts have been crucial to the development of forms of governance (pp. 12–15), and have provided for liberalism "particular conceptions of the objects to be governed" (Rose, 1996, p. 42). To scientists and intellectuals is granted a certain amount of autonomy to enable "action at a distance" and legitimate the workings of the State without direct intervention (Barry, Osborne, & Rose, 1996, pp. 10–11). Empowered with the authority to problematize the state of affairs, experts link technical knowledge with political practice in several ways: First, they provide government with new objects and subjects of governance and second, they legitimate political programs in the name of scientific authority. Governing partially operates through these expert reflections that are not just ideas: they seek to become practicable by connecting with governmental procedures and apparatuses (Rose, 1996, p. 41).

Lasswell's new expert, the "administrator-investigator," largely operates within this paradigm of liberal expertise. Politics is not a matter of State-oriented intervention, coercion, or mediation of conflicting interests. Rather, Lasswell's preemptive program, relies on the authority of "autonomized" scientists and researchers who "will be intimately allied to general medicine, psychopathology, physiological psychology, and related disciplines" (p. 203). In Nikolas Rose's words (1999), these preventative governing operations include "the calculated modulation of conduct according to principles of optimization of benign impulses and minimization of malign impulses" (p. 234). The administrator-investigator belongs to a politics of "primary prevention . . . a whole programme of political intervention to educate authorities and lay persons so as to act on the conditions which exacerbate the possibilities of . . . problems occurring in the first place" (p. 235). In a move that foreshadows future conspiracy panics (and a general shift in governance), Lasswell's techniques of managing dissent have less to do with repressing or eliminating dangerous deviants from the social body than with producing experts who could assess the conditions necessary for the prevention of agitation. As a form of dissent management, the goal is to nip certain conditions' growth in the bud—to detect and thereby neutralize an emergence before it can coalesce, something Melinda Cooper (2006) later calls a war strategy of "pre-empting emergence." *Psychopathology and Politics*, then, can be seen more as a manual to prevent social agitation than an effort to demonize it, in other words a *preventive rationality*.

In this early work, the fusion of psychology and politics hinges on the ability of experts to bring it about. Lasswell's preliminary project sets the groundwork for a broader psychopolitics by searching for motives behind political actions, applying psychoanalytic interpretive skills to individual cases, and generalizing from individuals to traits that collectively contribute to social tension. This early research is designed to change the frameworks, methods, and problems with which experts engage. Lasswell's later work strives more explicitly to intervene into the production of proper political subjects.

While the "agitator" is an important focus of *Psychopathology and Politics*, Lasswell's (1948) *Power and Personality* discusses political types with regard to actual and potential leaders. The "general theory of political personality" represents research whose

> aim is to bring into being democratic leaders who share the basic personality structure appropriate to the elite of a society where power is subordinated to respect and to identifications with humanity. The chief difference between the "basic" citizen and the democratic leader needs to be mainly a difference of skill and not of values. (1948, p. 152)

The analysis of a "democratic leader" yields information about how to cultivate it. Of special interest in Lasswell's prescriptions are the "non- or antidemocrats who have rejected democracy after being extensively exposed to it, or who imagine that they conform to the democratic ideal when they are undemocratic in actual conduct" (p. 152). Understanding antidemocrat types enables strategies to discourage this development: The process of developing "character, technique, and perspective" must include the creation and deployment of new and better political images for young people, especially through new media technologies (pp. 156, 172–173).

Lasswell repeats his earlier call for a cadre of experts, which now include both self-governing actors *and* institutions: "What I advocate is an act of institution building for the purpose of carrying on a vital part of the intelligence function essential to the science and policy of democracy" (pp. 168–171). Carrying out the assessment protocol developed in his earlier work, these "social self-observatories" would be "capable of exposing the truth about the hidden destructiveness of our cultural institutions, and of reporting on the effect of experimental efforts at reformation" (p. 173). Lasswell cites Jeremy Bentham as his intellectual precursor in this matter, though notes that in Bentham's time "the technical problems of measuring social trends were in a most rudimentary state" (pp. 238, 19f). Another name for these experts might be social watchdogs. Later this expert monitoring function, I argue, becomes commonplace within professions (like journalism) and even among dissenting groups.

With *Power and Personality*, Lasswell takes the arguments of *Psychopathology and Politics* as givens. No longer needing to convince readers to look for motives in political action, or the case-study methodology, or the pathologization of political personality types, Lasswell can effectively develop the articulation between politics and psychology. More positive and affirmative in tone, *Power and Personality* seeks strategies for developing proper subjects, rather than investigating why deviants exist. Through these two major works, Lasswell establishes the conceptual context in which the "paranoid style" emerges as a problem. In this nascent conspiracy panic, agitation is linked to a psychological state, begging for solutions that include prevention against dissent and cultivation of the reasonable.

A short and strange moment occurs late in *Power and Personality*, a moment whose brevity reveals much about the future trajectory of "political paranoia." The chapter "Leadership Principles: Reduce Provocation" elaborates the different "breaking points" in individuals. These are the subjective vulnerabilities that need to be met with external, institutional support to maintain the democratic personality. A few pages into the relatively detached discussion of manageable characteristics and useful techniques, a section called "The Menace of the Paranoid in the Atomic Age" suddenly interrupts the smooth flow of technopolicy discourse. Lasswell writes:

> In coping with our present-day difficulties in the hope of reducing provocativeness, we must not lose sight of the fact that even certainty of annihilation cannot protect us from the paranoid psychotic. If we knew that another war would actually eliminate us, we would not be safe from war. All mankind might be destroyed by a single paranoid in a position of power who could imagine no grander exit than using the globe as a gigantic funeral pyre. And the paranoid need not be the leader of a great state. He can be the head of a small state or even of a small gang.
>
> Even a modicum of security under present-day conditions calls for the discovery, neutralization and eventual prevention of the paranoid. And this calls for the overhauling of our whole inheritance of social institutions for the purpose of disclosing and eliminating the social factors that create these destructive types. (p. 184)

This remarkable little section is as anomalous as the paranoid type it discusses. The irrational announces itself irrationally: it interrupts the text, only to be followed by a return to the calm reflections on the minor provocations that need to be managed by experts. At this stage, Lasswell cannot codify paranoia; he cannot problematize it within politics (as a "type"). The political paranoid cannot be given the nuance and detail other pathologies are given: it is outside any type, a force whose power threatens to destroy not only all typology, not only all politics, but also quite literally the world itself. Lasswell still feels compelled to address this extremity, even if it demands a different tone of writing. He provides an extremist response to extremism. Paranoia here cannot be incorporated—as pure pathology, it can only be eliminated.

This conceptually unmanageable force does not remain unrepresentable for long. It eventually comes under the scrutiny of problematizers; only now, it does not appear as a personality type, but as a *style of thought*. With this I move forward fifteen years, to the germinal work of Richard Hofstadter.

HOFSTADTER AND THE SEARCH FOR A MIDDLE

Hofstadter's classic essay "The Paranoid Style in American Politics" first appeared in *Harper's Magazine* in 1964 (a year after the assassination of John F. Kennedy). It was later expanded and reprinted in the collection called *The Paranoid Style in American Politics and Other Essays* (1967). This text has influenced generations of political scientists and historians, and any serious attention to conspiracy theories must cite it—pro or con. According to Mark Fenster (1999), Hofstadter's essay is emblematic of a postwar liberal consensus approach to domestic political unrest, in which the pathologization of dissent prevailed. Fenster's analysis of Hofstadter is excellent, and along with Jodi Dean's (2000b) writings on him, comprises a devastating critique of this pathologization model. I will refer the reader to their writings and concentrate here on how Hofstadter links a style of thought to political action.

Hofstadter's conceptual debt to Lasswell is clear: He searches for motives behind political action (specifically the "agitator's" activities), he defines these motives as psychological (though tempers them with political history), and he abstracts particular psychological motives into collective and generalizable traits. Finally, he pathologizes them. Most importantly, Hofstadter *assumes* the legitimacy of linking psychology to politics, never feeling obliged to argue for it as Lasswell did. Indeed, political psychology has become such a dominant discourse that Hofstadter is compelled to distinguish his work from its typological research. He argues that in

> using the expression "paranoid style," I am not speaking in a clinical sense, but borrowing a clinical term for other purposes. I have neither the competence

nor the desire to classify any figures of the past or present as certifiable lunatics. . . . It is the use of paranoid modes of expression by more or less normal people that makes the phenomenon significant. (pp. 3–4)

He calls this the paranoid style "simply because no other word adequately evokes the qualities of heated exaggeration, suspiciousness, and conspiratorial fantasy that I have in mind" (p. 3). Hofstadter can secure this loan in the already-accepted articulation between psychology and politics. His casual adoption of political psychology may seem to empty the paranoid style of its clinical connotations but it still carries the *authority* of psychology. His diagnosis isn't clinical, but it is social; carrying the legitimacy of the psychopathological category out onto the social field.

For Hofstadter, it is not the content of beliefs that matters, but the *style* of thought. Style "has to do with the way in which ideas are believed and advocated rather than with the truth or falsity of their content" (p. 5). This style does not refer to particular ideas, since "any system of beliefs can be espoused in the paranoid style, [it's just that] there are certain beliefs which seem to be espoused almost entirely this way" (p. 5f). The paranoid style is not merely the belief in a conspiracy theory—it is a worldview: "Not that its exponents see conspiracies or plots here and there in history, but that they regard a 'vast' or 'gigantic' conspiracy as the motive force in historical events" (p. 29). The distinction from ordinary political beliefs is not in "the absence of facts, but the leap of imagination at critical points" (p. 37). This emphasis on a worldview and a style of thought begins to give generic traits and formal coherence to a multiplicity of dissenting knowledge claims.

There are important differences from Lasswell, then. The turn from personality type to style is a shift in problematization. Problematization no longer seeks to categorize individual actors, but to establish a manner of thinking that could be taken up by *any* political actor. The pathological is no longer an easy distinction to make from the normal: As Hofstadter notes, it is "intensely rationalistic" and an "imitation of the enemy" (pp. 36, 32). The paranoid style both possesses its own characteristics and approximates the normal. It is a *mimic* of reason and thus needs constant vigilance.

Hofstadter focuses on this mimicry and proximity, and we need only go to paranoia's etymology to see it in operation. The spatial position of the *para* is *beside* or *beyond* the noid. After all, the paranoid is not antinoid, nor exnoid, nor xenonoid. It touches the mind, being both proximate yet quite dissimilar (along similar conceptual lines as paramilitary, parapsychology, paraphrase, parallel, paranormal). The paranoid style in its domestically populist form is not simply exiled to the outside of normal political discourse; it is a danger that constantly threatens from within. While it is banished to the fringes of official thought, it is also among us, lurking within the nation, in the heartland, among the populace. It is not one of "us," but it could be anyone. This proximity of the paranoid style to normal thought sets the conceptual stage for future experts.

Contemporaneous with, and in some cases influenced by, Hofstadter's essay are a range of other texts: *The Politics of Unreason: Right-wing Extremism in America, 1790–1970* (Seymour M. Lipset & Earl Raab, 1970), *The Strange Tactics of Extremism* (Harry Overstreet & Bonaro Overstreet, 1964), and *Extremism USA* (John Carpenter, 1964). More recent problematizations influenced by Hofstadter include: *Conspiracy! The Paranoid Style and Why It Flourishes* (Daniel Pipes, 1997), *Political Paranoia: The Psychopolitics of Hatred* (Robert S. Robins & Jerrold M. Post, 1997), *American Extremists* (John George & Laird Wilcox, 1996), *Extremism in America* (Lynn Sargent, 1995), and *A Culture of Conspiracy: Apocalyptic Visions in Contemporary America* (Michael Barkun, 2003). This is of course a small sample, limited to the book-length treatments. Myriad newspaper stories, journal articles, and short essays draw from Hofstadter (especially in the *New York Times* and *Washington Post*; Applebome, 1995; Johnson, 1995; Rich, 1995; Leiby, 1995; Charney, 1995; Achenbach, 2004). In various ways, these texts link conspiracy theories to domestic political extremism, forms of dissent, and dominant styles of thought. Together they comprise the conceptual dimension of conspiracy panics.

Populism/Domestic Con-fusion

Many of these panics appear to respond to conjunctural moments of political destabilization, with particular emphases on unruly populism and political confusion. Beginning with Hofstadter, the paranoid style is intimately linked with populism. Hofstadter accounted for the booming popularity of conspiracy theories in the 1960s by tracing them through U.S. history. Dating back to the American Revolution, these irrational thoughts accompanied populist grumblings, leading to paranoid social behavioral patterns, such as the formation of the Anti-Masonic Party in the early 19th century (pp. 14–19). While present at the founding of the nation, the paranoid style is not a constant presence—it has "successive episodic waves" of heightened activity (p. 39).

Even while Hofstadter claims that the paranoid style is not exclusive to American politics, his essay can be seen as a moment in a lineage of reflections on "The American." From the impressionistic interpretations of Crevecoeur around the time of American Independence through Alexis De Tocqueville's classic *Democracy in America* and onward, meditations on "The American Character," the "American Style," and the "American Identity" have preoccupied analysts. This brief history of European intellectuals defining and appraising "the American" eventually gets taken over by "internal" reflection, continuing through such research as "culture and personality studies" in the social sciences and "American character" studies in the humanities (McGiffert, 1964).

More than just establishing the content of "Americanness," the very fact and form of the problematizations may themselves be a feature of Americanness. Taking the American as object and subject of reflection is itself part of political identity formation. Often, this evaluation includes the identification and location of the "un-American" within, especially when discussing the limits of dissent (as a "balancing" of liberty and security). The un-American is not necessarily an "alien," though it has been historically defined as such. At various times, this internal transgressor is a traitor, rebel, subversive, defector, insurgent, seditious dissident, rabble rouser, or sympathizer.

While there are a few examples of research done on extremism and political paranoia from an international perspective (most notably Pipes), the vast majority of problematizations articulate the paranoid style and political extremism to an American context (George & Wilcox, 1996; Halpern & Levin, 1996; Gardner, 1997; Sargent, 1995; McGiffert, 1964; Schlesinger, 1962; Archer, 1969). With titles like *Extremism USA, American Extremists, Extremism in America, The Extremists: Gadflies of American Society,* and Hofstadter's essay (which is the first to articulate extremism and Americanness with paranoia), one can see the preoccupation with the national quality of extremist dissent. The refrain in these works, that extremism and the paranoid style have existed in America since its inception, makes it easy to argue that the problematizations on extremist dissent and conspiracism are bound up with the self-reflection that composes the "American" style.

For Hofstadter, the cold war 1960s was another moment when America's paranoid style was spiking. But he located something peculiar to this reemergence: This is a "new phenomenon; the threat is not foreign, but homegrown" (p. 24). While Hofstadter is speaking about the enemies constructed within the paranoid style, we can flip this to include the ways the paranoid style itself is turned *into* an enemy." The paranoid style is not traceable to a "foreign" element.

Much of the dissent-management strategies of the 20th century, or as Michael Rogin (1987) calls them "countersubversive practices against dissent," worked via xenophobia (p. 4). They were directed at an alien other, whose potential for infiltration into the native has been used to justify crackdowns on subversives. From the repression of immigrant working-class movements (where the immigrant was defined as an agent of foreign interests) to the more obvious Red Scares (in which an external communist force was targeted), domestic dissent has been typically problematized around the security of national borders from external invasion. In the case of the paranoid style, however, no outside force is culpable: it is domestic and popular. Once the threat is located *within* national political identity, a new countersubversive framework is required to render this danger intelligible.

And what exactly is the danger? According to the Overstreets (1964), the primary threat is that "too many moderates will be pulled from the center" (p. 14). This "working impatience with dissent" betrays a fear not of external invasion, or even of a well-mounted movement by an already formed group (Lipset & Raab, p. 3). Rather, the fear is that otherwise normal political actors will be drawn *away from* the moderate center and into more radical forms of politics. The concern is both with extremism as such and with its potential attractiveness to moderates.[3]

A foreign invader can more readily be demonized as Other, as its very alienness places it outside the political system *from the outset*. But a domestic political paranoid or extremist is harder to position as Other given that they are "one of us." Domestic extremists are considered too close to, yet alienated from, normal political processes. They resemble the people, while at the same time threatening to *become* the people. Whereas the xenophobic discourse focused on *infiltration* (the external masquerades as internal, They pretend to be Us), these new conceptions stress *division* (the internal is split, the middle is replicated in extremis, some of Us menacingly resemble the rest of Us). One can begin to see how a panic forms around this boundary confusion and the camouflaged indeterminacy of the new extremism.

More recent problematizations of the paranoid style also articulate it to populism, but with new inflections. In the late 1990s, the term *conspiracism* began to gain currency (see Daniel Pipes, 1997). Conspiracism sheds some of the psychological connotations of a term like paranoia in favor of a pejorative link to political ideas and practices (Marxism, fascism) and dangerous sentiments (racism, anti-Semitism). Conspiracism is at times used interchangeably with the paranoid style (including Pipes, 1997). The paranoid style as conspiracism is linked to four developments:

1. new motivations (hate speech, resentful backlashes, histories of oppression)
2. new targets (globalization, new surveillance technologies),
3. new kinds of groups (African Americans who believe that AIDS and the crack epidemic are genocidal strategies against them, and militia organizations who fear a New World Order enough to take up arms in defense), and
4. new visibility in popular culture (Hollywood films, TV shows, magazines, websites, books). (Pipes, 1997, p. 17)

Conspiracy panic texts that focus on populism often highlight the fact that conspiracism permeates both the Left and the Right. In the 1960s studies (including Hofstadter, Lipset and Raab, and the Overstreets), the paranoid style is deemed to be primarily a right-wing phenomenon, while the Left is merely susceptible to it. The more recent analyses of both political paranoia and extremism stress a bipolar condition. Perhaps most famously captured in Michael Kelly's (1995) term *fusion paranoia*, the convergence of political wings in the conspiracy theory milieu marks the research of the 1990s (Nina J. Easton, 1995). George and Wilcox (1996) chronicle this tendency and signal it in their book's title, *American Extremists: Militias, Supremacists, Klansmen, Communists and Others*, and Pipes (1997) analyzes it systematically (especially pp. 154–170).[4]

I will briefly note here that there is a more interesting fusion of Left and Right going on, one at the level of the problematizations themselves. When it came to panics over the militia movement, concern about conspiracism produced strange bedfellows, positioning Left/liberal commentators with the state in calling for stricter regulations and increased surveillance powers. But this is not that unusual if one recognizes that the "opposition" shares the same form of thought, or problematization. I explore this convergence of Left and Right in conspiracy panics, and ultimately in contemporary political rationality, in chapters 4 and 5.

The concern over "fusion paranoia" is not primarily about the Left/Right binary, however, but about center/margins, or mainstream/fringes. The problem is not in a given conspiracy theory's political affiliation, but rather in the moment when elements gravitate from the mainstream to the extreme *at either end*, and then return to infiltrate and seduce that mainstream. The anxiety is over "popular confusion," a troubled political spectrum, a once-legitimate categorizing system disrupted (Carpenter, 1964, p. 1). In general, this scenario of destabilization represents unruly political populism that requires innovative governing strategies. As mentioned above, the domesticity of the paranoid style and extremism requires an incessant *division*—conceptualizing paranoia by distinguishing it from the mainstream. It is this internal, self-reflexive sorting procedure to which I now turn, examining in some detail the definitions, themes, and characteristics assigned to the paranoid style, political paranoia, and conspiracism.

The Exaggerated Masquerade: Problematizing a Style of Thought

Hofstadter, as I have discussed, notes that political paranoids are not clinically deranged: it is the very "use of the mode by more or less normal people that makes it significant" (p. 4). The paranoid style can be isolated as an object of thought, but its difference is one of degree not kind. Differentiated by its form, the paranoid style remains close enough to commonsensical ideas as to be able to house their contents and *de-form* them.

Numerous other commentators take up this proximity. For the Overstreets (1964), extremism is an "nth degree *exaggeration* of traits common among us in gradations" (p. 20, italics added). For George and Wilcox (1997), the "difference between the average person and the political extremist is largely one of degree and not of kind" (p. 9). Following this line of thought, Robert Robins and Jerrold Post (1997) describe the paranoid as "not having fully departed the world of reality. Rather, the paranoid clings to a part of that world . . . it is a pathological *exaggeration* . . . a *form of adaptation gone wrong*" (p. 19, italics added). The political paranoid is "perfectly normal except for delusions of conspiracy and victimization" (p. 4). Hofstadter concurs with this when he defines the paranoid style in relation to normally functioning rationality: the paranoid style can be seen as an "imitation of the enemy. . . . It is nothing if not coherent [and] intensely rationalistic" (pp. 32, 36). What emerges again and again in these texts is the theme that political paranoia is a hyperbolic mimic of mainstream thought.

In addition, these problematizers warn that this mimicry can return to the mainstream and *masquerade* as legitimate. According to the Overstreets, it is the "nature of extremism to go in for protective coloration. It disguises itself as moderate" (p. 15). This imitation is more pernicious than "blatantly delusional thinking" since it is "far more dangerous . . . when the *delusional thinking is borderline* and consequently not easily recognized" (Robins & Post, pp. 19–22; italics added). We again find ourselves at the boundary between the noid and the paranoid: not noid/paranoid, but noid/noid, where the / is the para.

Robins and Post provide an example of this masquerade, comparing two people they encounter on a Washington D.C. intersection handing out pamphlets (pp. 20–22). On one corner, a follower of Lyndon Larouche distributes literature on an international conspiracy. On the other, a man wearing a sandwich board warns about the evils of government mind control. The latter is easily recognizable as a delusional paranoid, while the former pretends to be a legitimate political actor. Once again, the problem of differentiation is posed: the paranoid style is not essentially different from the normal, but is both a fantastic exaggeration of it (in its form) and a simulation (in its masked appearance).

Pipes (1997) also has much to say about this mimicry. In the chapter "House of Mirrors" he borrows a definition of the paranoid style as the "secret vice of the rational mind" and argues that it is seductive because it takes the form of "pseudoscholarship" (p. 34). The entire chapter addresses the "difficulty in distinguishing the real from the imaginary" and how it is "maddeningly difficult to keep [conspiracism] in focus" (p. 20). Pipes begins to perform a sorting operation upon the problem: "Reader and author alike need markers to distinguish the solid ground of fact from the swamp of fantasy, for it is this insidiousness that permits conspiracism to spread from the extremes to the mainstream" (p. 38).

Pipes embodies the normal or noid style of thought, one that seeks division between the rational and its simulated excess but does not concern itself with distinguishing true from false (that is to say, with falsifying conspiracy theories). To do so would place conspiracy narratives squarely within the regime of truth (in the sense that they *could be* true or false). To paraphrase a line from scientific dismissals of pseudoscience, conspiracy narratives are "not even false" (Hitchens, 2005).[5] The goal, rather, is to differentiate a style of thought from the very style that *composes* the regime of truth (the rational style that *can* distinguish true from false).

Most significantly, this differentiation is difficult to accomplish because the paranoid style is in seductive proximity to the noid style—a deformation, an excessive mimicry, a phantasmic exaggeration of the ordinary. This exaggeration is akin to what Gilles Deleuze (1990c) calls the "unjust pretender." Unlike the copy (which even if it fails to resemble the model is a just pretender), the simulation operates without reference to the model:

> It is built upon dissimilarity, implying essential perversion or deviation. . . . That to which they pretend, they pretend to underhandedly, under cover of an aggression, an insinuation, a subversion, "against the father" and without passing through the Idea. Theirs is an unfounded pretension. (256–257)

That is, the simulation does not resemble, it dissembles, it is an image without resemblance.

Metaphysical thought, in Deleuze's reading, has as its mission "to distinguish the true pretender from the false one" in order to assure the "triumph of the copies over simulacra, of . . . keeping [simulacra] completely submerged, preventing them from . . . 'insinuating themselves' everywhere" (pp. 254, 247). And why does the simulacra need to be detected and domesticated? The simulacra "places in question the very notation of copy and model" (p. 256). It "harbors a positive power which denies *the original and the copy, the model and the reproduction*. . . . The same and similar no longer have an essence except as *simulated*" (p. 262, italics original).

What the simulation does is reveal the sorting procedure itself to be simulated (as an unfounded and unfixed activity). This is the threat to a regime whose authority is founded on these distinctions (i.e., true/false, but more importantly, inside/outside true). Banishing the simulation would thus erase the *simulatedness* of the regime, because simulation would be defined as an activity that is "other" to the regime.

This concept of simulacra gives us a better sense of conspiracy panics' problematizations of political paranoia as a style of thought. The copy, or the just pretender, can be contained within the mainstream regime of politics and truth. It is a false knowledge that can be debunked through the official procedures of distinguishing truth from falsity.[6] The model is preserved and even invigorated as the copy is still measured up against it (as failure). But paranoia, whose proximity and ability to mimic normal modes is its precise threat, is "not even false." It has no measure—it suspects even the system that would measure. And this proximate masquerade becomes acute when we examine these panics within liberal political rationality.

The etymology of the term *paranoia* even speaks to this characteristic. From the Greek *para* and *nous*, paranoia is defined as *beyond* or *beside* the mind. It is out there, yet adjacent to here. It resembles the noid, while at the same time threatening to *become* the noid. This nearness spurs the conspiracy panics and the problematizations it engenders.

LIBERALISM'S EXAGGERATION

Skepticism

In the accounts above, what is it precisely that gets hyperbolized in the paranoid style? Seymour Lipset and Earl Raab (1970) locate a paradox in political extremism: "The same values and moral commitments that have been the constant strength of our democratic life (individualism, antistatism, egalitarianism) . . . provide the substance of extremist threats to that democratic life" (p. 30). According to these researchers, "extremist movements have been powerfully spawned by the same American characteristics that finally reject them" (p. 30). Lipset and Raab are content to leave this shared set of characteristics as a "paradox" and a curious contradiction.

According to Robert Robins and Jerrold Post the "primary distortion is of the necessary suspiciousness in American politics," an "exaggeration of the tried political style of alert suspicion" (pp. 5, 18). They go on to claim that political paranoia "distorts conventional and useful responses to danger. . . . It is a malignant distortion of an otherwise adaptive response, a useful mode of behavior that has misfired, a dangerous and destructive parody of prudent coping behavior" (p. 18). Robins and Post, in the panic rhetoric over mimicry, assert that what is at stake is the preservation of a particular degree of skepticism. Healthy political suspicion must be saved from its parodic deformers who threaten to take it away to the extremes.

For Daniel Pipes (1997), this excess reaches its pinnacle in the conspiracist statement "appearances deceive," in which even "the most benign governments in human experience (the British and the American) [are turned] into the most terrible" (p. 48). What emerges from his pages is the sense that skepticism turns into suspicion, into a lack of trust in the basic integrity of Western governing.[7] Pipes argues that it is ironically those nations "with a substantial body of opinion that suspects . . . its own government [which are] most targeted by conspiracism" (p. 174). But this is more than irony—it returns us to the logic of exaggeration, excess, and simulation at the heart of conspiracy panics.

In a twist on Pipes's assessment of the Americanness of conspiracism, Jodi Dean (2000b) argues that conspiracy thinking was present as a foundational suspicion that produced America as a nation and people. During the revolutionary phase, conspiracy theories were the lingua franca for understanding tyrannical political machinations. Only later, with the postrevolutionary rise of consensus politics and pluralist values did conspiracy narratives become associated with irrationality and extremism. In order to expand Dean's assessment, we can explore the centrality and persistence of skepticism within liberal modes of governance, especially as it is modified in accordance with limits and excess.

The Moderate Ethos of Self-Reflection

Political suspicion is a component of liberalism's ethos of permanent self-criticism. To be free in liberal governance one must employ a vigorous skepticism upon governmental activities. According to Michel Foucault, liberalism is not a theory or an ideology, but "a practice . . . regulating itself by means of a sustained reflection" (Foucault, 1997a, p. 74). Its principle of reflection is that "one always governs too much, or, at any rate, one always must suspect that one governs too much. Governing should not be exercised without a 'critique'" (p. 74). Liberalism is "a tool for criticizing reality," and "a form of critical reflection on governmental practice" (pp. 75, 77). It is a "constant reflection on and criticism of what is. Its internal regulative principle is seen as the need to maintain a suspicious vigilance over government so as to check its permanent tendency to exceed its brief in relation to what determines both its necessity and limits—society" (Burchell, 1991, p. 143). As a mode of governing defined around self-reflection, liberalism takes its own activity and its limits as objects of concern. Liberalism has an ingenious suppleness because of this, as it allows for a self-modification through perpetual self-problematization.

And how does it do so? At least since John Locke, governmentalized freedom has been linked to the "use of Reason" (Barry Hindess, 1996, p. 129). Liberalism is concerned to ensure that people's public and private behavior will be conducted according to appropriate standards of civility, reason, and orderliness, without state regulation (Cruikshank, 1999; Gordon, 1991). In Hindess's view, developing "appropriate habits of thought and behavior" is crucial to liberalism's "indirect regulation" (pp. 129–130). This political subject would become responsible through reasoning, especially through responsible reasoning. And via this self-reflexive subjectification, the political actor locates its source and parameters for freedom. Liberal political rationality thus signifies both a form of governing (governing at a distance, indirect regulation) and its content (a subjectification that relies on the exercise of reason and thought).

In his classic work *The Public Philosophy*, Walter Lippman (1955) explicitly acknowledges this double meaning, claiming that "a rational order is not only an attractive and a sublime conception but . . . a necessary assumption in the government of large and heterogeneous states" (p. 83). Reason does not transcend its material conditions, but is immanent to the mode of governance that finds it useful. This is a specifically liberal reason, highlighting procedural matters in a pluralistic society: "It is not possible to reject this faith in the efficacy of reason and at the same time to believe that communities of men enjoying freedom could govern themselves successfully" (p. 102–103).

The liberal arrangement of freedom and rationality also entails a certain relation to a regime of truth. According to governmentality studies scholar Nikolas Rose (1999), the mechanisms of "the conduct of conduct that have taken shape in the West, and those strategies that contest them, are ineluctably drawn to rationalize themselves according to a value of truth" (p. 24). Conducting oneself as a citizen is thus not simply a behavioral matter; it requires an active and persistent self-problematization, one that is operable only through a certain style of thought (a relationship between truth and reason). Self-criticism is not just tolerated—it is a motor of liberalism's flexibility, "polymorphism and its recurrences" (Foucault, 1997a, p. 75).

A *reasonable* skepticism is thus a crucial element in liberalism's mode of governing. But an exaggerated and deformed one can threaten the very political structure that requires critical reflection. Robins and Post's "Save Our Skepticism" campaign, as a type of conspiracy panic, calls for a *moderate* suspicion, one well within the boundaries of a regime of truth. It is this set of acceptable limits for skepticism (and thereby dissent) that is at stake in these problematizations (the paranoid style, political paranoia, and conspiracism) within liberal political rationality.

Reason, the Regime of Truth, and the Marketplace of Ideas

For Lipset and Raab (1970), it is "an American article of faith that because of the ultimate efficacy of human reason, error is legitimate and tolerable. A direct attack on the popular properties of human reason has never been politically possible in America" (p. 6). Extremism, as a politics of unreason, is precisely defined as this attack on reason. Lipset and Raab here are also staking a claim on a *popular rationality* (the widespread properties of human reason), which may be different from a *populist* rationality (in Foucault's sense of subjugated knowledges being popular knowledges). The governmental link between rationality and dissent was forged even before the terms *extremism* and *conspiracism* were coined. In a section of The Public Philosophy titled "The Limits of Dissent," Walter Lippman (1955) argues that the "borderline between sedition and radical reform is between the denial and the acceptance of the principle of the public philosophy: that we live in a rational order in which by sincere inquiry and rational debate we can distinguish the true and the false" (p. 102).

Conspiracy theories refuse to recognize "error" and instead ascribe evil intentions to political actors (Lipset & Raab, pp. 7, 14). Through their hypersuspicion, conspiracy theories attack the liberal model of reason as they are "designed to legitimate the closing down of the ideational market place" (p. 17). Their tactics employ "not the usual methods of political give-and-take, but an all out crusade" (Hofstadter, 29). Extremism is "antipluralism" (Lipset & Raab, p. 6), a monism in which "paranoids do not have adversaries or rivals or opponents; they have enemies" (Robins & Post, p. 5). In a sense, the loyal opposition has become alienated and agitational: they "share a contempt for rational political discussion and constitutional legal solutions" (in this quote, the characteristic is ascribed to 1960s campus leftists). (Lipset & Raab, p. 12).

In these texts we can see a close connection forged between political action and rationality: Extremism as such is not violent action or conflict with particular values (individualism, freedom, or equality). Rather, extremism is the very refusal to subscribe to a faith in reason, to the procedures for distinguishing truth from error in opinion, and to the marketplace of ideas. Since politics is characterized as rational contest and negotiation toward consensus, Lipset and Raab can call extremism and conspiracy theories "antipolitics" (pp. 12–17). Conspiracy theories go "beyond the limits of the normative procedures which define the democratic political process" yet those procedures are being defined by the problematizers (p. 5).

It should be apparent here that conspiracy panics are not merely about ideas. They involve, at their heart, the procedures of governing. As Jodi Dean (2000b) notes, pluralist conceptions need to shore up their standing via this marketplace and its gatekeepers. In fact, as the State Department's Strategy for Combating Terrorism makes clear, defeating terrorism involves bolstering consensus: "In place of a culture of conspiracy and misinformation, democracy offers freedom of speech, independent media, and the marketplace of ideas, which can expose and discredit falsehoods, prejudices, and dishonest propaganda." The desire to contest the very process of contestation removes conspiracists from the field of politics and into the realm of pure threat.

Extremism is positioned as that which lies beyond the limits of the regime, yet as that which subverts the regime. Once again the issue of proximity is paramount. The other to reasonable politics is never just outside— it is at the borders, simulating and blurring the lines; it is a para-site. The panic over boundaries and viral intruders/mimics resonates well with what some have called the more pervasive "security culture" (Crandall & Armitage, 2005; Knight, 2001).

The problem is not that extremists do not share a consensual truth, but that they do not subscribe to the *regime* of political truth, where sorting truth from error is the required procedure in the marketplace of ideas. This is not about a consensus in outcome (agreement, uniformity in opinion) but consent to the rules, procedures, and forms of dissent and difference.

While liberalism's style of thought is an ethos of self-criticism, it only allows a moderate kind, one that will dissent within the regime of truth. There are thus limits to liberal self-critique and on the problematization of the political sphere. In the experts' reflections, discussing the metamarketplace (the contest over the rationale of governing procedures) is not allowable— the sphere is apolitical. Once the regime of truth is taken as an object of dissent, it automatically places the critique in extremis, as unreasonable. Reason, as an "American article of faith," is liberalism's procedural technique (i.e., the regime of truth operates through reason) *and* its authorizing force (i.e., the regime of truth itself is reasonable). Reason becomes the operation guiding the *immanence* of rule where the effective performance of a rule becomes its immanent justification (Hardt & Negri, 2000).

The conspiracy panic problematizations agree that the self-critique that defines liberalism has gone awry. Political paranoia's skepticism has gone "too far"; it is an unjust pretender. The paranoid style subverts faith in the marketplace of ideas, in the link between freedom and rationality, and in the regime of truth itself. Liberal self-problematization has hypertrophied; the turn to the self has exceeded the kind of rationality required to make responsible turnings. Only a reasonable criticism is allowable, only a moderate form of modulation.

REASONABLE RESPONSES

Once this excess of skepticism has been problematized, what responses are proposed? What is interesting in all of these conspiracy panic texts, from Hofstadter to Pipes, is the fact that coercive measures (punishment, detention, repressive measures against speech) are actively disavowed. Mark Fenster (1999) argues that the pathological model of Hofstadter and his inheritors easily leads to a repressive response. However, these analyses explicitly argue that repression should not be carried out upon the paranoid style.[8] Two reasons are given to avoid these harsh measures.

The first is tactical, as coercion "would split society even further, and thereby give extremism further draw" (Overstreet & Overstreet, 1964, p. 21). Suppressing conspiracism would create a scenario where the "paranoid person feels cast out by society, which increases their paranoia" (Robins & Post, 1997, p. 40). If "alienation from normal political processes" is a reason why paranoia flourishes, then direct suppression would only inflame the problem (Hofstadter, 1967, p. 39).

The second reservation against repressive techniques is, at first glance, less about strategy than it is about moral national integrity. Brute censorship, according to the Overstreets (1964), only happens "in totalitarian systems . . . there is an obligation to defend extremism's constitutional rights, so we cannot use coercion"; prohibition is "un-American" (p. 21). And for George and Wilcox, there is a "certain danger in the notion that we should be 'intolerant of intolerance' " (p. 10). But this is indeed a matter of strategic efficacy, as the "net effect of domestic extremism has been negligible [while] the net effect of attempts to exterminate it have been quite telling, a legacy that haunts us to this day" (p. 48). Strategies of dissent management must, thereby, be more supple and differentiated than simple repression. This is not surprising, since in a liberal art of governing "political rationality . . . replaces violence as a mode of governance" (Wendy Brown, 1998, p. 43). Given these reasons, two responses are suggested.

The First Response. One tactic advocated is to refold the extremists into the mainstream: "[We are] not trying to ostracize or liquidate extremists—we want to bring them to the center" (Overstreet & Overstreet, p. 292). George and Wilcox define their work not as an attempt "to provide a rationale for persecuting or doing away with certain 'extremists' . . . [but] to provide understanding of a human problem" (p. 9). A number of these problematizations refer to the usefulness of this "understanding," from the detrimental effects of pathologization (Sargent, 1995; George & Wilcox, 1996) to the reinvigoration of the center that the challenge of extremism provides (Gardner, 1997).

This domestication would entail reaffirming a proper form of "Americanism" at the social and political level. Stabilizing forces are not in operation for society as a whole as they are for the party coalitions, ideology, and rhetoric of the American political system (Lipset & Raab, p. 508). Renewal would take place at the grassroots level, in community activism (Overstreet & Overstreet, pp. 282–287). These local and partial experiments include refamiliarizing citizens with the founding American political tracts that elaborate the "principles of government" (Carpenter, p. 203). Other suggestions include becoming active in the political process, reading the news to get acquainted with problems of the day, participating in local hearings, reaffirming religious foundations, and finally, "knowing" your enemy (Carpenter, pp. 203–208). In a way, these 1960s suggestions prefigure the 1990s calls for increasing civil society cooperation and bolstering community participation (examined in chapter 2).

Along with this rejuvenation of micropatriotism, there are calls for a macro political flexibilization. This means creating responsive institutions and a malleable political structure to absorb extremist movements (e.g., preserving the two-party system to prevent them from organizing into a third party or some other broad-based organization) (Lipset & Raab, pp. 503–504). It would also mean ensuring that the political system is "conducive to normative change—and to the orderly discussion, dissent, and conflict which are attendant on normative change" (p. 504). The key is to rejuvenate proper forms of political reason. Make room for dissent: not to eliminate it altogether in favor of consensus, but provide the authoritative framework by which to dissent and to recognize proper dissent (that is, within pluralist negotiation).[9] At the same time, the political system must continue "ruling out direct challenges to legitimacy" (p. 504).

In addition, a key technique that would ward off the dangers of "counterextremism" is the formation of the "democratic personality" (George & Wilcox, pp. 88–91). Echoes of Lasswell's fusion of politics and psychology can be heard here, as fostering a "nonextremist" personality would "show a better way" to extremists and their potential seductees (p. 91). The objective here would be to induce higher "levels of democratic restraint," primarily through education, to produce "cadres of opposition to undemocratic excess"

(Lipset & Raab, p. 507). We once again see preventive rationality at work here. If the political immune system is bolstered and vigilant attention paid to potential symptoms of deviance, the styles of thought leading to extremist behavior can be modified in advance of it engendering a crisis.

In sum, this first strategy, incorporation, seeks to bring the alienated back into the fold as a way of reinvigorating the center. The management of dissent is accomplished through making the social and political body capable of absorbing challenges and by reinvigorating the sectors characterized as vulnerable. Through a strengthening of national patriotism, a revitalization of education, and flexibilization of the political structure, extremists can find a space of action within the center, *but no longer as extremists.* By definition, extremism is a rejection of that marketplace, of the center, and of the structure that attempts absorption. Thus, the attempts to tame extremism as a form of "error" cannot exhaust the possible responses to the paranoid style.

The Second Response. There is a more prevailing nonrepressive tactic in these texts. Calling for similar techniques (bolstering of education, rejuvenation of citizenship through grassroots activity and refamiliarization with America's foundational political tracts), this response strengthens the norm by incessantly positioning the dissenter as an alien, as not one of us. Rather than bringing the outsider back into the mainstream, this conceptual strategy seeks to turn the domestic dissenter *into* an outsider, and keep it at bay. Rather than making extremism disappear (via prohibition or absorption) it is made to appear incessantly as "not-Us." Problematization is a production of visibility, a perpetual visibility that allows a continuous renewal of judgment in the name of the mainstream (the proper American). We have shifted tactics from making dissent invisible (the totalitarian strategy) to making it visible, but only as a spectacular scapegoat.

We can see this at work in the 1995 congressional hearings on militia activity. Mark Fenster succinctly and persuasively argues that the "metaphors of exposure and release" that framed the hearings comprised a rhetoric of pathology (pp. 22–51). In this case, the scapegoat is made to appear in a public, official forum in order to "clear the air" and prevent this kind of thought and activity from festering in the dark. In a conjoining of the aural and the ocular, this "hearing" makes the unknown "visible," working as an immunizing agent and antidote to the unclean and disease-ridden political body. The scapegoating of domestic dissent is a ritual whose goal is much like the one described by James Frazer when he describes tribal scapegoating: to secure a regime's integrity by "cleansing the ills that are infecting a people" (1922, p. 666). Ramifications of this ritual, according to Fenster, limit the responses to populism to "strategies of containment, legislative enactments, surveillance, and policing" (p. 23). In other words, pathologization and scapegoating are not the same as direct repression: they make a problem visible in order to deploy other more nuanced strategies of neutralization.

Focusing on militias by clearing the air seeks to detect a national problem before it emerges fully blown. While easily defined as extremist, their populism was another matter. Panic over patriot populism had to walk a fine line. On the one side, the militias had to be widespread enough to constitute an actual threat. On the other side, they could not be so extensive as to be truly popular. Like a viral circulation on the verge of becoming a mature pandemic, militias had to be prevented from becoming a full-blown populist movement. The militia hearings, the most public version of this preventive rationality, sought to cut off and isolate the viral spread of the militia movement. Distinguishing it from the "public" (for instance in myriad appeals by Arlen Specter) took a potential Us-versus-Them populism and rerouted it as a consensus We who stand in judgment of a minority outsider group. Turning the militia movement from potentially popular to discursively antipublic, official problematizers (having been scolded for not detecting this "gathering storm" before the Oklahoma City bombing) now led the conspiracy panic charge with a coordinated, bipartisan, institutional preventive action.

This preventive rationality should remind us of Lasswell's writing. An irrational dissenter is not confronted with a coherent rationality (as logical argumentation). A "return to common sense" is more than an acceptance of dominant ideas or a consent to authorities. Daniel Pipes (1997) argues: "Sound logic and superior leadership do not of their own appear sufficient to make the paranoid style fade away; more profound changes need to take place . . . *a thorough reevaluation of self*, plus fundamental changes in *thinking processes* and social perception" (pp. 184–185, italics added). The influence of Lasswell here is clear. New subjects are needed, ones that can operate reasonably on their own after being trained in proper styles of self-reflection. There is an important difference from Lasswell, however. The "social self-observatories" he prescribed are no longer simply in the hands of experts—they now become every citizen's duty.

Governing at a distance, while requiring expertise to prescribe new techniques, cannot simply rely on it. These conspiracy panic texts are attempting to fuse reason and politics in a way that promotes a liberal technology of citizen subjectification. Reason must become part of the *ethos* of the self, a work of the self on the self. The nonrepressive responses to conspiracism are not just about making people reasonable, but making reason a *people's enterprise.*

PROBLEMATIZATING AS A STYLE OF THOUGHT

Conspiracy panic experts define conspiracy theories as a style of thought, but do so as a way of disseminating their *own* style of thought as a model. What these problematizing texts offer is not so much a set of beliefs that require agreement, or consent to their authors' authority. These texts do not just promote a certain value (reason) over its deviant (paranoia). They do not demand the reader's identification with a classificatory scheme. Rather, these problematizations offer up their *own* styles of thought. They display the very style of thought that the readers, as citizens, should take up when they encounter political paranoia. These are "practical" texts, "functional devices that would enable individuals to question their own conduct, to watch over and give shape to it, and to shape themselves as ethical subjects" (Foucault, 1985, pp. 12–13). It just so happens that the reason-training manuals here take as their object the very style of thought needed to be a proper citizen. The practical texts provide prescription through example, presented as scholarly description. These are turns to thought, where thought works on thought to provide a manual for turning.

Even more, these styles are preventive; designed to encourage individuals to *detect* and *identify* political paranoia, to sort out the noid from the paranoid. To be reasonable does not just mean identifying with the "reason" side of the binary. The ability to discriminate between reason and political paranoia *is itself the rational act*. The capacity to differentiate "us" from "them" is a rational capacity, and its decentralized enactment makes it part of a political rationality. What we have here is a self-justifying performance, since proper turns are performed at the very moment the paranoid style is detected. Problematizing style is itself a style of problematization.

And what is this official style of the conspiracy panics? As noted earlier, this style involves a serious devotion to differentiation, in which false pretenders and excessive mimics can be distinguished from proper moderate reasoning. Pipes (1997) offers "tools . . . to identify conspiracy theories" that include "common sense, a knowledge of history, and the ability to recognize distinct patterns of conspiracism" (p. 38). It is crucial that he defines these as tools, rather than conceptually asserting them as expert truth-claims, as this sorting procedure is a "subjective process" (p. 37). What kind of subject are we talking about here? The goal is not a subject's obedience or agreement, but the willing and reasonable choice to embrace the noid style as one's own. Sorting out is a procedure—an invitation to take up a style of thought as a practice of the self on self, to adopt it as an ethos.

Producing a subject is not done once and for all. In an update of Lasswell for a more decentralized era, Pipes locates personality-type detection (and the social observatories) within the processes of subjectivation; that is, within the self. The paranoid style "manages to insinuate itself in the most alert and intelligent minds, so excluding it amounts to a *perpetual struggle*, one in which the reader is invited to join" (Pipes, p. 49, italics added). Like the incessant need to distinguish and expel the simulation, the sorting mechanism needs persistent renewal. The political subject needs continuous modification; prevention never ends. Pipes is essentially encouraging, through himself as example, a liberal technology of subjectification, where permanent self-criticism is necessary for governing through freedom. It is one in which subjects turn on themselves properly, with a modicum of rationality that will turn *against* liberal rationality's excesses.

The conspiracy panic experts problematize conspiracism, but in order for subjects (as citizens) to perpetually perform their own problematizations. Thus, these training manuals present a new set of questions for consent. These manuals for thought prescribe an object to be problematized, but what makes *this* particular turning appealing, as opposed to other kinds (even paranoid ones)? In other words, what makes these positive mechanisms of ethical formation stick? Can the authority of these problematizations and prescriptions be "consented" to? Perhaps consent, rather than being a deliberative rational submission, can be defined as an "attachment," an affirmation of a technology of subjectification (Butler, 1997, p. 102).[10]

Consent, on the one hand, to the parameters of dissent, to the distribution of proper political positions and forms (moderation). Consent, as well, to the regime of truth that underpins this distribution. Consent, finally, to the particular technologies of subjectification which, in their incessant turning upon the self to differentiate and upon others to monitor, produce those parameters and rejuvenate that regime. To put it another way, the goal of scapegoating the paranoid is consent to the very ritual of scapegoating.

CONCLUSION

This chapter has worked through a number of texts to examine how the problematization of conspiracy theories is linked to conceptions of politics and reason. These texts are a series of meditations that link political forces to styles of thought. In these conspiracy panic works, we can see an intertwining of two themes or problems: first, a pathological style of thought (outside the boundaries of the regime of truth), and second, an extremism in political activity (beyond the pale of normal political discourse).

Through a transposition of a clinical term to the field of politics, "paranoia" and "extremism" are conceptually fused into new intelligible objects: the paranoid style, political paranoia, and conspiracism. Once this object is given comprehensibility, pronouncements are made upon the possible effects of this phenomenon and remedies are prescribed.

Through the work of experts, a style of thought is made visible, intelligible, and amenable to intervention as a means of moderating dissent and securing consent in contemporary liberalism. And what is peculiar to this relationship between liberal governance and thought is that the object of problematizations (conspiracism) is an exaggeration of liberalism's own ethos of skepticism and self-problematization.

The texts examined here are not the only experts involved in the conceptual production of political paranoia. These include academic researchers, "independent" scholars, journalists, citizen watchdog groups, public intellectuals, and private intelligence-gathering organizations. Their technical expertise in the fields of political psychology, sociology, political science, intelligence, history, current affairs, and cultural analysis are not directly tied to the State, but they can still serve the interests of good government.

More than labeling, these problematizations are productive, as they construct objects and subjects for intervention, for thought, and for governing. Problematizations do not just exist as abstract objects or ideas. They are conceptual practices, "a kind of intellectual machinery or apparatus," that makes the field of politics intelligible and "understandable" (Nikolas Rose, 1996, p. 42). Within liberal styles of governing, problematizations

> have an epistemological character, in that they embody particular conceptions of the objects to be governed—nation, population, economy, society, community—and the subjects to be governed—citizens, subjects, individuals. And they deploy a certain style of reasoning: language here understood as itself a set of "intellectual techniques" for rendering reality thinkable and practicable, and constituting domains that are amenable—or not amenable—to reformatory intervention. (p. 42)

At times, this technical knowledge gets linked with State practices. Conspiracy panics provide the common sense upon which more concrete activities (especially state activities) can justify themselves. With the appearance of conspiracy theory experts in the news media and at congressional hearings, the conceptualization of conspiracism as a threat can lead to explicit state intervention into dissent (regulation of hate speech, increased surveillance, the State Department's *National Strategy for Combating Terrorism*).

The perpetual project of taking conspiracy theories as a "problem" has two tasks: a hermeneutics of differentiation that sort out the simulation of rationality from the authentic and the copy, and avoids the seduction of the simulation; and a hermeneutics of suspicion that targets and expels those styles of thought that cannot be co-opted and redeemed. Because the paranoid style can potentially be taken up by anyone it is critical to focus on the proximate: domestic paranoia. As Paul Virilio (1990) argues: "The reasons for alarm . . . are not important. What is essential here is that, by turning first suspicion, then hatred, onto one's neighbor, one's comrade, they destroy any trace of social solidarity" (p. 80). This "administration of fear" around conspiracism promotes a mistrust among people, encouraging amateur and professional political psychologists to monitor other citizens as way of reaffirming investment in a commonsensical people (p. 76).

The cohesion of liberalism's political rationality comes with this injunction: to modulate thought and behavior with an eye toward limits and extremes. Responsible thought is an ethos as *modus*: a modulation through moderation, and vice versa.[14] Within this will-to-moderate, dissent itself is problematized, and reasonable skepticism and rational critique are promoted.

Skepticism is moderately enacted, mistrust is itself mistrusted, and distinguishing the authentic American from the pretenders becomes a citizen's duty. These are the conceptual conditions established by conspiracy panic experts, ones that find expression in a number of institutional and discursive problematizations. The next two chapters examine one of those discourses, professional journalism, as it participates in conspiracy panics in the service of making politics reasonable again.

2

POP GOES THE PROFESSION

Journalism, New Media Culture, and Populism

I n early 2004, the unlikely pairing of Bill Moyers and Jack Valenti took public action against a television station. Coinciding with the fortieth anniversary of JFK's assassination, *The History Channel* broadcast an 11-hour, multipart documentary called "The Men Who Killed Kennedy," exploring the various conspiracy accounts surrounding the event. What incensed the pair was one particular account, the one that implicated Lyndon B. Johnson in the planning and coverup (Moyers and Valenti were both Johnson aides). They demanded that the channel launch an independent investigation into the charges and provide a rebuttal to the claims.[1] Here we have a preeminent journalist and the head of the Motion Picture Association banding together against a televisual text. If we consider the History Channel's series to be a hybrid of sensationalist popular culture and investigative journalism, then it could have no more appropriate mirror adversaries than Valenti and Moyers. But this is just a recent example of a vociferous response against popular culture for telling historical and journalistic narratives, especially when they involve conspiracies.[2]

This chapter begins a two-part focus on one institutional support of conspiracy panics—professional journalism. We begin to explore the concrete enactment of a political rationality via conspiracy panics. Journalism has been decried in many sectors for being a vehicle for dominant ideology and elite interests. While this has produced many critical insights, I wish here to explore the specificity of journalism as a discourse with its own rules and articulations. This method is not done to exonerate professional journalism by seeking to circumscribe its operations within "internal" or occupational practices. Rather, it seeks to link its discursive properties to the broader spheres of a regime of truth and political rationality. First, a brief summary of journalism as a profession is in order.

JOURNALISM AS A PROFESSION

How rigidly can the category of "profession" be applied to the various practices that compose journalism?[3] While the definition of a profession remains a contested subject (see Larsen & Olsen, 1996; Abbot, 1988; Starr, 1982), considerable scholarship tracks the *effort* by journalism to constitute itself as a profession. Michael Schudson (1978) traces the historical emergence of "objectivity" as the journalistic ideal that gave journalism coherence as a profession. Schudson, examining Walter Lippman's writings, argues that this concept of "objectivity" was an attempt by journalism to professionalize itself through the scientific method. Training procedures, barriers to entry, and recognized credentialization processes were other features used by journalism—as by all other true professions—to achieve professional sovereignty or autonomy. This self-conscious process of "autonomization" consumed journalism's leaders in the first half of the 20th century.

Journalism also sought autonomy through the development of an ethical vision. Douglas Birkhead (1984) argues that journalism took on a moral and ethical component, since a "vision of responsibility could distinguish a profession even in an industry" (p. 10). But this project would never be fully realized, according to Birkhead. Instead, "journalism would be destined to a perennial state of semi-professionalism, to a continuous dynamics of emerging professionalism, to a faith in a 'spirit of professionalism,' rather than in the exact example of the established professions" (p. 11). It is this very flexibility, this incessant self-modification, I argue, that allows journalism to adapt to such new conditions as the Internet, and thus to persist.

As an ongoing exercise in professionalization, journalism engages in a form of self-reflection: it takes itself as an object of concern. These self-problematizations take place through a variety of mechanisms and institutional sites. Among the more formal mechanisms are professional associations (newspaper guilds, editors' societies, publishers' associations), conferences, codified guidelines for reporting and editing, journals and reviews, in-house manuals, popular books, trade publications, and pedagogical training programs in institutes and academic departments. More informal, everyday occupational practices also contribute to this professionalization. Among these are the daily ad hoc editorial decisions in any given newsroom, memos, self-regulated procedures of reportage, layout and design decisions, the exertion of publisher controls, unstated assumptions about the role of corporate advertisers, and debates about these matters on editorial pages.

At stake in these sites is the collective definition of journalism as a profession. As a profession, journalism seeks to develop a series of competencies, a technical expertise, a professional acumen (e.g., "news judgment"). The result is a set of relatively coherent practical techniques that come to constitute professional consistency (no matter how loose and alterable). Journalism *rationalizes* itself, giving itself cohesion, integrity, and a purposeful social function. These reflections may revolve around the profession's social and political role. They may also focus on its relationship to its readership, to citizens in general, and to government and corporate interests. Reflection is often organized around the First Amendment to the U.S. Constitution, creating an ongoing series of defenses of "freedom of the press" and free speech as a way of preserving the profession's autonomy. Regardless of the content of these reflections, this process of self-problematization itself acts as a *form* of professional self-constitution in which journalism gains autonomy through rationality (both as reasonable truth telling and as self-regulating institution).

In other words, professionalism is a discourse. It is an ensemble of statements and practices, one that produces both knowledge and subjects. This includes what has been called "professional ideology," which usually refers to the values espoused by the profession. But a discourse analysis also highlights how the profession defines and organizes itself around those values; in other words, the debates *about* professional ideology, identity, and integrity. It involves statements about professionalism as well as statements made within professional ideology.

To think of professional journalism as a discourse means addressing not only its internal components (its "occupational" elements) but how it relates to other discourses and institutions. Journalism has a tension over autonomy. The profession-as-discourse is not reducible to an instrument of other forces (as reproduction of ideology formed elsewhere, for instance). At the same time it is not simply an independent field or social force. This project argues that professional journalism circulates within a larger regime of truth and political rationality that prevents it from being merely an occupational force. This will become more evident as the profession's contribution to conspiracy panics becomes clearer. In addition, a discourse often produces an "other" or a foil. For our purposes here, this other will be defined as popular culture, or more accurately, the "popular."

Numerous critics lament the decline of journalism, especially insofar as it has sunk into the depths of popular culture. But these lamentations usually equate the popular with sensationalized style, tabloidization, oversimplification, and reliance on melodramatic narrative. Demonization of the popular is standard fare for hand wringing about the profession, but it is only a narrow definition. Here, I will be using the popular in three senses:

1. As pop culture in its commonsensical usage: widespread, commercialized culture (Hollywood).
2. In reference to *populism*: How does popular culture speak to, and in the name of, "the people"? This highlights the political character of the term, especially as populism refers to creating an Us/Them. (Fenster, 1999)
3. As the bottom-up uses and appropriations of technology: Here we can think of the history of the amateur (Douglas, 1987), grassroots,

and radical media (e.g., microradio/low-power FM, deep-dish TV, paper tiger, community access, radical press) (Kahn & Kellner, 2004; Dyer-Witheford, 1999; Juris, 2005), youth and technology, subcultural competences (Packer, 2002), tactical media and hacktivism (Lovink, 2003; McCaughey & Ayers, 2003), and blogging (Deuze, 2003).

This nuanced conception of the popular will be explored via three examples where professional journalism encounters conspiracy theories as a question of popular culture and political rationality. The following chapter will focus on one case, the 1996 controversy surrounding Gary Webb's "Dark Alliance" series and its relationship to the then-emerging World Wide Web. In this chapter, I examine two of professional journalism's conspiracy panics: over the Oliver Stone film *JFK* and over political extremism in the form of militia populism.

In one case, journalism tried to reestablish "cultural authority" against a popular cultural text (*JFK*) (Zelizer, 1992). In the other case, journalism attempted to revive its own relevance via an experiment in civic or public journalism. This notion of the "people" to be represented and integrated is counterposed to an extreme populism, via a problematization of conspiracy theories and popular media.

JFK

Twelve years before the History Channel flap, a more famous controversy erupted over the Kennedy assassination, professional journalists, and popular culture. Oliver Stone's film *JFK* came at an important moment for both journalism and conspiracy panics. Opening in 1991, it kicked off what was called the "conspiracy decade." Just as the Kennedy assassination inaugurated modern conspiratology, so its 1990s filmic representation, and the controversy it engendered, kicked off a conspiracy panic.[4]

Stone's film is a three-hour sprawling narrative anchored on protagonist attorney Jim Garrison's investigation of the Kennedy assassination via prosecution against one of its Dallas players, Clay Bertrand. Ultimately, with the narrative helper figure of shadowy insider Mr. X (Donald Sutherland), the film posits a conspiracy network composed of anti-Castro Cubans, paramilitary and government black ops agents, the mafia and Dallas police at the operational level, and a specific group of cold war hawks in the Pentagon and State Department along with big oil magnates who set the plan in motion. The film's aesthetic experimentations (mixing documentary footage with recreations with fictional scenes while playing with chromatics; rapid editing) were matched with an extensive research process, drawing on a number of conspiratological sources. In a rare move for a Hollywood film, Stone released an annotated and documented version of the screenplay. *JFK: The Book of the Film*, was published a year after the film's release, and included almost 100 articles and commentaries from the controversy surrounding the film.

The vehement criticism of the film began while it was still in production, with pieces appearing in the *Dallas Morning News, Washington Post*, and *Time* (Margolis, 1991; Lardner, 1991; Zoglin, 1991). Perhaps the most persistent and fervent attacks came from the *New York Times*, "ordinarily the grayest and calmest of newspapers, [which] devote[d] nearly thirty articles, op-eds, letters, notes, addenda, editorials and columns to the most savage attacks on the film" (Mankeiwicz, 1992, p. 187). As Frank Mankeiwicz asks, why would such a wide array of prominent journalists (including Tom Wicker, Dan Rather, George Will, Anthony Summers, George Lardner, Jr., David Ansen, among numerous others) "devote so much destructive energy to the task of turning Americans against this film," even against "the idea of the movie" (p. 187)? To begin answering this question, we can place the film in the lineage of Kennedy assassination conspiracy accounts.

JFK was only the latest contribution to the visual representations of the Kennedy assassination. On November 22, 1963, President John F. Kennedy was assassinated. This much is accepted, with little debate.[5] But this statement of fact opens a Pandora's box of conflicting accounts, competing visual narratives, and an ongoing research project that continues to this day.[6]

For the vast majority of these researchers, multiple shooters carried out the assassination—the very definition of a conspiracy. While the identity or affiliations of the assassins may have been disputed (candidates included the Mob, the CIA, the FBI, Castro's Cubans, anti-Castro Cubans, LBJ, the KGB, and the military-industrial complex), what was agreed upon was that the official version was, at best, sloppy research and, at worst, a cover-up. These alternative assassination theories, though marginalized by mainstream journalism, must nevertheless be considered *coconstitutive* of the JFK assassination event.

More than 40 years after the assassination, myriad texts, actors, and institutions continue to weave the fabric of the JFK event.[7] More than 2300 articles and books take up some aspect of the assassination and track its investigation (Simon, 1996, p. 7). Novels, songs, and theatrical productions narrativize the multiple accounts. Films (from the Zapruder film to Bruce Connor's mid-1960s avant-garde film *Report* to Oliver Stone's *JFK*), documentaries, and television dramas (e.g., *X-Files* and *Dark Skies*) give visual credence to these accounts. Ritualized media reenactments and digital simulations of the assassination keep the assassination in the public eye (e.g., *Court TV Forensic Files* 2004, *ABC News* Presents, 2003). In the assassination researcher community, anonymous and pseudonymous documents continue to circulate (e.g., *Nomenclature of an Assassination Cabal, The Gemstone File*). Even official bodies legitimate the alternative accounts: The House Select Committee on Assassinations in 1979 produced findings that support the multiple-shooter scenario, and opinion polls routinely find 70% of the U.S. populace doubting the official lone-gunman version. Public lectures, conferences, and tabloid newspapers reanimate the memory of the event as well as the debate over its definition. The Conspiracy Museum is located (where else?) in Dallas, Texas.

In sum, there have been plenty of popular cultural, visual depictions of various assassination accounts. So what made Oliver Stone's film so controversial? Its massive popularity was certainly a factor—a major Hollywood director using a large cast of big-name stars. Also, the film foregrounded the very techniques of representation employed. As Art Simon argues: "The commission critics . . . splintered the forces that mediated the event and the government's account of it. They elevated this process to a level at which its mechanisms of construction, its gaps, silences, contradictions, and representational strategies, became acutely visible" (p. 27). Conspiratologists contested the official account not just by positing another, "truer" account but by challenging the methods and forms of constructing that official narrative. The subjugated knowledges foreground the power relations infusing the production of assassination knowledge. Stone continues this provocation by mixing settled facts with speculation, documentary footage with recreations, black/white with color stock, forcing the viewer to confront their own trust in the visual. Critics argued that this mixture of visual images confused the viewer and was a breach of trust regarding the accurate visualization of events.

More damning than this fusion of aesthetic techniques was the claim that Stone had overstepped his bounds as a filmmaker. Even before its release, *JFK* initiated a vicious offensive by many journalists who argued that popular culture had no business treading on journalism's professional turf. It was journalism, not filmmaking, that was supposed to interpret news history and contribute to collective memory (for an analysis of this turf war see Zelizer, 1992, and Simon, 1996). The criticisms rested on a conception of a public whose formation depends on information flows from authoritative sources like historians and journalists. The "popular" sphere could be tolerated (as entertainment) as long as it did not cross into the realm of political history. The anti-*JFK* attacks were less about what the film had to say and more about its right to say it.

But the journalist critics' logic here is disingenuous. Popular renditions of the Kennedy assassination have been a frequent occurrence, whether as made-for-TV movies or recreated segments for news magazines, cable channel documentaries, or retrospectives. Popular culture had thus taken on political history without this kind of controversy. Had Oliver Stone produced a blockbuster that conveyed the Warren Commission's findings, there would likely have been no controversy.

More than just being pop culture, then, *JFK* was part of the lineage of conspiracy theorizing about the Kennedy assassination. Pundits hurled "conspiracy theory" epithets at Stone's work. We can say here that *JFK* was popular in two senses: It was a successful Hollywood film (the first meaning of popular); but it was also popular in the second sense laid out above—linked to an Us/Them populism.

Mark Fenster (1999) provides an excellent discussion of conspiracy theories in their articulation to political populism. For Fenster, "conspiracy theory is a nonnecessary element of populist movements, but is itself necessarily populist in its evocation of an unwitting and unwilling populace in thrall to the secretive machinations of power" (p. 63). It operates by "interpellating believers as 'the people' opposed to a relatively secret, elite 'power bloc'" (p. 67). Drawing from the work of Stuart Hall and Ernesto Laclau, Fenster identifies this populism as part of a counterhegemonic project: It is "not entirely a misrepresentation of a real antagonism, in that the very impreciseness of the term 'the people' enables it at times also to be used in liberation movements" (p. 64). Ultimately, Fenster closes down this openness when he categorically states that, when articulated to populism, conspiracy theory "is an ideological misrepresentation of power relations" whose "successful incorporation within a large populist movement would most likely occur in authoritarian or fascist regimes" (p. 67).

As a number of critics noted, JFK was a populist tale, one that ultimately divides the country into an innocent and manipulated democratic people (represented in their right to know by Jim Garrison and, politically, by their fallen king Kennedy) versus a corrupt and crypto-fascist elite (a shadowy network that includes Clay Shaw and David Ferrie) (Stone & Sklar, 1992). JFK's Hollywood delivery of a populist tale places it at the heart of an emerging crisis in journalism, one that cuts to its core mission as a profession.

In a well-known 1992 Rolling Stone article "Rock, Rap and Movies Bring You the News," Jon Katz announced a new turning point in journalism. Katz declared that a new generation of Americans was increasingly turning away from professional journalism (what he called "old news") as a source of knowledge. Young people were turning to popular culture (or "new news") to get information about society. The article was pivotal because it did not add to the litany of hand wringing over a "lack" of news or information gathering by young Americans. Instead, Katz simply asserts that there are alternative sources (without passing judgment on them). Katz lists three major cultural examples of new news: the TV show The Simpsons, the hip-hop group Public Enemy (a self-described "black CNN"), and Stone's JFK.

One can see why the film took on special significance for mainstream journalism. According to Barbie Zelizer (1992), JFK challenged the "cultural authority" of professional journalism. Which medium or social force will take the lead in telling stories of culture to itself? Journalism has positioned itself as this official storyteller. For Zelizer, the Kennedy assassination was a pivotal event for professional journalism's cultural authority, a moment of glory especially for broadcast journalism. JFK instigated a clash over cultural authority by challenging professional journalism's interpretation of one of its watershed events. To question the official account meant undermining journalism's privileged position (founded in part on that account). I would add that the film further inflamed journalists by implicating them and visual media in the assassination's official account (for example, showing the camera as weapon and the role of newspapers and *Time/Life* in disseminating cover stories).

But to understand the full significance of the *JFK* controversy, we need to push the analysis past the Kennedy assassination to the very origin of professional journalism, expanding the discussion from conspiracy panics to more general panics over popular irrationality.

THE POPULAR AND THE PUBLIC: PROFESSIONALIZATION AND RATIONALITY

A number of journalism scholars have written about the rise of professionalism in the field (Birkhead, 1984; Carey, 1988; Ewen, 1996; Schudson, 1978; Zelizer, 1992). This emergence, especially the attending value of objectivity, did not appear whole cloth. The press, newspapers, even journalism had obviously existed in the United States even before there was a United States. While reporting and newspapers has a long and rich tradition, professionalization emerges at a particular moment under certain circumstances.

Michael Schudson (1978) traces the historical emergence of "objectivity" as the journalistic ideal that gave journalism coherence as a profession. This ideal functioned to distinguish journalistic practices from their dependence on corporate interests and governmental influence, as well as from popular will. Objectivity also arose as a way of overcoming subjective biases and their undesirable public consequences (loss of faith by readers, general disintegration of democratic consent) (Schudson, pp. 156–158).

One of the leading public figures in the movement to professionalize the field was Walter Lippman, who furnished "the most sophisticated rationale for objectivity as an ideal in journalism" (Schudson, 1978):

> Lippman's prescription for the ills of journalism was science. He believed that the pursuit of scientific method in journalism would make the press not only more professional, but also more liberal and heroic. Liberalism meant openness, he wrote—remaining free in mind and action before changing circumstances without being paralyzed by skepticism. The person taking on the liberal spirit makes an effort "to remain clear and free of his irrational, his unexamined, his unacknowledged prejudgments." (pp. 154–155)

The process of professionalization, one that accelerated in the second decade of the 20th century and became fully institutionalized in the 1930s (Schudson, 1978), thus depended heavily on a liberal political rationality, one whose freedom of thought depended on a moderate skepticism.

Lippman's call for scientific objectivity as a unifying method didn't simply affirm rationality for its inherent noble qualities. Journalism sought a superior status to the "disreputable, tawdry model" of tabloid journalism (Haas & Steiner, 2002; Soderlund, 2005). Professionalism was a *response* to particular types of progressive-era news reporting, especially to what was then called "new journalism" (Soderlund, 2005). One component of this new journalism is what has come to be known as "yellow journalism." A term of derision, yellow journalism referred to the sensationalized styles of reporting (banner headlines and large typeface, increase in illustrations and color supplements, and an emphasis on salacious vice and crime stories, as well as simple human-interest tales). Most famously embodied in the competing New York papers Joseph Pulitzer's *New York World* and William Randolph Hearst's *New York Journal American*, yellow journalism was seen as pandering to the lowest instincts, the emotional and affective cheap thrills of scandals and scares—in a word, all those human characteristics considered "irrational."

At the same time, new journalism referred to another genre of newsmaking popular at the time, namely muckraking. Muckraking, as an early form of investigative reporting, focused on government corruption and corporate greed. It appeared in different media outlets than yellow journalism (magazines like *Cosmopolitan, McClure's, Munsey's Magazine*, novels), it came through freelance rather than staff writers and had a more consistent political bent (progressivism, even socialism). Some scholars examine the intertwinement of the two seemingly separate news genres (Olasky, 1991; Campbell, 2001). Yellow journalism's emphasis on the underdog and everyday life could be seen as a populist backbone to the more progressive muckraking, as a combination of "storytelling and reform" (Miraldi, 1990).

As Gretchen Soderlund (2002) notes, the rise of professionalization based on a rational-information versus irrational-sensation model is tied to a moral panic, specifically over white slavery. The sensationalist reports by muckrakers were depicted as the dregs of journalism. Professionalization cannot be said to arise on its own, with internally generated values. It emerges on the back of a demonization, or at least a polluted other. The irrational haunts journalism.

Walter Lippman's notion of the irrational was linked to the "crowd" or the "mass," common concepts of the time that can be read as synonyms for the "popular." Armand Mattelart notes that the rise of the social sciences was predicated on studying a new force in history, directly articulated in Gustav Le Bon's *The Crowd*. For many early social scientists, this subjectivity (forged via urbanization, massification, industrialization, and immigration) was an irrational one, susceptible to manipulation, impulsive group behavior, and violence. For Lippman, the crowd was an irrational subject most attracted to, and pandered to by, yellow journalism. This seething mass of impulses was the bane of democracy. For journalism to take on its new professional social function, a different subjectivity would need to be proposed.

Lippman finds this new subject in the "public." As opposed to the irrational, impetuous, and unpredictable crowd, the public was rational, contemplative, and deliberative. Unlike the bodily mass concentrated in the city streets (the image underpinning the concept of the mass), the public was spatially dispersed across a vast U.S. geography, lending itself to an easier abstraction (Anderson, 1991; Warner, 1990). For Lippman, the "people" was invisible, inaudible, and largely nonexistent. He acknowledged that the "public" is a mere phantom, but a necessary one (1955). There was no *materiality* to the public, since that came in the form of private self-interest. The "public interest," then, was what humans would choose if they saw clearly, thought rationally, and acted disinterestedly and benevolently. The public transcends any collective but is also out of that collective's reach and comprehension (Ewen, 1996).

How to manage this seeming contradiction—a public that depends on a collective but transcends it and is not accountable to it? Lippman's solution is simple: We need a sector of society trained in understanding the public, a strata of experts charged with *cultivating* a public through scientific methods. Much like Harold Lasswell's call for social observatories examined in chapter 1, Lippman argued that the United States needs social engineers and social scientists to do the work of shaping the public will and opinion. We can hear resonances here with Habermas's notion: the public as departicularization or transcendence above self-interest via the use of Reason. The major difference is that, unlike finding the public through a collective decision-making process, Lippman argues that people cannot be trusted to transcend their petty self-interest to form a public. People (paternalistically defined as "innocent bystanders") are deluged with propaganda and cannot be expected to have the time nor the resources to understand their conditions. How, Lippman asks, can they distinguish the public from the private-disguised-as-public?

The public, then, is a result of a series of debates among informed experts, agents charged with the special purpose of defining the public interest. The rest are interested spectators, who often need to be kept away from affairs of specialists. These masses can intervene when a maladjustment or crisis in governing occurs, but for the maintenance of norms, specialists are required. Professionalization (in a variety of social spheres) is thus crucial to a production of a public, yet, like other modern sciences, insulated from a wider population.

Journalism plays a major role here for Lippman. The lingering elements of yellow journalism during his career (he even worked for the *New York World* and is famous for reforming it) were depicted as part of the problem. Rather than helping inform people, it was hindering development of a public via its sensationalism, even propaganda. The other component of yellow journalism, muckraking, had also gone too far. Lippman opens his classic work *Drift and Mastery* with a meditation on the excesses of muckraking:

The sense of conspiracy and secret scheming which transpire is almost uncanny. "Big Business," and its ruthless tentacles, have become the material for
the feverish fantasy of illiterate thousands thrown out of kilter by the rack and
strain of modern life. It is possible to work yourself into a state where the world
seems a conspiracy and your daily going is beset with an alert and tingling
sense of labyrinthine evil. (p. 1)

In this early expression of a conspiracy panic, Lippman ties a news genre to
its detrimental effects (the "smear of suspicion") as well as to the appetites
that seek it out (p. 1). The dominant forms of journalism, for Lippman,
pandered to the basest impulses, keeping people tied to their irrationality.

On the other hand, journalism's potential professional form could provide the solution to this scenario. With a commitment to scientific objectivity as a method, journalism could take on the new social function of
representing and constructing a "public." They could become the social
engineers necessary for the public interest. Information, then, is the scientific
unit for the debate around the public. Journalists, supplying a forum and
channel for experts to formulate the public good, could thus contribute to
democracy. But the *demos* here is itself a phantom, an imagined community
in which the public is articulated to rationality and transcendence over
against the irrational people.

We can see this change in conceptions of the press' social role if we
think about the marketplace-of-ideas model of political knowledge. As John
Nerone (1995) argues, with professionalism the press moved away from its
partisan roots. The partisan press, in Lippman's formulation, would be seen
as self-interested, propagandistic, thus stunting the populace's capacities for
becoming a public. In the partisan form, each newspaper could be seen as
one agent or booth in the marketplace, offering its idea-wares among competing agents. With professionalization, journalists come to define themselves as professional *gatekeepers* for the marketplace of ideas. They no longer
put forth claims but allow some claims to participate in the marketplace
while excluding others (Nerone, et al., 1995).

Here is where we can weave journalism's professionalization into a
broader political rationality. Lippman's call for a professional journalism
grounded in scientific principles and against irrational impulses is designed to
make journalism an autonomous practice. Refusing dependence on the state,
on advertisers, or on the whims of an irrational mass, journalism could take
on a dignified and noble cause, the public interest.

This conception of freedom based on detachment from the irrational
and attachment to scientific principle should remind us of liberal political
rationality. As elaborated in chapter 1, this style of governing contains a
notion of freedom that is not "equated with anarchy, but with a kind of well-
regulated and 'responsibilized' liberty" (Barry, Osborne, & Rose, 1996, p. 8).
Crucial to liberal political rationality is "the question of the relation between

the mutations of politics and the history of systems of expertise" (p. 7). In a liberal ethos of governing,

> the activity of rule must take care to observe and maintain the autonomy of the professions and the freedom of the public sphere from political interference. Thus, in the process in which intellectuals and scientists act as critics of the State, they can none the less serve to act in the interests of good government. (p. 10)

A profession, then, is not isolated and purely autonomous: it is *autonomized*. This autonomy is not opposed to governing; it is a crucial component in its calculation, producing a self-organizing machine, but within a regime of truth and a political rationality.

Journalism's professionalization can be seen as an institutionally specific enactment of this liberal ethos. Incessantly clamoring for freedom from direct forms of state intervention, and historically attempting to carve out its own sphere, journalism autonomizes itself through the techniques of professionalism. Nevertheless, because its freedom is well regulated (by its own professional protocols) and responsibilized, its autonomy is still well within the liberal art of governing. As Michael Schudson (1978) argues, Walter Lippman's faith in science had a political valence: "As absolutism falls . . . science rises. It *is* self-government" (p. 125).

As a scientific endeavor, the journalistic profession is self-monitoring and self-regulating such that recourse to state intervention is rarely needed.[8] Through its incessant self-problematizations, the journalistic profession can still claim its moral function as the "agency for integrating a complex society" (Birkhead, p. 4). Douglas Birkhead's thesis that this professionalization is never fully realized makes it all the more effective as liberal governance, which requires flexibility and adaptability to new circumstances. The recurrent self-reflective ethos of professional journalism provides an incompleteness that makes it more effective as a self-governing institution. Journalism's professional sphere is therefore not simply an in-house affair of occupational concerns.

Even more important for my argument about the profession's role in conspiracy panics is that the genesis of journalism's liberal ethos is bound up with a relation to an *other*. Specifically named "yellow journalism," we could more accurately widen it to say "popular culture" (as the debased realm of affects, base impulses, appeals to self-interested motives, and sensationalism). The profession's rational ethos is founded on a panic, one that is revived each time journalism seeks to reestablish its authority through similar panics. It is this professional-discursive context that informs the *JFK* controversy. Only this time popular irrationality arrives as a blockbuster film and delivers not just gossipy sensationalism but an irrational political knowledge—a conspiracy theory.

Ultimately, this is no real departure from the profession's origins. As I mentioned earlier, yellow journalism involved sensationalism as well as forms of investigative reporting (muckraking). Conspiracy theories, now coming in the form of Hollywood pop culture, signal a particular kind of investigative narrative. Popular forms of information transmission then and now become problematized. And it's not as though sensationalism has actually disappeared from professional journalism. Professional journalism remains firmly entrenched in scandal mongering, though often by depoliticizing it.

The goal of professionalization, then, cannot simply be attributed to its internal desire to represent a public autonomously. It was a form of liberal political rationality, one whose autonomization was designed to govern at a distance more effectively. When it needed to "manage the multitudes" (as Armand Mattelart [1994] puts it) via scientific reason, it did so.

The skirmish over *JFK*, while inaugurating the conspiracy decade, is also a ritual reenactment (and reenactment is seemingly the paradigm performative trope regarding the assassination trauma). First, it resurrects a crucial modern moment in journalism's cultural authority, namely televisual journalism's power over the Kennedy assassination interpretations. Second, it rehearses the earlier founding of journalism's professional authority, especially insofar as it was established against the popular. Journalism reenacts its autonomization (the source of its legitimacy) by problematizing popular culture. Just a few years after the *JFK* event, however, a more significant conspiracy panic occurred, and with it came a revised conception of journalism's mission, especially its formulation of a public.

POLITICAL EXTREMISM/MILITIAS

In 1995, the United States witnessed a landmark event that permanently changed the form of conspiracy panics. On April 19 of that year, the Murrah Federal Building in Oklahoma City was bombed, killing 167 people. After initial speculation that Islamic fundamentalists were responsible, mainstream news outlets changed their framing device with the arrest of Timothy McVeigh. Journalists and pundits honed in on the tenuous connection between McVeigh and the burgeoning network of militias and armed populists.[9] Even though no evidence (especially early on) could demonstrate a direct link to this movement, within a day the militias became the focus. Here was a newly emergent crisis, according to pundits; a very active and organized rumbling that went unnoticed until the Murrah Building bombing.

Militias were typically linked to conspiracy theories, especially around a perceived dawning of a New World Order (NWO) (signified most explicitly by the sightings of black helicopters). The confiscation of weaponry, roundup of U.S. citizens and containment into camps by UN troops, the criminalization of dissent, and even the deliberate bombing of the Murrah

Building to usher in these repressive measures were all strongly connected to the "militia worldview." Militias were identified as the concrete embodiment of conspiracy theorizing (Egan, 1995; Rich, 1995b; Rosenberg, 1996). As perennial conspiracy panicker Richard Cohen put it, "These groups drill to the muffled cadence of bizarre conspiracy theories" (1995).

Conspiracy panics now could attach a clear and present danger to conspiracy theorizing. This was not like *JFK*, where the effects of a conspiracy theory could undermine an institution's authority or create error in historical belief. Conspiracy knowledge itself was dangerous because it could lead to violence. In the conspiracy panic discourse, paranoia about the NWO leads to the formation of armed groups who commit terrorist acts. During McVeigh's trial, for example, the prosecution introduced into evidence a video (allegedly watched "religiously" by McVeigh) detailing a conspiracy account behind the government siege and destruction of the Branch Davidians.

Thought and action are tightly fused in this conspiracy panic, as conspiracy theories can lead to terrorism. Conspiracy theorizing no longer had the status of a harmless, if obsessive, pastime of a few pathetic loners. Since the Oklahoma City terror, conspiracy theories have become identified as dangerous knowledges and their popularity deemed a social menace. We have moved from buffs to bombs. The paranoids are really out there, we are told. In the militias, we find the concrete realization of all the fears of the conspiracy problematizers. It's as though Lasswell's textual outburst 60 years earlier about the paranoid getting hold of a bomb had finally been vindicated.

This development in conspiracy panics is also notable because it marks a common ground shared by mainstream journalism and progressive journalism. There is near unanimity on the characterization of militias. While a few leftist journalists (like Alexander Cockburn, 2005, and Sam Smith, 1995) stand out for their more nuanced analyses, most define the militias as an acute threat to democracy. Part of this ideological harmony is due to similar patterns of sourcing and reliance on the same pool of experts. In this case, these experts are not just government officials but a small range of "watchdog" organizations and their spokespeople. Among these commonly cited "hate monitors" were Morris Dees (and others from his Southern Poverty Law Center), Chip Berlet, the Anti-Defamation League, John George and Laird Wilcox, Kenneth Stern, and makeshift monitors like the Center on Hate and Extremism. Rather than relying on state institutions, these private intelligence groups took on the burden of watchdogging the populace, a kind of outsourcing of social surveillance.

But even as militias were problematized as a clear and present danger, soon a related but more diffuse phenomenon would be articulated within conspiracy panic discourse. It is this transmutation from the militia problem to a problem with "extremism" that is of particular interest here.

The mid-1990s problematizations of militias were part of a lineage of meditations on political extremism that had been going on since the mid-

1960s (described in the previous chapter), especially extremism's links to populism. Militias, the armed wing of populism, were defined as a specific threat. But the crisis over populism found itself dealing with a representational problem. Conceptually, the militias were easily definable and contained via an articulation to the right-wing, white, religious, and supremacist elements of American reactionary culture (regardless of the actual amount of these elements among militias). But the broader populism that spawned and supported the militia movement (a populism often called the "Patriot movement," and composed of underground publications, shortwave radio programs, conventions, paraphernalia, etc.) was not as easily represented. This indeterminacy in problematization is endemic to populism, as Fenster, drawing from Ernesto Laclau, notes (1999, especially pp. 52–76).

Problematizers were faced with the familiar dilemma: The populist rumblings had to be seen as widespread enough to constitute a social menace, but not big enough to actually constitute something common or widely accepted. The resolution was formed via a problematization that synthesized the two into what could best be described as the "unspecified enemy." As discussed in the introduction, the unspecified enemy only rarely takes the concrete form of an action/actor but is instead considered dangerous because it can virtually appear at any time. Like a permanent sense of unease, the indeterminate enemy strikes without warning and comes in many guises. The climatological and meteorological metaphors applied to conspiracy theories now were transferred to extremism (climate of hate, atmosphere of hate, soil of extremism, a force upon the plain, wildfire). This vague threat perhaps found its best configuration in the film *Arlington Road*, whose tagline was "Your Paranoia Is Real." Tim Robbins's character is a conspiracist whose terrorist actions are attributed to white resentment and paranoid thinking. Yet his embodiment is not enough for this parable, for it could easily play out as a simple morality tale, solved with the elimination of the corrupt individual. Instead, as Robbins's character states on more than one occasion, there are "millions of us." The phrase is notable both for its populist sentiments (us vs. them), and for its lack of specificity even while citing numbers. The image of a teeming mass, but one rendered *invisible* in the film is the best example of populist allusion.

This domestic unspecified enemy has another telling quality. Robbins's character moves to the suburbs as protagonist Jeff Bridges's neighbor. It is his very proximity to the normal that makes him so menacing (the para/noid). Robbins, like populist extremism discussed in chapter 1, masquerades as the center, which provides protective cover. Robbins is an unjust pretender whose threat lies in his potential to unmoor the moderate and turn it toward the extreme. The dangerous populist is virtual: it could be anyone, even your closest neighbor. "Political paranoia" is as far away as possible from normal thought, yet as close as our neighbor's thoughts. Thus while "their" paranoia is not real, *your* paranoia about them is. After all, there are millions of them among us. We don't have to rely on Hollywood for this image; we can see it in the titles of Timothy McVeigh biographies: *One of Ours*, *American Terrorist*, *All-American Monster*.

As a final remark on this diffuse populism, we should note that as much as the militias were articulated as a right-wing phenomenon, extremism and conspiracism did not belong to one side of the spectrum. As discussed in chapter 1, "fusion paranoia" signaled that extremes on each end of the spectrum find common ground in conspiracy theorizing and merge in the paranoid citizen-subject.

The most ludicrous and chilling moment of this formulation came a few days after the Oklahoma City bombing, when CNN ran a segment on the history of "hate speech." For an example of right-wing hate speech, they showed 1920s footage of Klan marches. For the Left? Clips of demonstrators in the 1960s getting clubbed by police. Regardless of whether being on the receiving end of baton blows constitutes hate speech, the point here is that the "problem" of populist extremism very quickly encapsulated multiple political positions.

This then is the first effect of journalism's panic over militias: Their problematizations crucially link irrational knowledges (conspiracy theories) to political extremism and acutely present the recurring problem of U.S. domestic populism. The Oklahoma City bombing at one level inspired a concern over right-wing paramilitary groups. But at a broader level, within the lineage of conspiracy panics it reinvigorated an *antiextremism*. This antiextremism (a part of political culture at least since Hofstadter's 1960s) is founded on a conception of the norm and a moderate consensus that composes the body politic. This moderate body is otherwise known as "the public."

The second effect speaks to journalism's relation to popular culture more specifically. And here the third definition of the popular comes into play, as we focus on professional journalism's relationship to technologies and formats. Framing the emergent populism of the Patriot movement entailed tying it to the use of then-emerging technologies (fax and Internet), the renewed uses of old minor ones (shortwave radio), and the rise of talk radio.

Conspiracy culture in general was linked with the Internet (Mashberg, 1995; Timko, 1995; McClellan, 1995; Leiby, 1995; and, for a transatlantic perspective, Westley, 1995). Within days of the Oklahoma City bombing, militia uses of the Internet were a hot topic in journalism (see especially Egan, 1995; Glass, 1995; Rich, 1995a, 1995b; Thomas, et al., 1995; Easton, 1995; Sauer & Okerblom, 1995; as well as the 1995 network news segments "Terrorism Over the Internet" on ABC *World News Tonight*, and "Militia Groups Use TV and Internet to Spread Their Message" on CBS *Evening News*). The Net was claimed to be the newest technology used to spread terrorist and militia messages (along with more traditional means like magazines, pamphlets, videos, books, and particularly shortwave radio). Concern over online militia threats was not limited to mainstream journalism; such publications as the *Village Voice* chimed in on the post–Oklahoma City debate (Davis, 1995).[10]

"Hate speech" (the kind of conspiracy theorizing done by militias) was thus not an abstract speech act but performed in close connection with particular media. Hate speech joined with sensational stories, gossip, and untrustworthy information as the perceived content of nonprofessional channels. And this form of conspiracism was not just relegated to the spectacular forms found in militia newsletters and patriot shortwave radio shows (what the *New York Times* called the "new medium for the far right" [Rimer, 1995]). Consistently, mainstream journalism connected right-wing talk radio (for example, G. Gordon Liddy and Rush Limbaugh) to the militias ideologically (Egan, 1995; Hinckley, 1995; Raspberry, 1995; Tierney, 1995; Russakoff, 1995). *The Washington Post* carried an editorial by William Raspberry with a headline that summed up the articulation: "Bomb Throwers and Broadcasters" (1995). Bill Clinton elliptically referred to the angry words "regularly said over the airwaves of America today" that "spread hate" (Clinton Rips Hatemongers 1995). Seen as linchpins between the Newt Gingrich–era Republican Party and the Patriot movement, talk radio became a "preferred medium" for extremist thought.

While often discussed in terms of the shrillness of the host-personalities, the very format of talk radio was part of the problematization, accused of encouraging hate speech (Friedhoff, 1995). It was equivalent to "hot air" according to prominent *Washington Post* media critic Howard Kurtz (1996). Talk radio is "overheated" and "enables little people to make a very loud noise" (Yardley, 1995). Unlike print news, talk radio's purpose was not to "provide edification or enlightenment or even debate, but to feed red meat to their audiences" (Yardley, 1996). It is irrational (Gosier, 1995; Suber, 1997), filled with an emotion fueled by hatred and resentment (Yardley, 1996) and contributes to the "dark side" of radio (McCoy, 1996). At times, even calling in "regularly" was enough to warrant attention (Bridges, 1995; FAIR in Pogrebin, 1996; Roush, 1996; editorial, *Boston Globe*, 1996).

With a mélange of metaphors drawn from the zeitgeist of epidemics and bombings, Diane Rehm calls the "infectious world" of talk radio "volatile," where "hot mouths" provide "pathways for the spread of information and opinion, accurate or otherwise" (1996). These "rhetorical excesses" comprise a "virus [that] continues to spread" (1996). Talk radio was defined as irresponsible and demonizing while Clinton's response to it was described as a "reasoned plea for self-imposed restraints on electronic hate speech" (Hoagland, 1995).

Lumped in with daytime tabloid TV, talk radio signaled the destruction of reasoned debate and democratic dialogue in favor of high-volume opinion and demagoguery. Mort Zuckerman, in an article titled "Beware of Adversary Culture," called it trash media and differentiated the kinds of people drawn to it: "The public may seem to abhor this out-of-control media, but mainstream America still cannot seem to stop watching or reading the stuff. The consequence is a subversion of the moral authority of everyone, from pope to president" (Zuckerman, 1995). Zuckerman's problematization of popular media (using the old elitist chestnut about trash) tries to differentiate, in good Lippmanian style, between the public and its other, the popular-as-mass or crowd.

For Zuckerman, the solution rests in action-on-speech: "Our rhetoric must be toned down, our words more carefully weighed, even while we expose and correct the evils of the day. We cannot allow divisiveness and anger to replace *e pluribus unum* as America's national theme" (1995). But lest we think this a partisan statement, Jeff Cohen, executive director of Fairness and Accuracy in Reporting and described as a "hate speech" monitor, claimed that "the problem with talk radio is that there isn't enough anti-hatred offered so people could choose between the two" (Albrecht, 1995, June 18).

Concern over talk radio was not limited to its white conservative rage sources. As we'll see in chapter 5, African American radio programs were key venues for discussion and dissemination of AIDS genocide accounts. As University of California-Berkeley Professor Jewelle Taylor Gibbs put it, "Black-oriented talk-radio shows are rife with conspiracy stuff" (Marin & Gegax, 1996). In addition, talk radio was blamed for spreading the Hale-Bopp comet theory that led to the deaths of Heaven's Gate members. Ultimately, talk radio was "the technology of hate" (Albrecht, 1995, June 11), filled with "political passion" that constituted "a danger to public dialogue" (Rehm, 1996).

Talk radio's call-in format was notable for the fact that, in an age of withering appeal for old news' mass broadcasting, it encouraged the participation of its listeners. Talk radio was, if anything, interactive, but this didn't necessarily mean it was democratic (see also Fallows, 1999). For others like Arthur Schlesinger (1997), it contained the potential for too much democracy (a technological amplifier for what James Madison called "the common passion"). In either view, talk radio was an *improper form of interactivity*.[11] Interactive populism was recognized for its participatory potential but needed a proper form. It just so happened that professional journalism was developing this proper form around the same time. To make sense of this populism management and conspiracy panic within journalism, we need to examine this proposed form, called variously *civic journalism* or *public journalism*.

Public Journalism

During the time between late 1994 and 1996, we see a growing concern within professional journalism about its status and drawing power (though some, like Howard Tumber [2001], point to a crisis in journalism in 1999). By 1994, two years have elapsed since the controversy over *JFK* and Jon Katz's *Rolling Stone* provocations about new news. The rise of the internet and talk radio as popular media for information transmission provoke numerous articles both in newspapers and in the profession's trade journals. One response to the crisis took the form of incorporating the emergent technology of the Internet and reaffirming professional codes of rationality (discussed next chapter). Another, competing set of values and practices were beginning to be proposed as a curative to the profession's ills. In the pages of *Columbia Journalism Review*, *American Journalism Review*, *Quill*, and other venues, the proposed remedy came under the names *civic journalism* or *public journalism*.

Before defining what it is, we can look at what it is *not*. John Dinges, NPR's then editorial director, gives us a clear demarcation:

> It's not talk radio. When people talk to each other as citizens and form an opinion, that's a different opinion from one that is not based on dialogue. We try to convey citizen opinions that are the result of them talking with other citizens. It's really pretty encouraging, because they don't say off-the-wall things. People talking together use common sense." (in Hoyt, 1995)

For Judith Sheppard (1995) public journalism was, "in this age of talk radio and cyberspace chatter, a last refuge for reasoned, informed opinion and the powerful institutional voice" (p. 18). Public journalism was thus aware of the interactivity erupting into public media discourse and its promise, as "the new technologies break the journalist's monopoly, making some of the new news an unmediated collaboration between the sources and the audience" (Ellen Hume, quoted in Fulton, 1996). However, it wouldn't be easy for journalists to harness this promise:

> We like to celebrate the idea that we're open to the community. But, in truth, print newsrooms control the nature of the dialogue. We're the professional communicators, the readers are passive recipients of content created by experts, and if you have a complaint, well, write a letter to the editor. (Noth, in Lasica, 1996)

Professional journalism would have its work cut out for it with harnessing this power of interactivity, and the task was partially taken up by the burgeoning civic journalism campaign.

Jay Rosen (communication professor) and Davis "Buzz" Merritt (former editor) are generally considered the founders and main spokespeople for public journalism. Some of its other more prominent supporters include deans and distinguished chairs from around the United States. It quickly became an academic subfield in journalism studies, with numerous books and conferences over the course of a few years, as well as a series of projects that linked scholars with working journalists.

A number of websites, blogs, and interest groups were established around the project, including *Civic Journalism Interest Group (AEJMC)*

http://www.has.vcu.edu/civic-journalism/; *Community Journalism Project*
http://www.rtndf.org/resources/cj.shtml; *Pew Center for Civic Journalism*
http://www.pewcenter.org/; and Rosen's own blog *PressThink* http://www.
journalism.nyu.edu/pubzone/weblogs/pressthink/. Finally, the *J-Lab* (http://
www.j-lab.org/) is a site devoted to the technological developments that
might assist civic journalism. In 2003, PJNET, a network and professional
association devoted to the topic was launched, with a charter that encapsulates the various components of the agenda (http://www.pjnet.org/
charter.shtml).

Various definitions of public journalism have been offered, but some of
its basic features are:

- Responsibility to nurture civic commitment and citizen participation in the democratic process.
- To take ordinary citizens' perspectives and avoid insider talk that
  comprises much of mainstream journalism.
- To rethink professional values of neutrality, objectivity, and the
  conflict model of reporting. Specifically, to encourage interpretive
  analyses that put raw facts in context to foster dialogue.
- To report solutions and not just problems.
- To *provide* solutions and thus serve an integrative function rather
  than just a representative one. For example, some news organs set
  up mock legislatures, townhalls, and juridical rituals.

In sum, civic journalism was designed to help improve the quality of public
life. In this way, journalism could revitalize its mission by reconnecting to its
putative representational source, the public. Some have criticized public
journalism as a new marketing tool, as being a cynical ploy to keep corporate
journalism viable (for an account and assessment of these critiques, see Haas
and Steiner, 2002). This reductionist approach ignores all discursive effects
outside of the bottom line. It also disregards those within journalism who
seek to rescue the profession from these very commercial interests—an
autonomization that I have been arguing has been part of the profession's
birth. If public journalism was primarily a marketing strategy, it was a disaster, as the sensationalized corporate journalism model eventually won out.
Instead of this cynical narrative, I want to treat the public journalism movement as a discourse that was attempting to regain a waning authority.

THE WANING OF CIVIL SOCIETY; THE PROMISE OF VITALITY

Journalism expressed a wider contemporary concern over civil society. As
Mark Fenster notes, the 1990s context was one of crisis in the public sphere
(pp. 68–74). The waning of affect, the decreasing participation in civic ac-

tivities (emblematized in Robert Putnam's *Bowling Alone* argument), and the perceived "apathy" in voter turnout all were signs of the disappearance of civil society. When the context was articulated in this manner, defining and renewing civil and political engagement became paramount. Renewal meant figuring out ways to get people connected with each other again, and by default, connected to the discourses and institutions of classic liberal society (local associations, political groups, cultural institutions). The civil society revivals entailed more attention to community groups (and to community governing), with more emphasis on dialogue, rational debate, and ultimately consensus. A number of Foucauldian governmentality studies scholars assessed this crisis as a transitional moment in modes of neoliberal governance (Barry, Osborne, & Rose, 1996; Dean, 1999; Rose, 1999; Bratich, Packer, & McCarthy, 2003; Morison, 2000). Key in this process was the development of "cultural citizenship" (Miller, 1998; King, 2006).

Journalism could find its niche here, since it is an institution within civil society, whose own authority and participation was waning. Seen as contributing to the malaise of public life, journalism could likewise become a catalyst for its revitalization (Tumber, 2001; Stein, 1994a). And this meant not just reporting on the civic renewal campaigns, but *actively participating* in them. Journalism could contribute to this larger movement of reviving civil society by mobilizing people again as citizens and community participants.

Some of the concrete proposals within civic journalism demonstrate this. For many, the prime relationship that needed to be reestablished was between citizens and government via the media. For David Holwerk, "readers' frustration with the power of government can be addressed by newspapers, which can create a 'new civic trust'" (quoted in Stein, 1994a). Public journalism's major spokespeople reiterated this idea: For Jay Rosen, "Citizens are frustrated with the political system. . . . Public life is in an advanced state of decay and journalism must do something about it" (quoted in Stein, 1994a). The news profession, according to Buzz Merritt, has the ability of "re-engaging citizens in public life" (quoted in Stein, 1994a).

But this public life was not relegated to voting or lobbying. It referred to the spheres of civil society, as well. One of the main commitments in public journalism was to put people in touch *with each other*. Fostering interactivity included promoting ballgames, civic associations, adult classes, political meetings, and neighborhood social events (Rosen, quoted in Stein, 1994b). Thus public journalism, while becoming the dominant name, was also synonymous with civic journalism, citizen journalism, and community journalism (Meyer, 1995). "Community," a highly popular concept in rethinking governance, also became a mantra for the public journalism movement. For Philip Meyer (1995), the concern over "loss of community" (found in the writings of Robert Bellah, Robert Putnam, and Amitai Etzioni) was exactly the grounds from which public journalism emerged, and which could potentially be rectified. One can hear echoes here of the various calls in the

1960s antiextremism literature for increased civic participation, local asso-
ciational groups, grassroots patriotism, only now the government was not the
primary agent fostering these publics. Perhaps civic journalism could be one
of Lasswell's social self-observatories, one that would foster proper democratic subjects and minimize antagonism.

Public interaction with governing institutions was not explicitly about
reviving the state, but it did fit well into a political rationality of liberal
governance. In a keynote talk about public journalism and new media, S.
Yelvington plainly stated: "Individual empowerment doesn't mean the end of
the organization of the state" (1999, in Tumber, 2001). As Foucauldian
governmentality studies scholars argue, neoliberal governing procedures rely
on increased civic or community relations to govern more efficiently. The
populace, once autonomized and responsibilized, ties its self-regulated behavior
to traditionally state-centered governance. Whether it be through community
culture (Coffey, 2003), urban design (Hay, 2003), self-help discourse
(Cruikshank, 1999), safe driving (Packer, 2003), gaming (Miklaucic, 2003),
homeland security (Hay & Andrejevic, 2006), or charity and volunteerism
(King, 2006), the self-governance of the populace (especially through cultural
practices of everyday life) becomes intertwined with destratified strategies of
good governance delinked from the state. For James Hay (2003; 2005), the
growing discourse of communitarianism, including the work of Putnam, is
precisely how this new mode of governing was being implemented.

Journalism, via its new civic form, would assist in bringing people together as a mode of good governance. This included practices such as conven-
ing focus groups to help orient political coverage, creating preelection forums
for a discussion of issues, and sponsoring regular meetings for people to discuss
local or community problems (crime, waste management, failing schools).
Journalism becomes a "public actor," one that balances autonomy and participation: "At its best [it] is independent . . . and also connected" (Rosen, 1996
p. 4). In this case, it does not *represent* a public out there, but seeks to *constitute*
it. It would "build community" (Cochran, 1995) and would "add to public life
rather than just reflecting it" (Mclellan, quoted in Stein, 1994b). If not activists, public journalists are committed actors; they "see themselves as conveners
of public talk, aids to a more active citizenry, modelers of deliberative dialogue,
supporters of a healthy public life" (Rosen, 1995).

The vitalist rhetoric of health, rekindling, renewal, catalysis, connection, and mobilization is a rhetoric that doesn't belong to representation-as-
mediation. It puts journalism into a different kind of mediation, one that
actively works "in between" (citizens, community members, governors/gov-
erned) to join together in new and renewed ways. Being in media res no
longer means signifying; it is a *pragmatics*. It is no accident that numerous
proponents cite pragmatism as their philosophical bedrock. To put it another
way, public journalism was to be an actor working on connections: an articulatory force.

How would this conjugation machine work? For one thing, interactivity would be accomplished by the *medium* itself. Remember that the calls for civic journalism primarily involved print journalism. Some did look to the burgeoning Internet for its interactive qualities (Pavlik, 2001). Ironically enough given the next chapter's argument, the *San Jose Mercury News* (publisher of the Gary Webb CIA/crack story a year later) was noted for its innovative potential in fusing technology with public journalism (Cochran, 1995). But most of the outlets involved in the practical movement were print based. Newspapers, tied to the older forms of journalism, would be more likely to accomplish the civic tasks. In a paradoxical image, print could produce a new face-to-face relationship. Opposed to the debased and commercialized broadcast news and more importantly to the popular media of talk radio, print journalism would remediate print itself with new connective powers.

And what form would this interactivity take? Interaction takes the form of a dialogue, according to Rosen, and thus a vital public sphere depends on "better conversation" (Stein, 1994a, 1994b; Rosen, 1995). Democracy rests on deliberative dialogue and journalists are obliged to provide conditions for it (Rosen, 1995). Philip Meyer (1995) was explicit about how this dialogue could be undermined even within public journalism. According to Meyer, the philosophical lineage of the public journalism movement is in the "easily perverted field of critical theory" (http://www.unc.edu/%7Epmeyer/ire95pj.htm). It is this same theory that spurs "extreme advocates of various causes—radical feminists, for example" and could lapse into advocacy journalism whose practitioners "don't mind coloring the facts or even making them up." Interaction, lest it fall prey to extremism, should be moderate, rational, dispassionate, and respectful of the discursive procedures; in other words, it needs to subscribe to the regime of truth.

And this moderate conversation has an affinity with particular mediated forms. Desensationalized dialogue is best accomplished via print. We see a writing-oriented medium being given properties associated with orality, which echoes early notions of print and the public sphere (see Michael Warner, 1990). Print's moderate conversation is starkly contrasted with the interactivity found in contemporary media forms: talk radio, shortwave, and the Internet, where hate speech, dangerous talk, and shrill irrationality dominate. New media and formats, the home to conspiracy theory-fueled patriots and hateful speech, functioned as the Other by which to define public journalism.

Occasionally this was made explicit, as when the *Chicago Sun Times* editorial page editor stated: "In contrast to talk radio, where the aim is to vent, the goal of public journalism is to listen and to help readers connect to their communities" (Hornung, 1994). Other times, public journalism's potential danger lay in making "an editorial page editor . . . the print equivalent of talk radio" and thus needed distinguishing (*New York Times* editorial page editor Howell Raines, quoted in Sheppard, 1995). But more often, this scapegoating and discrimination didn't need to be spelled out so directly in order to work. The simultaneous promotion of public journalism and pathologization of hyperactive populism are enough to show the connections were "operational but not articulated within the discourse" (Grossberg, 1992; 1995).

AGAINST APATHY, AGAINST HYPERPATHY: PUBLIC VS. POPULAR INTERACTIVITY

In sum, civic journalism would actively participate in constructing a public. The "public" of public journalism converged harmoniously with the broader campaign of civic renewal: it essentially consisted of mainstream consensus politics. This included electoral participation, closer proximity to community leaders, and increasing interaction with already existing institutions. Any transformation of U.S. society and politics was at bottom a renewal of core values and should take place via orderly and juridical procedures. The fundamental core value at stake here was *trust*. It was a metavalue, one whose preservation conditioned other possible values. Institutions needed to win back the trust of its constituents, as a way of rebuilding relations. The civic renewal project was founded on an assumption of the basic legitimacy and authority of the political institutions. The problem, defined within this project, is the unresponsiveness of those institutions, but more importantly a lack of public engagement with them. The public must be won over.

What better way to win over that public than via journalism? Journalism as "media" took on its etymological roots, functioning "in between" governors and governed. Professionally speaking, it was beholden to the interests of neither. But its historic mission authorized it to be the best representative of the public (in Lippman's sense of being experts in the public interest). Journalism could reintegrate citizens (more precisely, the populace *as* citizens) into governing institutions, thereby restoring trust in basic political discourses and procedures. At the same time, professional journalism could regain its own authority as a representative of the public, restoring trust in its own operations.

The contextual moment of mid-1990s professional journalism contained an experiment in constructing a public accompanied by an acute demonization of emergent popular forms. One hybrid of thought/action (moderate, consensus) sought to revitalize its subjects by triumphing over another hybrid (irrational, extreme). Public interactivity, composed of community-based activities assisted by print journalism, was encouraged. *Popular* interactivity, an excessive passional politics through media like radio and the Internet, was considered "antidialogue." Anger, frustration, vehemence, passion: Instead of being motivation to act, these became reasons to pacify. In fact, they were often considered "antipolitics" and they needed to be quelled as a condition of proper, moderate action.

In other words, the civic renewal project (especially within the public journalism experiment) depended on conspiracy panics. Militias, the broader populism that nourishes them, the conspiracy theories that fuel them, and their mediated communication forms, became emblematic of a populist version of engagement. This popular interactivity (a version of the third type of popular culture) was depicted as pathological and inimical to the public project. Conspiracy panics turn the openendedness of populism into extremism in order to install a powerful moderate, the public.

Journalism is crucial to this civic renewal project predicated on antiextremism. Extremists, as examined in chapter 1, are intolerable because they do not presume the legitimacy of fundamental institutions, or they depict them as irrevocably corrupted. Like the conspiracy theories that fuel their actions, extremists exercise an excess of skepticism toward institutions. This is unacceptable to the civic renewal campaigns of journalism, whose conspiracy panic anchors a will-to-moderation.

Interestingly enough, journalism even engaged in its own populism, its own Us/Them. Public journalism called for taking "ordinary citizens' perspectives" rather than the perspectives of political elites. Public journalism did recognize citizens' frustration, alienation, and cynicism. Faced with these populist rumblings, public journalism (in tandem with pundits and politicians) continued to explicitly bemoan apathy or implicitly demonize *hyperpathy*. The latter term, while not uttered, underpinned the conspiracy panics: *Too much action* was a problem. The masses, when defined as apathetic, were a resource to be tapped; a milieu of potential publics. Popular culture, however, was hyperpathic, an excess that required a different series of responses (scapegoating and pathologization).

Subjective activity was either lacking or excessive; either way it had to be reorganized into a moderate and acceptable form.[12] Civic journalism, unlike the traditional Lippmanian form, would not simply act as expert problematizers, providing objective facts on conspiracy theories to inform the public. Rather, their participation in conspiracy panics would be as advisors and guides. Public journalism would act as *watchdogs* for the public. However, rather than being monitors of governmental corruption, these would be watchdogs against extremists. They would keep an eye on the populace in the name of the public. In other words, they would monitor those, like the militias, who appropriated the watchdog role against government. Public journalism's mission ultimately preserved governing discourses by protecting them against excessive critique, and seeking to restore public trust in them.

The public, so often assumed to be equivalent with universal values and desubjectified interests, comes to have a very specific valence within public journalism. It consists of reformist politics, moderate thought, dispassionate dialogue. It can be formed and expressed through some media and not others. Seeking to activate political subjects, the forms of acceptable behavior are fully within liberal conceptions of what democracy looks like. Other experiments and other potentials are quickly demonized or tamed. These extremist, conspiracy-fueled voices have no place in the public as imagined during the crisis of the civic. Public journalism, as a crucial player in the conspiracy panics that accompany this crisis, proposes a solution that will simultaneously revive its own flagging powers. Regardless of the ultimate success of this proposal, its momentum and drawing power for many remains a symptom of the conspiracy panics and broader political rationality of the late 20th and early 21st century.

CONCLUSION

The 1990s found professional journalism in a quandary. It, like other public-oriented institutions, was losing credibility and audiences. The attacks on JFK and the emergence of public journalism demonstrate two attempts to revive journalism amid this crisis. In each case journalism sought to redefine itself in relation to the "popular" (in one case a Hollywood film and in the other a populist use of new media formats). Most significantly, the popular culture being "othered" was wrapped up with conspiracy theorizing.

The two instances offer competing strategies of professionalization, marked by different conceptions of the "public." With the JFK controversy, we saw a notion of the public that hearkened back to the early foundations of the profession. The public transcends collective individuals (the popular as mass): This is Walter Lippman's rationale for the rule of experts, especially journalism. Journalists would be specialists in the public good, determining the public interest through a scientific relationship to political knowledge. By gatekeeping the marketplace of ideas, journalists would assist in creating an informed public while not being beholden to the popular. Like Harold Lasswell's call for social observatories, journalism's expertise is designed to ensure a stable governing function. Professional journalism, as an autonomized sphere, could provide preventive doses of reason to ward off potential antagonisms.

In the JFK event, journalists tried to shore up this cultural authority by claiming the turf of political history as theirs, and pillorying unofficial narratives emerging via unofficial channels (or "new news"). Popular cultural conspiracy theories, much like early yellow journalism in their combination of sensationalism and investigation, became the irrational counterpoint to the rational public and its representative: professional journalism.

Public journalism also sought to ground itself in its genetic source, the public, but with a different valence. At times public journalism explicitly argued against the more traditional model, with the latter's impersonal style of objectivity and thin notion of the public. Instead, it offered a public that emerged out of, and through, the interactions that composed citizenship and civil society. In other words, the Lippmanian version was a transcendent category, formed in opposition to concrete interactions (defined as mob, crowd, or mass). With public journalism, the public is produced *immanently*. Print journalism, rather than being associated with separation and impersonal abstraction, now means face-to-face proximity and conversational interaction.

The new public is a result of the dynamic process of enhancing interactions among concrete subjects. The profession should "follow them down," becoming an agent in this *self*-organization. Print is "a medium through which citizens can inform themselves and through which they can discover their common values and shared interests" (Glasser & Craft, 1998, p. 205). Notice the lack of representation here—journalism is the immanent instrument through which a public (in)forms itself. The new civic/public is defined by community, local, and regional affiliations as well as national ones: It is both a set of abstract capacities (dialogue, national citizenship, reason) and local interconnections (community, neighborly interactions, specific audience needs).

Journalism is not an external sector mediating between a public and government, but an immanent guide for a public to regulate itself, an internal amplification mechanism to provide the civic interactions necessary for good neoliberal governance. However, immersing into networks takes on particular forms: rational, moderate, and reformist. In addition, the immanent public still has outsiders, subjects who in their conspiratological claims and amateur uses of technology became "remainders" (Honig, 1993). When it came to conspiracy theories (and their resulting dangerous extremist populism), journalists helped political subjects sort out moderate from extreme views on their own. Much like the broader conspiracy panics going on in the United States, public journalism took on Daniel Pipes's injunction to fight the perpetual subjective struggle against conspiracism.

While the two major events in the 1990s involving conspiracy panics, journalism, and popular culture differed in their inflections of the public, they thus converged as a discursive practice. Public journalism often positioned itself as a counter to traditional professional standards, but both were connected as strategies within political rationality. The scientific, instrumental reason of classic professionalism as a transcendent sector of expertise was giving way to the immanent, deliberative, reason of civil society.

What appears to be an opposition between two forms of professionalization shares something foundational—a notion of the public as moderate and as formed through reasoned truth telling. The civicmindedness of the public, whether formed via the rule of experts or immanently in dialogic citizen interactions, was intimately linked to rationality. Whether in the name of science or civil society, journalism's discursive strategies of publicity sought to subjugate knowledges that didn't subscribe to the regime of truth.

The public was inseparable from its distinction from popular culture, be it Hollywood film or populist uses of emerging technologies. In each case pop culture became coded as the space of irrationality, sensation, passion, and paranoia. Two different publics, the same rejection of the popular. And both strategies were part of governing at a distance, either via scientific rationality or a political rationality based on moderate communitarianism.

The next chapter continues the analysis of the recent matrix of journalism and popular culture via conspiracy panics. In addition to assessing how the conspiracy panic worked to subjugate particular political knowledge claims, it examines the effects of a conspiracy panic on the very meaning and organization of an emergent technology.

3
TRUST NO ONE
(ON THE INTERNET)

*Gary Webb, Popular Technologies,
and Professional Journalism*

INTRODUCTION

I n the initial weeks after September 11, 2001, numerous commentators called attention to the swirling rumors and conspiracy theories about the attacks (see for example O'Leary, 2001, and Tyrangiel, 2001). While official rumors (health panics, specific warnings about vague new attacks) were spread by mainstream news outlets, popular rumors were attacked by those very outlets. In particular, the Internet was cited as a catalyst for the wide and rapid circulation of unreliable information. The articulation between untrustworthy narratives and this new medium could be made so smoothly because it had already been performed for a few years. This chapter examines one of those earlier moments where professional journalism, the Internet, and conspiracy narratives converge. This chapter continues the previous one's focus on journalism as a significant force in conspiracy panic discourse. But while the previous chapter examined what might be considered "external" agents (popular culture and popular uses of media), this one finds journalism facing an "internal" problem, namely its own subjects mired in conspiracy narratives. The particular conspiracy involved here is the CIA/Contra/crack story.

DARK ALLIANCE

On August 18–20, 1996, the *San Jose Mercury News* published a three-part investigative series called "Dark Alliance" authored by award-winning reporter Gary Webb. The series was simultaneously posted on the *Mercury*

News website, with links to court transcripts, photographs, other investigations' results, and congressional reports. In the series, Webb reported that throughout the early and mid-1980s, Nicaraguan cocaine traffickers Oscar Danilo Blandon and Norwin Meneses, high-ranking agents of the reactionary antigovernment Contra movement (formed, trained, and financed in part by the CIA), sold cocaine in the United States through "Freeway" Ricky Ross and funneled profits back to the Contras. Webb argued that the crack explosion in Southern California was significantly propelled by the activities of Meneses, Blandon, and Ross (who became one of the largest crack distributors in Southern California) and thus indirectly by the Contra movement. The direct role of the CIA in this sordid endeavor was left to suggestion: the agency would not return Webb's requests for information, and he was content to establish its supervising relationship with the Contras.

The general narrative linking the CIA to the Contras and both to cocaine trafficking was nothing new.[1] However, the Webb series introduced a number of new inflections. First, Webb brought this foreign policy story home, tracing the disastrous effects of the CIA/Contra/crack nexus on one U.S. city, Los Angeles. In addition, Webb's access to Ricky Ross, the LA drug dealer who provided key distribution networks for the suppliers, gave the story an insider dimension unseen before. During Ross's trial, Webb also convinced Ross's attorney to ask certain questions of Blandon on the witness stand, yielding sworn testimony that Webb could use as evidence in his series. These developments contributed to the detail and thoroughness of Webb's story, but more important than the power of the narrative itself was that a well-respected regional daily newspaper published the narrative. A well-publicized three-part series in the *San Jose Mercury News* gave the account a potential legitimacy and circulation it did not previously have.

In this chapter, I assess the "metastory" surrounding Webb's series as a concrete example of conspiracy panics (Kornbluh, 1997, p. 33). Webb's series came during and contributed to a moment of crisis in mainstream journalism. Two forces converge in Webb's series and its aftermath: (1) establishment journalism confronts and manages the reemergent phenomenon of conspiracy theory; and (2) establishment, print-based journalism attempts to organize a relationship with the emergent medium of the Internet. When these two forces collide in the profession, conspiracy theories and the Web end up mutually defining each other. This problematization of a conspiracy theory goes beyond disqualifying the story. It also reshapes the profession of journalism in its relation to new technology. As Mary E. McCoy (2001) argues, the controversy around Dark Alliance provoked a paradigm repair of journalism's professional authority.

Webb's story, as an object of concern, is a portal into the public anxieties over the popular emergence of the Internet. In this case, professional journalism's conspiracy panic manages cultural anxieties over the disruptive character of new technologies. New media, then, partially receives meaning and organization through an already existing discourse, journalism.[2] Once again, we are examining how a specific institution or professional discourse enacts political rationality; specifically in this case how professional journalism operates as technical expertise of "governing at a distance."

PILING ON THE COUNTERATTACK

When the Dark Alliance series was first published, there was resounding indifference on the part of the major dailies including the *Los Angeles Times*, the *Washington Post*, and the *New York Times*. According to media critic Ben Cosgrove (1996), "the only thing more chilling than the story itself is the East Coast media establishment's stunning inattention to this still-unfolding debacle" ("Cocaine Import Agency," www.netizen.com/netizen/96/37/ special4a). Rather than expanding on the *Mercury News* series and pursuing its leads, major newspapers ignored it. Instead of disputing Webb's claims as "false," which would mean bringing the claims into a regime of verifiable truth, the print media generally employed a tactic of neglect. The *Los Angeles Times*, *Washington Post*, and *Time* posted their first stories almost a month after the original series—around the time Webb started making the rounds on CNN and CBS *Morning News*—while the *New York Times* took almost two months.

What happened during that period is crucial to this event. The story began to circulate in nontraditional sites of news production, or what Jon Katz (1992) calls "new news" (p. 33). Talk Radio (primarily African American oriented), tabloid television shows (Montel Williams did a two-part series), and the Internet extended the story's life; the Internet, especially, was host to newsgroup discussions, email listservs, and an ever expanding network of web links. As journalist Peter Kornbluh (1997) argues, the

> wildfire-like sweep of Dark Alliance was all the more remarkable because it took place without the power of the mainstream press. Instead, the story roared through the new communications media of the Internet and black radio—two distinct, but in this case somewhat symbiotic, information channels. (p. 34)

The *San Jose Mercury News* website began receiving an extra 100,000 hits per day, at one point having 1.3 million (Kornbluh, p. 34). Mainstream journalism, in this case, did not give the story "legs" (the active efforts by professional individuals, institutions, and media outlets to extend a story). Normal channels of news transmission were superceded by user interactions with the Internet.

Mainstream disregard for the story could not last for long. The increasing visibility of Gary Webb, the growing new-media-fueled outrage in African American communities, and the prominent media campaign by U.S.

Representative Maxine Waters began a groundswell that could not be ignored.[3] At that point, establishment journalism's tactics largely shifted from neglect of the story to attacks on the agents of its production (Webb and the *SJMN*).[4] Deeming it a journalistic "pacification program," Alexander Cockburn and Jeffrey St. Clair (1998) called the denunciation "one of the most venomous and factually inane assaults on a professional journalist's competence in living memory" (p. 29). In the following sections, I examine two main targets of this counterattack: (1) how the story violated truth-telling protocols of journalism, to the point of being labeled a conspiracy theory, and (2) its online presence.

CONSPIRACY THEORY AND REASONABLE TRUTH-IN-REPORTING

Much of the criticism of Webb and the *San Jose Mercury News* was directed at the alleged "shoddy" reporting and editorial practices that went into producing the story. Webb's story was depicted by the *Washington Post*, *New York Times*, and *Los Angeles Times* as lacking evidence, and being unfounded (see Heyboer, 1996; Solomon, 1997; Cockburn & St. Clair, 1998). Webb and the paper, critics charged, violated journalistic responsibility by implicating the CIA without a "smoking gun" *definitively* proving the agency's complicity in the drug smuggling (Cockburn & St. Clair, 1998, p. 395). Far from carrying out their own investigations, many newspapers made a priori judgments on Webb's findings, dismissing them even before the CIA and Department of Justice conducted their own in-house investigations.[5] Reverting to the professional protocol of relying on official sources, the major dailies now cited those "close" to the story, even if unnamed (Golden, 1996). According to a *New York Times* statement, "our best sources say that the CIA was not a major factor in the crack epidemic" (Katz, 1996, www.netizen.com/netizen/96/41/katz4a.html). Their "best sources" were identified as CIA officials.

Official denials and lack of facts were the major counteroffensives indicting Webb's narrative. No critique interrogated the conditions of truth telling, including uncooperative official sources, vested interests, and generalized institutional secrecy. Even though Webb's published findings were tame compared to his original version (the story went through massive editing and toning) and to others' more dramatic claims about the CIA's role, the story was still dismissed as speculation, "fantasy" (White, 1996; Massing, 1999), "myth" (Britt, 1996), and a revamped "rumor" (Beato, 1996; Cohen, 1996). Conjecture, the argument ran, was not the investigative journalist's job.[6]

Even more fatal were denunciations of Dark Alliance as a "conspiracy theory" (Fletcher, 1996; Mitchell & Fulwood, 1996; Yoder, 1996; Morris, 1996; Wood, 1996; Maxwell, 1996; Lane, 1996; Roeper, 1997), even "political paranoia" (Kazin, 1996). Webb's speculations were more than violations of journalistic protocol, they were now depicted as the irrational fantasies of a political paranoid. After "Dark Alliance" was published, House Representative Maxine Waters, who spearheaded the demand for a formal congressional investigation into Webb's claims, was called a "conspiracy theorist" (Parry, 1998b, www.consortiumnews.com/ consor26.html). And Howard Kurtz snidely remarked in one of his numerous attack pieces on Webb and the *Mercury News*, "Oliver Stone, check your voice mail" (Kurtz, 1996). Attacks often attributed claims to Webb's investigation that the series never made, like that the CIA was directly responsible for the crack epidemic; or that the agency deliberately introduced it into African American communities.[7]

The most explicit way Webb's story was marked as a conspiracy theory was through the claim that "Dark Alliance" incited "black paranoia" (Cockburn & St. Clair, 1998; Naureckas. 1997; Knight, 2001). This black paranoia was not simply defined as a collective psychological condition—it was given historical and social underpinnings (Terzian, 1996b; Claiborne, 1996; Editorial, 1996; White, 1996; Kempton, 1996; Lane, 1996; Mitchell & Fulwood, 1996; Britt, 1996; Maxwell, 1996). Because of this history, argued Richard Cohen (1996), "a piece of black America remains hospitable to the most bizarre rumors and myths—the one about the CIA and crack being just one" (p. A21). In general, these mainstream accounts treated the belief systems of African Americans as "sociological curiosities" (Naureckas, 1997). Such appeals to social and historical contexts made the CIA/Contra/crack theory intelligible and worked to explain the occurrence of prima facie misguided theories. As I have argued elsewhere (Bratich, 2001), this is a cultural approach in which African American conspiracy accounts are still symptoms to be read as expressions of frustration—oversimplified and channeled in the wrong direction. And, for Gary Webb, fanning the flames of "race paranoia" was further evidence of an egregious violation of journalistic protocol. This racial coding of conspiracy theories is not just endemic to Webb's story. As we'll see in chapter 4, problematizing conspiracy theories through race is done especially with AIDS genocide theories, and performed by the Left as well as the Right.

Ultimately, the mainstream press, according to *New Times Los Angeles* journalist Rick Barrs (1996), argued that "Webb had overstepped the bounds of journalistic ethics and fueled genocide theorists in black communities" (http://cgi.sjmercury.com/drugs/ postscript/controversy/controversy1031.htm). The response to Webb's story was geared toward discrediting him as well as the *San Jose Mercury News*, as their "procedures were unacceptable" (Adams, 1998) and they "went too far" (Rieder, 1997b). "Lack of evidence" was not interpreted as an investigative opportunity but as a transgression of journalism's codes of conduct and truth-telling procedures. In sum, any dispute over facts was imbued with the defense of journalism's professionalism.

The attack on Webb's evidence had less to do with the truth-value of the claims than with the very forms of truth telling allowable in professional journalism. As Peter Kornbluh (1997) argues:

> The furor over "Dark Alliance" and the mainstream media's response to it
> dramatically raise the issue of responsible and irresponsible journalism—par-
> ticularly in an era of growing public cynicism toward both government and the
> institutional press. For many in the media, Webb's reporting remains at the
> core of the debate over journalistic responsibility. (p. 39)

What counts as evidence and responsible reporting? The answer depends on
the "game of truth" situated in the professional setting of journalism, hence
depends on such factors as the reliance on official sources for credibility and
the permissible boundaries of reporters' speculation (Foucault, p. 297). While
journalism is not isolated in its practices (i.e., it is embedded in relations
with corporate interests and the state), its self-defined occupational concerns
about autonomy shape knowledge conditions specific to the profession. I
have discussed in the previous chapter how this commitment to a professional, "autonomized" expertise is an important dimension of liberal governance.[8] Now, I turn to how Webb's story was linked to a rise of "conspiracy
theorizing" in the 1990s, and in turn this theorizing became intertwined with
the very definition of new technologies.

CONSPIRACY THEORIES AND THE INTERNET

The discrediting of Webb's account as conspiracy theory came at an interesting moment in mid- to late 1996, when conspiracy theories were a hot
topic in journalism. The crash of TWA Flight 800 had occurred only one
month before, sparking numerous alternative accounts of the plane's demise.
Even before the joint investigation by the National Transportation Safety
Board and the FBI was fully underway, the official story was that mechanical
failure had caused the crash off Long Island. Others speculated that a bomb
on the plane caused the crash, or that Arab terrorists shot the plane down
with a surface-to-air missile (Hidell, 1997). The most publicized counter-
narrative was promoted by one of journalism's own eminent representatives,
Pierre Salinger.[9] Armed with a portfolio of documents, Salinger held press
conferences where he hypothesized that U.S. naval exercises off the Long
Island coast had gone awry, with an errant missile hitting the plane. Salinger's
early evidence was drawn from a document circulating on the Internet and
confirmed by unnamed intelligence sources.
    "Dark Alliance" and Salinger's TWA Flight 800 story were linked in
numerous articles and broadcast news segments (Beato, 1996; Alter, 1997;
Witkin, 1997; Roeper, 1997; Canon, 1997). These and other "paranoid"
theories were declared "emblems of the times" (Berg, 1997) and part of an
"age of conspiracy" (Alter, 1997). Joel Achenbach (1996), in the Style section of the Washington Post, wrote that the Salinger and Webb stories were
examples of a "time besotted with Bad Information." At this historical,

premillenial juncture, the pundits claimed, it had become difficult to distinguish good information from bad, as even conspiracy theories could appear seductively logical and objective (echoing Hofstadter). To avoid this seduction, Achenbach drew from the conspiracy panic discourse described in chapter 1 when he pleaded for a "controlled skepticism." This rational subjective faculty would be required to distinguish legitimate knowledge producers (especially journalists) from pretenders and "information manipulators" (Achenbach, 1996).

Of significance here is that the Salinger and Webb cases involved the profession's *own agents*. The conspiracy panic was over an internal problem. It was harder to reject a conspiracy narrative as "other" when respected journalists—themselves experienced adherents to journalism's truth-telling practices—were its authors. So the object of concern quickly turned to the Internet, and transgression went beyond the individual responsibility of Webb and Salinger to implicate digital media's involvement in the construction and dissemination of conspiracy narratives.

For instance, the "African American paranoia" that Webb's story allegedly fueled was linked to the increased usage of the Internet to spread the story. Jack E. White (1996) claimed that, while black conspiracy theories were long standing, what was new was that the CIA/crack story "spread via a new black lane on the information superhighway" (p. 59). White went on to make sense of the Internet *through* these conspiracy theories, stating that the " 'Black telegraph'—as some African Americans call the informal word-of-mouth network they've used to keep in touch with one another since the days of slavery—has moved into cyberspace" (p. 59). White defined the black telegraph, which includes both talk radio and cyberspace, as "a font of bizarre fantasies" (p. 59). The Internet here takes on the characteristics of an already-subjugated "informal" communications or rumor network, the home of "conspiracy mongers . . . fanning the flames" (p. 59). This new technology, then, was rendered intelligible as a space of rumor, gossip, urban folklore, and fantasy.

Salinger's story also involved the Internet. According to Jodi Dean (2000), "[c]onspiracy's haunting of some media accounts of the Internet" begins around the time of the Salinger story (p. 66). While Salinger himself argued that his account and the evidence for it came from a French intelligence source, news accounts focused on the prior circulation of the narrative on the Web. Tom Teepen's (1996) Cox News Service article, calling the friendly-fire scenario absurd on its face, blamed the Internet: "Certainly the media explosion, its new vents often unstaffed by sober gatekeepers, is a vast petri dish for growing foul cultures. Even legitimate journals wind up reporting wildfire charges because their currency in other media becomes news" (p. 17A). Salinger's persistence continued to provoke responses from mainstream journalism. In early 1997, 60 *Minutes* presented a segment on the Salinger story. Journalist Cathy Young (1997) called the broadcast "an alarmist report on the Net as a haven for conspiracy buffs" promoting "a new

flurry of concerns about whether the Internet is a source of valuable information or of paranoia-fueling junk" (p. A7). In essence, mainstream accounts argued that while a conspiracy theory may in itself be based on "bad
information," it is made even more "foul" because it circulates through an
untrustworthy medium. Salinger's story thus joined Webb's CIA/Contra/crack
story to create a moment where journalism problematized conspiracy theories, the Internet, and above all their mutual affinity.

Even before the Webb and Salinger stories, the articulation between
conspiracy theories and new technologies had already been made in journalism. Conspiracy culture in general was linked with the Net (Mashberg, 1995;
Timko, 1995; McClellan, 1995; Leiby, 1995; and, for a transatlantic perspective, Westley, 1995). The articulation between conspiracy accounts and the
Internet continued after the Webb controversy. The speed with which conspiracy theories surrounding Princess Diana's death emerged and spread were
attributed to online circulation (see Belsie, 1997; Colker, 1997). The life and
death of Heaven's Gate members was also added to this mix as another
example of cyber perniciousness (see *New York Post* staff, 1997). But the
Webb story is different insofar as the *confluence* of these two phenomena
became the very defining feature of the Dark Alliance series. It is to this
simultaneous attack on Webb and the Web that I now turn.

A number of journalists went beyond criticizing Webb's story by finding
fault with the story's online presence (Cohen, 1996; Golden, 1996; Kurtz,
1996; Achenbach, 1996; Shaw, 1997; Canon, 1997). According to G. Beato
(1996), newspapers did not go far enough in criticizing Webb's story. They
attacked it only at the level of evidence, overlooking "one of the most
significant aspects of the Dark Alliance series: that it achieved at least as
much of its impact from its presentation as it did from its content" (http:/
/www.feedmag.com/ 96.11beato/96.11beato.html). Beato specifically cited the
Web incarnation as the problem, disparaging it as something "you might find
on the Fox network." The *Mercury News* article contained "twenty-some-
thing grunge typography and . . . free-wheeling sensationalism," producing
an "x-appeal and a decidedly tabloid TV sensibility" geared toward "post-
Cronkite conspiratainment buffs." The *Mercury News*, according to Beato,
was "savvy enough to capitalize on" the Web's penchant for housing conspiratorial rumor mongering, mentioning that the paper had been a pioneer
in moving print-based journalism into cyberspace (it was the first U.S. daily
to establish a significant online presence). It is no accident, Beato claimed,
that the paper used the CIA/Contra/crack story, "so pregnant with newsgroup
innuendo, to serve as the foundation for its most ambitious online presentation to date." Once again, conspiracy theories and the Internet inextricably
form an organic synthesis, in which the characteristics of each resonate with,
and determine the qualities of, the other.

This connection was continued in a *Los Angeles Times* article called
"Cyberspace Contributes to Volatility of Allegations." According to Eleanor

Randolph and John M. Broder (1996), Webb's story was "a case study in how information caroms around the country at whiplash speed in the digital age" and the use of "the World Wide Web to disseminate the story's material may have contributed" to the misinterpretations (p. 14A). The article even quotes the *Mercury News*'s Internet director asserting that conspiracy theorists "are well represented in the online world," as if to anchor the articulation between conspiracy narratives and the Internet through one of the accused agents in this articulation (p. 14A). Randolph and Broder warn that this "volatile effect of combining reporting, high-decibel promotion and the global reach of the World Wide Web" will need to be confronted by news producers (p. 14A).

Beato echoed this warning when he claimed that the story's "official nature, as well as its sheer bulk, gave [it] a mantle of well-documented legitimacy" (www.feedmag.com/ 96.11beato/96.11beato.html).). For Beato, this "information overload has always been a standard technique of conspiracists."[10] Because of its capacity to spread and increase info-glut, the Web is "the conspiracist's medium of choice." The Internet "reduces an investigative journalist's ethical responsibilities" and therefore the "new capabilities of this medium—its speed of transmission, its capacity for targeting receptive audiences, and establishing real dialogue—are powerful attributes that call for unusually high levels of responsibility and restraint." Beato can make this technologically determinist statement, however, only after saturating the technology with intelligibility through its link to conspiracy theories. Defined as a "hotbed" (Fallows in McChesney, 1997), "fertile ground" (Lasica, 1996), or "medium of choice" for conspiracy theories, the Internet is in this way made meaningful for the profession of journalism.

THE NET AND JOURNALISM: CRISIS ONLINE

Rendering the Internet intelligible was a primary concern for journalism at this time. According to Cockburn and St. Clair (1998), "Webb's series coincided with the coming of age of the Internet," when the establishment press had to "face the changing circumstances of the news business, in terms of registering mass opinion and allowing popular access" (p. 30). Webb's story was a sign of the "looser standards" that came with online journalism, and constituted a danger to traditional investigative journalism (Hanson, 1997; Weinberg, 1996). Just a few months after Dark Alliance was published, J. D. Lasica (1996) wrote an extended piece for the *American Journalism Review* on the crisis of going online. Lasica posed quasi-apocalyptic questions like "What will be the role of journalists when anyone with a computer and modem can lay claim to being a reporter? Will professional journalists be needed in an era when people can get their news 'unfiltered'?" (p. 20). But by the end of the article this threat of extinction subsides, as Lasica finds not just hope for survival but a chance for the profession's renewal. Because the Internet offers new interactivity and interconnectedness, "[j]ournalism needs to look at the Net not as a threat but as an opportunity to repair our strained public relations" (p. 30).

The Internet as both threat and promise is reiterated in 1997 by David Shaw of the *Los Angeles Times:*

> There is no clear agreement among editors on how best to capitalize on—but not be cannibalized by—this powerful new medium. This is a problem . . . of how to maintain the core function, values, and identity of a newspaper while taking advantage of the interactivity, synergy, graphic display and unlimited space the Internet offers. (p. A1)

This double valence, I argue, is resolved through a reinvigoration of the profession's authority. Specifically, what is proposed is a reaffirmation of its gatekeeping function in the public sphere of rational knowledge.

In 1995, Louis Boccardi, the president and CEO of the Associated Press, gave a keynote address at the Interactive Newspapers Conference emphasizing the need to establish trust online; a sentiment echoed by other editors (Fitzgerald, 1995a). Journalists "must not let themselves be seduced into dropping their own standards" Boccardi argued, because "journalism still carries the responsibilities that journalism has always carried" (Fitzgerald, 1995a, p. 31). To avoid technology's allure and preserve the profession's credibility, *Interactive Week* editor-in-chief Gary Bolles called for journalism to reinvigorate its filter function by creating "trust circles" amid the flood of new digital information (Fitzgerald, 1995b). An advertising framework was suggested, in which newspapers (and even individual journalists) would function as "brand names" with high trustworthiness quotients, producing brand loyalty to retain newspapers' credibility (Fitzgerald, 1995b).

Even after the Webb story's peak, J. D. Lasica (1997) argued that "in the still-evolving conventions of this young medium, we should embrace the enduring standards and values of traditional journalism: editorial integrity, balance, accuracy, respect for others and fairness" (p. 52). Staci D. Kramer, then chair of the Society of Professional Journalism's Task Force on Online Journalism, argued that the

> organization's traditional code of ethics is a good place to start. Its tenets are direct and clear: Seek truth and report it; minimize harm; act independently; and be accountable. . . . We need to remember: Common sense doesn't leave the room when online journalism comes in. (in Lynch, 1998, p. 42)

It is not surprising that the profession would affirm its basic principles. The important point here is that the threat of new technology was being handled through an even stronger affirmation of the profession's values and codes, as a way of reestablishing a waning authority while avoiding being "cannabalized."

The metastory around Gary Webb's exposé emerged when journalism was experiencing a crisis of legitimacy. As discussed in the previous chapter, this crisis involved not just a waning readership but a deteriorating social function concomitant with the perceived decline in civil society. This was a self-problematization in which the profession reflected on how its codes and protocols would encounter the new technology of the Internet. Mainstream journalism, concerned and even anxious about its relation to the new medium, charges it with being the chosen medium for unreliable fantasies of conspiracy theories. Reciprocally, the untrustworthiness of these theories' information is not just inherent in the theories themselves—they are untrustworthy precisely *because of* their circulation on the Internet.

CODING THE NET

The Internet in this professional narrative is coded as anarchic, turbulent, and disorderly. Just before the Webb series was published, *New York Times* staff writers declared that "the Internet is a medium defining itself, an untamed universe that has yet to be domesticated by any of the newspapers, magazines, television networks and other entities experimenting with online products" (Randolph & Broder, p. A1). In a similar vein, Philip Terzian (1996a) asserts that "the Internet . . . refuses to be tamed" (p. 31A). His editorial (which mentions the proliferation of conspiracy theories) describes the Net as

> essentially subterranean, a kind of drainage system. It seems to be a sort of space-age labyrinth: slow, overweight, haphazard and confusing, leading to no concrete destination. Its aptitude for good has yet to be proven; its power to do harm is still brimming with potential. (p. 31A)

And Catherine Ford (1997), discussing the relationship between the Internet and conspiracy theories, claims that

> much of [cyberspace] is raw copy—unedited, uncensored and unfiltered. It is the perfect forum for liars, cheats and megalomaniacs; the perfect outlet for those whose opinions are so beyond the pale that no reputable publication would touch them. . . . If television is entertaining into ignorance, cyberspace is informing us into anarchy. (p. B3)

The Internet is thus both excess (too much information careening with wild abandon) and lack (of ethics, filters, trustworthiness). Cyberspace is an untamable, irrational world, swirling with disorderly forces and dangerous, unlimited possibilities.[12]

In a curious way this new medium was defined as a "state of nature," an unrestrained and therefore ungovernable form of freedom. We can see this articulation between ultramodern technology and undomesticated nature in the mid-1990s proliferation of "Wild West" metaphors applied to cyberspace and the Internet. Coding the Internet as the Wild West had numerous semiotic valences: from the generally positive views of the Internet as a site of experimentation (Elrich, 1995; Impoco, 1996; Crowley, 1996), business prospecting (Verity, 1994; Elsworth, 1996; August, 1997), and libertarian frontier possibility (Leo, 1995) to the panic rhetoric around business dangers (Reuters dispatch, 1995; Pegoraro, 1997) and cybercrime (Myer, 1995; Editorial, *Newsweek*, 1994; Reynolds, 1995; Miller, 1996; Editorial, *Washington Post*, 1995).

By late 1996, however, there were calls to abandon the Wild West metaphor in favor of more ordered and lawful cyberspace (Humphrey, 1996) and by 1997 declarations were made that announced the end of the Wild West mentality (Neuwirth, 1997; Editorial, *Washington Post*, 1997; Richtel, 1997; Campbell, 1997). Even then-President Clinton employed the trope in declaring that "our task is to make sure that it's safe and stable terrain" (for e-commerce) (Baker & Chandrasekaren, 1997). For an account of how this metaphor operates with regard to hackers, see Taylor, 1999.

The Wild West metaphor was especially apt for analysts looking at how journalism would deal with the new technologies (Markoff, 1994; Randolph & Broder, 1996; Rieder, 1997b; Blumenthal, 1997; Shaw, 1997). "[B]ringing the gray lady to the Wild West Web," as journalist Laura Italiano (1996) eloquently put it, would mean taming the unbridled information flows through the application of professional protocols. Lacking the reasoned responsibility that has come to define modern rationality, the Internet functions as the ghost of the premodern that liberalism has constantly tried to ward off. In this case, coding the Internet as "out of control" smoothly leads to a conception of it as *needing* control. The wild world of cyberspace (particularly wild because of the unfiltered, even irrational, theories abounding in it) requires professional taming.

For journalism the development of the Internet was not simply a technological breakthrough in a history of progress. It was also a disruptive force, a threat not only in the usual sense (the hand-wringing sentiment "no one will read print journalism anymore") but also to the very *integrity* of journalism as a profession.[11] But these understandings were not simply a technophobic reaction by print-based establishment journalism. Mainstream journalism exhibited not an aversion to the new technology but an attempt at a controlled incorporation of it. What is at stake is *how*, not *if*, these new technological practices would be incorporated into journalistic practices. This annexation requires a set of problematizations of the technology in order to make it intelligible and therefore manageable.

These problematizations affect the very material, organizational relationship between journalism and the Internet. It is an articulation that both gives a meaning to the technology and reorganizes the profession itself. The problematization of the Internet *by* journalism, then, is also the self-problematization *of* journalism. By constructing the Internet in this way, journalism also authorized itself to intervene and to articulate itself to this new technology. Faced with a new development in the amateurization of news and information circulation, and fearing the loss of credibility as a filtering function, this unbridled technology was domesticated through the reaffirmation of the reasoned truth-telling protocols of journalistic practice.[13]

FREEDOM AND RESPONSIBILITY

The problem then is how to code the journalism-Internet coupling as a public space, as a free space in the marketplace of ideas, yet one still isolated from the seductive wild world of technological excess. Autonomy of the profession must be preserved, while thwarting the unbridled anarchy of unregulated thought and action. To this end, freedom itself is rejuvenated as liberal rights and responsibilities.

The value of "freedom" attached to technology is still "freedom of the press," in its classic liberal sense. First is the negative definition of freedom in which freedom *from* state intervention is a given: The profession's leaders never suggest that a responsible Internet will come from state regulation (see Fitzgerald, 1995a, 1995b; Lynch, 1998; and Lasica, 1996, 1997). Reviving journalism's position in public affairs thus requires not only "that the rational order of civil society be contrasted with the irrational disorder of natural society . . . [but also] between civil society and political society, that is, between civil society and the State" (Hardt, 1995). The freedom of the cyberpress is defined in a predictable way, as an *internal* issue, not an issue for legislation or censorship. Journalism, in this way, remains protected from external encroachment.

With freedom defined as an in-house matter, a second, technically positive version of freedom can be promoted. Embedded in the profession's protocols, codes, and rules for professional conduct, this notion of freedom provides a range of possible actions for subjects as long as they operate by the rules. As journalistic agents carry out their duties, professional freedom is intertwined with "responsibility."[14] Taming this unruly cyberspace requires the bolstering of professional protocols of truth telling and the cultivation of journalism's responsible subjects.

Freedom and responsibility are likewise intertwined in concepts like "journalistic ethics," "news judgment," and "professional conduct," which all work to produce a kind of reporter who operates through authorized procedures of knowledge production. As Michael Parenti (1993) argues, among others, reporters do not need direct censorship. By treating their "self-censorship as a matter of being 'realistic,' 'pragmatic,' or 'playing by the rules,' " reporters learn to regulate themselves (p. 41). By doing so, journalists recognize that their public duties "require the exercise of greater responsibility" (Nerone, 1995, pp. 51–52).

The notion of responsibility, endemic to journalism's historical professionalization, operates through everyday practices to produce self-monitoring journalistic subjectivities (autonomized reporters, editors, even readers). This applies to forms of journalistic truth telling as well, insofar as freedom entails truth and reason (in journalism's case, objectivity, balance, and the reliance on official sources). Journalism's agents are "responsibilized," which conditions the freedom espoused by the profession (Barry, Osborne, & Rose, 1996, p. 12).

Because of this entangling of freedom with reason under the sign of responsibility, untempered denunciations of the *Mercury News* story became possible, indeed mandatory. Being an irresponsible account irresponsibly connected to an irresponsible new medium, Webb's story functioned as a kind of test case for an Internet-journalism coupling. The test case revealed excess: excess that needed to be curtailed even as professional freedom through responsibility was reaffirmed and reinvigorated. Official journalism, via its articulation of the Internet to conspiratorial fantasy, reiterated its professional values by binding freedom to responsibility, and liberty to duty under the flag of reason. "Freedom," still defined by journalism's professional codes and practices, remained intact, as did those codes and practices themselves.[15]

BEYOND THE SECTARIAN: GOVERNING AND THE REGIME OF TRUTH

One could argue that the journalistic issues emerging in the CIA/Contra/crack metastory were simply a hermetic occupational debate, a cyber version of familiar, parochial intrainstitutional turf wars. By this account, professional envy—the fact that a regional newspaper scooped more prestigious ones—explains why established news organizations had to discredit the *Mercury News* (see, for instance, Barrs, 1996). But the CIA/Contra/crack metastory transcended the isolated concerns of a single profession to open a broader set of issues.

It is not enough to leave this analysis at the intrainstitutional level, an in-house approach that reduces journalism to an occupational activity rather than treating it as a social and political force. The professional regulation of, and struggles over, journalistic knowledge production are specific battles about wider truth-telling practices. According to John Tagg (1988), "what give such sectional actions a wider significance are their precise positions . . . in the 'political economy' of truth in our society, [in] . . . 'a regime of truth' " (p. 94).

Indeed, this wider significance extends even further. As discussed in the previous chapter, the professionalization of journalism is a kind of autonomization from the state. This meshes neatly with liberal political rationality, which seeks to govern at a distance. Required here is a sector of expertise that produces knowledge and creates responsible subjects, ones that circumscribe their conduct in accordance with reason. Conspiracy panics, here enacted by professional journalism, do the work of managing dissent and consent around these rules of reason.

In the case of the CIA/Contra/crack metastory, this professional autonomization operated successfully. There was no need for direct state intervention into the matter (e.g., preventing the *Mercury News* from publishing Webb's story). Instead, the responsibilized profession could act to dismiss the story via its protocols of truth telling. Labeled a "conspiracy theory," Webb's story violated both the rules of reportage and of reason and was therefore untrustworthy and unprofessional.

Autonomization and flexibility were at work in defining the Internet, as well. Through its provisional disruption and eventual restabilization, journalism bolstered its authority and integrity as a profession in the face of a technological "state of nature." Empowered with the innovative ability to destabilize itself to adapt to new conditions, professional journalism carried on its "action at a distance."

And there are even more explicit possibilities for professional journalism's general effects: For example, expertise "render[s] reality thinkable and practicable, and constitut[es] domains that are amenable—or not amenable—to reformatory intervention" (Rose, 1996, p. 42). Government does not take place on naturally given or unmediated objects: rather, "expertise plays a part in translating society into an object of government" (p. 13). With regard to the CIA/Contra/crack metastory, we can see the ability of expertise to create a governable domain. Journalism problematizes the Internet by attributing certain meanings to it; namely as a space of untrustworthy uncontrollable information practices and, more importantly, as the "medium of choice" for conspiracy theories. This problematization of the Internet contributes to ongoing crises and panics over new media and adds to the debate around state regulation of online media activities (around issues like pornography, pedophilia, peer-to-peer distribution, social networking, and hacking). As Laura Miller argued in 1995 (specifically with regard to the Wild West metaphor), "the way we choose to describe the Net now encourages us to see regulation as its inevitable fate" (in Taylor, 1999, p. 157).

Defining the Internet as the home for the menacing ideas of political paranoids can provide the conceptual conditions for policies and laws that boost intervention into cyberpractices, with the rationale of controlling dangerous extremist speech. The surveillance powers elaborated by the Patriot Act, for instance, are predicated on a conception of the Internet as a terrain where dangerous knowledges circulate and which needs to be secured. More specifically, the 9/11 Truth Movement has a significant online presence (examined in chapter 5), while "subcultures of conspiracy theories" are increasingly incorporated as targets of surveillance and detection. The conditions for defining cyberspace this way had already been established via, among other things, the conspiracy panics performed by professional journalism.

CONCLUSION

As Jodi Dean (2000) argues, the articulation of conspiracy rhetorics to the World Wide Web "places the question of the terms of truth and trust at the center of debates around the Internet and the World Wide Web" (p. 62). This was certainly the case when professional journalism dealt with the reemergent phenomena of conspiracy theories and the newly emerging Internet. As part of a conspiracy panic, the CIA/Contra/crack metastory represents a *crisis of trust* (especially in the social function of professional journalism). As portal, the conspiracy theory also displayed a broader cultural anxiety over the disruptive effects of new technologies. Journalism, by isolating and privileging certain cyberpractices, bestowed a meaning and coherence to the Internet congruent with its own historical ascendance as a profession. In doing so, the profession was able to reinvigorate itself as an autonomized practice in a liberal art of governing.

Reinvigorating the profession through new technology was only part of a larger strategy; namely to secure its function of representing the "public." The popular uses of technology examined here and in the previous chapter were one element of a broader campaign to distinguish the profession's mission (serving the "public") from popular culture and its hyperpathic populism (*JFK*, talk radio, *Dark Alliance*).

Ultimately, each journalistic event encountered an outsider; namely the rise of amateur journalists. This concern over popular journalism, especially in regard to new technologies, continued to inform debates about what constitutes journalism. A number of cultural analysts explored what a "popular journalism" might look like, outside of the public journalism movement (Hartley 1996). Recent controversies around the blogosphere, alternative sources of news (e.g., indymedia), and forms of citizen journalism raise this specter of the popular in the public once again. The phenomenon of blogging was able to break through the demonization of popular journalism by being taken seriously by professional journalists (even in one case having a concrete impact on the career of its stalwart, Dan Rather). As if outsourcing investigative journalism onto private individuals, bloggers garnered a quasi-legitimate status within public discourse. In addition, some professional news organs began to rely on "citizen journalists" for stories and photos (especially during dramatic crises). Yet we still can ask similar questions drawn from the above analyses.

In an age where technopolitical values like interactivity and audience integration abound, we have to ask, What forms of activity are rendered troubling and illegitimate? Some popular journalists are called "citizen journalists," as if their reporting was tied to a political subjectivity within the state. What is their cultural authority? How do they relate to the forms of truth telling deemed official and those that are subjugated? As for bloggers, they are generally given more leeway to have partisan viewpoints and opinions. But what are their limits, and when are they considered extremist or out of bounds? Those deemed "leftist" are often moderately liberal, while more radical perspectives are called "Bush-hating" or "America-bashing" extremists. A will-to-moderation still pervades the discourse about what counts as legitimate knowledge within the marketplace of ideas, and a particular rationality sets limits on popular participation in political knowledge production.

The long history of journalism's relation to the popular informs the 1990s. It takes on a particular hue with conspiracy panics. New and reemerging forms of populism (in popular culture, new news, in technological proliferation and usage) are met with "the professional-discursive," filtering the popular through a notion of the public. This allows journalism to renew its mission as marketplace gatekeeper as well as assist in the broader cultural-political crisis management of the withering of civil society.

Reviving professional protocols has a political and popular dimension, as the threat of amateurization comes to the foreground. In the previous chapter, the amateur came in the form of a Hollywood filmmaker (but amateur historian and political storyteller) and populist uses of radio and Internet. In this chapter we saw how professional journalism encountered the amateur in its ranks: not Gary Webb,[16] but the untrustworthy knowledge production, irrational truth telling, and irresponsible cyberpractices that followed Dark Alliance. This anxiety over the popular fueled the recent attempted stabilization of professional journalism, just as this anxiety marked the birth of the profession. Will science prevail in saving the public from themselves? Or will journalism become immanent to the internal interactions of the population, advising them on how to form their own moderate political body? Either way, journalism seeks to enhance both its own authority and the wider political rationality via acting as discursive agent in a conspiracy panic.

Professional journalism was a key discourse for conspiracy panics. Not only did it redefine and reorganize itself around neoliberal political rationality, it translated this rationality through various problematizations: popular culture, new technologies, forms of political knowledge. In doing so, professional journalism sought to create and revive a new public sphere or civil society, one in accordance with neoliberal rationality.

4

LEFT BEHIND

AIDS, Biowarfare, and the Politics of Articulation

The spring 1999 issue of *Paranoia: The Conspiracy Reader* featured an article entitled "The AIDS-ET Connection." This essay, written by Phillip S. Duke, PhD (we are not told in what), provides a "unifying scientific hypothesis" which purports to explain the simultaneous emergence of two different HIV strains in the geographically diverse areas of Africa and the United States (p. 51). Even more, this account claims to explain the phenomena of reported alien abduction experiences and cattle mutilations. Duke's unifying hypothesis is "the gray alien agenda," whose goal, in essence, is to rid the earth of human life and establish an alien settlement. AIDS has been deliberately introduced into the human population by these aliens as a way of freeing up space for colonization. In his conclusion, Duke, in good scientific fashion, limits his speculative claims by stating that the "AIDS-ET Connection must still be considered a hypothesis" (because there is not enough confirming data to render it a theory). He ends his article with a request for information, questions, and comments from the readership (pp. 51, 53, 54).

Splicing together different strains of conspiracy narratives (AIDS as biowarfare agent, the Ufological phenomena of abductions and cattle mutilations), "The AIDS-ET Connection" has the hallmarks of an AIDS conspiracy theory. In most commonsense approaches, this alone would be grounds for disqualification. But what element of the narrative is the crucial one that disqualifies it? Is it the interjection of the "gray alien agenda"? What if the agenda were terrestrial? Furthermore, if we categorize this hypothesis as a conspiracy theory, does that mean it is paranoid? And what does this have to do with the truth effects of Duke's claims?

In this chapter, I examine some of the political stakes involved in the production and problematization of AIDS conspiracy theories. AIDS conspiracy theories are widely disseminated and visible, and because of the urgency of life-and-death issues involved, perhaps the most fiercely debated. As Paula Treichler (1999) argues:

Meanings that can be loosely grouped as "conspiracy theories" warrant special attention . . . [they] are part of the larger "epidemic of signification" that the AIDS epidemic has generated—an epidemic that must be examined and interrogated, not eradicated. (p. 323)

Dismissing conspiracy accounts as "paranoid" would participate in this eradication by psychologizing the narratives out of their politics.

The special attention that AIDS conspiracy theories warrant includes the question, Can conspiracy theories ever be helpful in an ongoing crisis? As I show below, they are typically positioned as a distraction from real research and activism. But many of these conspiracy accounts *themselves* call for research and activism, hence dismissing them assumes that we know exactly what kind of knowledge, education, and activism is proper.

This is also the first of two chapters that will concentrate on conspiracy panics as they are enacted by what can loosely be called Left politics. I will therefore examine a progressive critique of AIDS conspiracy theories in order to foreground its political stakes and investments. What is threatened by AIDS conspiracy theories? Interrogating AIDS conspiracy theories insofar as they participate in an epidemic of signification entails, then, an interrogation of our own analytic frameworks and political identifications. Before taking on the conspiracy panic over AIDS conspiracy theories, I need to provide some general remarks about the Left's relationship to conspiracy research.

LEFT TURN

Thus far in this book we have been occupied with mainstream problematizations of conspiracy theories. But we cannot presume an already given politics in the theories and in the panics (e.g., that conspiracy theories are always oppositional and alternative, while dominant culture always seeks to problematize via a conspiracy panic). Thus, we continue to examine journalistic participation in conspiracy panics, but now with a focus on the alternative press. In this chapter and the next (on 9/11 and globalization conspiracy theories) we begin asking the following questions: How does the Left contribute to political rationality? How have conspiracy theories impacted progressive movements? What is the Left's role in conspiracy panics, and in liberal governance around fusion of thought and action?

The Left historically has had an ambivalent relationship to conspiracy research. Quite often it has been accused of trafficking in conspiracy theories. While almost any conspiracy narrative could have leftist implications or articulations, some are more easily identified as such. Among the research threads in this tapestry:

- The 1960s suspicion over state surveillance and agents provocateur (in COINTELPRO and other domestic spy programs)
- The research on various U.S. sponsored narcotics importation schemes (from Vietnam War–related importation of heroin to the CIA testing of LSD on citizens to the Iran-Contra drugs-for-weapons trade that spurs Gary Webb's CIA/Contra/crack story) (see Peter Dale Scott's work, Lee & Shlain, 1985, and Gary Webb, 1998)
- Narratives about 20th-century U.S. foreign policy involving assassinations, oppositional support, and coups (see much of Noam Chomsky's work)
- Elite control of media (though this is contested by people like Chomsky who argue that his is a structural analysis. But even political economic research gets *called* a conspiracy theory, which as far as conspiracy panics go is all that matters)
- Voter fraud (in the 2000 and 2004 U.S. presidential election)
- Hillary Clinton's "vast right-wing conspiracy" remark, which spurred broader research into the network of right-wing foundations, think tanks, and media outlets

This brief list doesn't include the various Left-leaning elements of other canonical conspiracy theories (e.g., U.S. domestic assassinations, UFO cover-up, New World Order, Gulf War cover-up, and subsequent Gulf War Syndrome).

But while a number of conspiracy theories are problematized as Left oriented, parts of the oppositional milieu explicitly disavow any association with them. Noam Chomsky is at pains to distinguish his "structural analyses" from "conspiracy theories" while often being accused of trafficking in them (more on this complicated relationship in the next chapter). The film *JFK* provoked a discussion among the Left in this regard. A few writers supported the premises as well as the political educational potential of the film (Parenti, 1992; Raskin, 1992). Others, like Alexander Cockburn and Chomsky, dismissed the film's politics, noting its lionization of Kennedy as leader and peacemaker, its blatant heterosexism, and its faulty central premise about Kennedy being killed for wanting to pull out of Vietnam rather than escalate. Amid the *JFK* film controversy, Chomsky claimed that conspiracy theories were tearing the Left to shreds (Parenti, 1996, p. 188). Michael Parenti (1996) responded that conspiracy theories could at times be useful supplements to leftist political research, even to structural analysis. This ambivalence over a popular cultural text continued later with conspiracy-laden texts like the *X-Files* and *Fahrenheit 9/11* (Kellner, 2002; Snider, 2004).

The problematization of conspiracy theories was taken up with full fervor in the wake of the Oklahoma City bombing, when conspiracy theories were articulated with militias (themselves located squarely in the right-wing camp). Ostensibly progressive analysts like Chip Berlet, Morris Dees, and

Kenneth Stern became expert sources for mainstream journalistic outlets, and outwardly leftist journalistic outlets like the *Progressive, Tikkun,* and the *Nation* led the charge against the dangerous knowledges that fueled militias. Chip Berlet, perhaps believing that it takes a conspiracy theory to fight a conspiracy theory, took it one step further by arguing that the Right was seducing and disrupting the Left with conspiracy narratives (e.g., 1994). Numerous others (Noam Chomsky, Michael Albert, David Corn, Alexander Cockburn, Peter Staudenmaier, Norman Solomon, David Gilbert, Joshua Frank, Diana Johnstone) have weighed in against the pernicious influence of conspiracy theories on the Left.

After September 11, 2001, conspiracy theories once again became a significant source of consternation and debate on the Left. These and other recent debates will be taken up in the final chapter, but for now I will end with an example that crystallizes the ambivalence and stakes of the Left's relationship to conspiracy panics; namely the contorted figure of Mark Crispin Miller.

In the late 1990s, Miller was a vocal problematizer of conspiracy theories. He, like many prominent academics and public intellectuals, distanced himself from conspiracy theories (Miller, 2000; 2003). However, in late 2005 Miller released a book on voter fraud in the 2000 and 2004 presidential races, promoting research that has been ridiculed as conspiratorial (Roig-Franzia & Keating, 2004; Zeller, 2004; Lubinger, 2004; Roeper, 2004; Varoga, 2004/2005). In a public presentation to 9/11 skeptics, Miller incredulously wondered why he wasn't being taken seriously about his work (even by the 9/11 conspiratologists). This once proud conspiracy panicker was now sharply exclaiming the truth of his subjugated knowledge. His earnest claims about evidence and proof of malfeasance make his enunciations all the more meager, as they do not recognize the context of reception that *he himself helped to weave.* This is why his is a tragic narrative, as his work set the stage for his own marginalization. His twist is an example of the Left's ills in the current predicament. Conspiracy panics thus belong to no political affiliation, and there is no necessary relationship of dissent to political rationality. Demonization in the name of reason can easily shift from being something done *by* a discourse to being done *to* that discourse.

RACE AND THE SOCIOCULTURAL APPROACH

The politics of conspiracy panics come into relief when we examine the issue of race. Recall that in the 1990s race was one of the most public of issues (e.g., affirmative action, identity politics on college campuses, the Tuskegee apology). We first visited this issue with the CIA/crack story in chapter 3, and we return to that moment now to elaborate the stakes of leftist approaches to conspiracy theories.

As discussed in that chapter, there was growing concern among African Americans over the ramifications of Gary Webb's *San Jose Mercury News* investigative series Dark Alliance (1996). Fearing that the story would incite the black community, then–CIA Director John Deutch made a personal visit to South Central LA to defend the CIA's activities to members of that community. In a town-meeting-style gathering, Deutch was met with resounding skepticism, jeers, and tough questioning.

Mainstream news accounts of the visit tended to applaud Deutch's efforts at reasoning with an unruly populace, as he "had confronted 'black paranoia' head on" (Cockburn & St. Clair, 1998: p. 90).[1] These commentaries emphasized the outrage expressed by the audience members, without furnishing the historical underpinnings or the specific details of Webb's story, which might have explained and justified that anger (Terzian, 1996a; Claiborne, 1996). Rather, African American anger was articulated as a byproduct of "race paranoia," of the irrational belief in a genocidal structure that targeted them (editorial, 1996, p. A14).[2] It was cited as an example of how African Americans are "vulnerable" to conspiracy theories (Mitchell & Fulwood, 1996, p. A1).

This should not be surprising, given the history of articulating African American identity to irrationality (e.g., associations with the body, animal nature, primitivism). This treatment of African American conspiracy narratives is a crucial practice within conspiracy panics and reared its head a few years after the Gary Webb story, regarding suspicion over 2000 presidential election fraud in Florida (Leo, 2000; Pierre & Morello, 2000; McFeatters, 2001; Brown, 2001) and over deliberate government sabotage after Hurricane Katrina in 2005 (J. Hicks, 2005; Russell & Donze, 2006; Thomas, 2005; Alberts & Voboril, 2005; Remnick, 2005; Thomas & Campo-Flores, 2005; Elliot, 2005). Some follow the lines of problematizers like Lasswell, Hofstadter, Pipes, Robins and Post, and Showalter, who use the clinical category of "paranoia."[3] What is common among almost all of these public discussions is the seemingly easy and commonsensical transposition of a medical framework to the field of politics. In essence, these approaches *psychologize* politics.

However, what is different about the reflections on African American conspiracy narratives is that this irrationality is no longer depicted as merely psychological. In addition to the traditional psychological approach, the more recent mainstream accounts of "political paranoia" also include what one might call a sociological or cultural approach.[4] This more nuanced analysis seeks not to dismiss conspiracy theories out of hand (as irrational), but rather searches for their origins in social, cultural, and economic conditions. This may not sound terribly problematic at first, as this framework pursues a more complex historical basis for these theories, even giving them a veneer of rationality (however misguided). In many cases, this approach has a sympathetic component, defining political paranoia as justifiable and sensible. However, as I argue here, these analytic frameworks are still disqualifying operations, as conspiracy accounts remain symptoms to be read, a result of social and cultural conditions rather than of a collective mental disorder. This kind of conceptualization does not only emanate from mainstream experts, it also infuses leftist approaches to conspiracy theories.

To begin understanding the sociocultural approach, let us return to the example of the CIA/Contra/crack connection. Commentators fleshed out this contextual approach. These "theories of conspiracy are articles of belief only for the powerless" and they "function as distraction from reality" (Kempton, 1996, p. 65). As Charles Lane (1996, p. 4) charges, "the black community is especially vulnerable" to those who would, in seeking their own "political prospects," manipulate "the understandable sorrow and frustration of people who have suffered cruelly from the drug epidemic." This black paranoia is similar to white militia paranoia, according to Cynthia Tucker (1995, p. A21), as "they boil up from the unreasoning fear and anger of people who are buffeted by forces they do not understand."

Because of this history, "a piece of black America remains hospitable to the most bizarre rumors and myths—the one about the CIA and crack being just one" (Cohen, 1996, p. A21). This appeal to social and historical contexts, while making the theory intelligible ("understandable"), works to explain the occurrence of prima facie misguided theories. "The litany of real injustices has spawned rumors that stretch the imagination" say Mitchell and Fulwood (1996, p. A1), and this history "makes the truth slide into rumor and then plummet into myth" (Britt, 1996, p. B01). For Bill Maxwell (1996, p. 32A), "black conspiracy theories should be called what they are: self-destructive traps that are bound in history." Maxwell goes on to assert that "too many of us blacks live squarely in the past . . . [s]uch an absorption with grievance prevents rational thought, making us susceptible to the most outrageous conspiracy theory or demagogue" (32A). These statements are indicative of the sociocultural approach, in which it is taken on faith that none of the claims being proffered are to be taken as credible; it is only the *emergence* of the claims themselves that need to be addressed.

In general, these mainstream accounts treated the belief systems of African Americans as "sociological curiosities" (Naureckas, 1997). That is, due to the understandable historical sedimentation of prejudice, African Americans lacked the rationality for political common sense. Historical oppression fuels the power of urban legends in the African American community, documented in Patricia Turner's *I Heard It Through the Grapevine* (1993). She does a thorough job tracing the different networks of information gathering and circulation. But by placing some conspiracy theories (governmental complicity with drug infusion, AIDS as biowarfare) into this mix with rumors, gossip, and innuendo (Church's Fried Chicken as KKK-owned sterility causer) and then contextualizing all of them as socially rooted, she ends up conflating all of these subjugated knowledges as social objects.

News media accounts drew upon similar assumptions. Rather than address the truth claims of those beliefs, these media reports went outside of the claims themselves to look for their rationale—in historical experience or social conditions. The knowledges are taken as phenomena that are to be understood through another discourse (not the one they are engaged in). They are to be *explained* not addressed, or addressed only by going behind them (dietrologically). One locates their "roots," unearthing their origins to account for the sprouting.

Conspiracy theories are not positioned as potential elements to be associated with (in terms of forging alliances) but are rather externalized as objects-to-be-studied. And how can rooted and muted objects respond? This question and its ramifications are at stake in this chapter. What is crucial here is that the sociocultural approach is a more sympathetic, but for that reason all the more effective, framework within conspiracy panics. Rather than find an acute threat (as in the case of the militias, for example), these panics seek to quell anxiety via a compassionate domestication. Political rationality employs more than one form of problematization, and it is important to see how the Left does or does not participate in them. In this chapter I explore one crystallized manifestation of the sociocultural approach on the Left, namely the response to AIDS-as-genocidal-warfare narratives.

AIDS, REAL GENOCIDE, AND REAL POLITICS

In introducing the conspiracy panics over AIDS conspiracy theories, I feel it necessary to enumerate some leading examples (see appendix). Though I have generally resisted describing conspiracy theories as such, it is important to show the formal and political heterogeneity of AIDS narratives that have been labeled "conspiracy theories." I have provided a chart that, while certainly not exhaustive, lists the most prominent versions of this account. The theories in the chart have either been problematized as a conspiracy theory (including the nonviral, nongerm warfare theories like Duesberg's), or have appeared in a forum that has been discursively positioned as a site for conspiracy theories (e.g., the zines *Paranoia* and *Steamshovel Press*, small presses like Adventures Unlimited and Feral House, or the websites *Conspiracy Nation* and *70 Greatest Conspiracies*).[5] The chart's variety of narratives allows us to recognize that any problematization requires *selection*. A conspiracy panic analysis often holds up a specific narrative as a synecdoche for conspiracy theories in general. This is especially true in the following case study.

GILBERT: DISTRACTIONS FROM REAL POLITICS

"Tracking the *Real* Genocide: AIDS—Conspiracy or Unnatural Disaster?" by David Gilbert, was the cover story of *Covert Action Quarterly* (1996). It was also republished as a pamphlet, along with reviews and discussion points (http://www.kersplebedeb.com/mystuff/profiles/gilbert/aids_rev.html). The author, we are told, has "been involved in the struggle against racism and imperialism since the early 1960s," is "currently serving a life sentence in New York State . . . as a white ally of the Black Liberation Army," and has been a "leading activist and educator on AIDS in prison" (p. 55).[6] Gilbert follows other political progressive and activist perspectives in theorizing about conspiracy theories. John S. James argued in 1986 that germ warfare conspiracy theories—then predominant—were not useful (James, 1986). "Even if proved," wrote James, "we could only punish the guilty, not save lives." Conspiracy theory "distracts from a better use of our energies," which is to inform the public about the "neglect and mismanagement of treatment research." For James, the conspiracy is a "conspiracy of silence," a pattern of ignorance about and mismanagement of AIDS treatment research by scientists, government officials, doctors, and journalists (pp. 1–5).

Simon Watney (1994) echoes this sentiment when he calls AIDS

> an ongoing massacre, quietly overseen and tacitly approved by the entire cultural and political system of the first world. Nobody may have set out with the intention that huge numbers of gay men should contract HIV, but that has been the inevitable consequence of government action, and inaction, all around the world. . . . This is not extermination by conscious policy, but by default, and the long-term consequences are not dissimilar." (p. 264)

This echoes Watney's critique of Peter Duesberg and other non-HIV dissidents: "We should scrutinize the 'anti-HIV' theorists very seriously indeed, for they consistently provide a gloss of pseudo-scientific respectability to profoundly irrational and usually homophobic forces" (p. 245).[7] While he does not explicitly position conspiracy accounts as distractions, Watney suggests that at that point in the epidemic (1994) origin stories may be irrelevant to the crisis. Moreover, at least in Duesberg's case, alternative origin stories have a strong link to oppressive reactionary agendas.

When the *New York Native* folded in 1997, the gay news magazine was credited with pioneering AIDS coverage in the early 1980s, as well as "criticized as a forum for conspiracy theories" (Pogrebin, 1997, p. 2). According to Troy Masters, then publisher of *Lesbian and Gay New York*, "It was a widespread community feeling that the *Native* had gone off on a long-winded, crazy, insane tangent that denied even the existence of AIDS, even while half of its staff died" (Pogrebin, 1997, p. 2).

David Gilbert's article makes a stronger claim: that conspiracy theories are *politically disabling* and *health endangering* (1996, pp. 55–64). But how does he end up with these positions? A close analysis of his argument is needed to understand how he arrives at the conclusion that in the contemporary AIDS crisis, conspiracy theories are antagonistic to leftist concerns. Gilbert opens by citing statistics that demonstrate that "the correlation between

AIDS and social and economic oppression is clear and powerful" (p. 55). He then argues that this pattern "meshes neatly with an extensive history of chemical and biological warfare (CBW) and medical experiments which have targeted people of color, Third World populations, prisoners, and other unsuspecting individuals" (pp. 55–56). He discusses here the genocidal use of smallpox-infested blankets against Native Americans, the Tuskegee experiment, and recent examples of vaccination testing fiascoes against African Americans. Because of this context, Gilbert argues, "there are good reasons why so many prisoners as well as a significant portion of the African American Community believe that government scientists deliberately created AIDS as a tool of genocide" (pp. 56–57). With the use of "good reasons" argument and the mention of Tuskegee, Gilbert signals early on that he'll employ the sociocultural approach (which was echoed elsewhere regarding AIDS, see Deparle, 1991; Hill, 1995; Gehorsam, 1991; Clark, 1992; Bock, 1994; and Asim, 1993).

Gilbert continues for the next few pages with a two-tiered critique of these beliefs—scientific and political. First, Gilbert announces that there is a "problem with this almost perfect fit [between AIDS and deliberate genocide]: It is not true" (p. 57). The splice theories of HIV's origin "wilt under scientific scrutiny" (p. 58).[8] To document the rigorous scrutiny that triumphs over the human-made splice-theory origin story, Gilbert cites two scientists. First, he defers to his friend Janet Stavnezer ("a professor of molecular genetics and microbiology specializing in immunology") who states that the "splice theory is scientifically impossible" (pp. 57–58). Second, he cites Dr. David Dubnau who, in a *Covert Action Information Bulletin* article nine years earlier, stated that the HIV splice theories "are simply wrong" (p. 58). No findings from any studies are produced. Rather, Stavnezer's statement comes from "personal correspondence and discussions" and Dubnau, whose specific scientific credentials are not given, is simply cited from a previous article (p. 59, n. 8).

This appeal to expertise is followed by a further scientific attempt to dismiss the human-made HIV origin story. Gilbert argues that the spacing and timing of the epidemic "eliminate the possibility that scientists deliberately designed such a germ to destroy the immune system" (p. 59). This claim assumes the fixed truth of certain scientific hypotheses that in 1996 remained contested. These include the geographical pattern of vaccination campaigns (linked in many conspiracy accounts to the spread of AIDS), and the "compelling evidence for the earlier genesis of HIV" (p. 59). While these claims were still being debated and researched (some of the "1950s AIDS cases" have remained highly questionable and certainly controversial), Gilbert asserts them as authoritative.

He also gives considerable credence to conventional renditions of scientific practice, claiming that until "the end of the 1970s the search for human retroviruses was propelled by speculation that they might cause cancer, not that they would target the immune system" (p. 59). Gilbert here consolidates retroviral research into a unified drive with a single-minded target, a consolidation that would certainly be disputed by practitioners at the time. Gilbert's faith in the stated goals of retroviral studies also ignores military biowarfare research, including the document considered a "smoking gun" in many AIDS biowarfare accounts. It is a transcript of once-classified testimony by Dr. Donald MacArthur, a deputy director of the Department of Defense, to a House of Representatives subcommittee on military appropriations. In it, MacArthur requests funding "to make a new infective microorganism which ... might be refractory to the immunological and therapeutic processes upon which we depend to maintain our relative freedom from infectious disease" (House Committee on Appropriations, 1969).

By asserting that HIV existed prior to U.S. chemical-biological warfare (CBW) research into it, Gilbert invests trust in the official record of science's history rather than the institutional secrecy endemic to CBW scientific practice. That is to say, Gilbert eschews his *own* critical sensibility, the one he employed when he earlier discussed the history of abuses by mainstream science and covert medical warfare. Instead he chooses to use mainstream science to discredit AIDS-as-genocide conspiracy accounts. Gilbert at times deploys science as part of the evidence for the Real Genocide, and at others to disqualify the False Genocide. This brings up the general issue of science in relation to both conspiracy theories and their critics: "When does science get questioned, and when does it get cited as evidence?"

By appealing to expertism and investing faith in the official record, Gilbert tries to use science's power to authorize his own position, ignoring even his own discussion of the complicity of science in a history of oppression. In other words, science's dirty history (biowarfare, genocide) is separated from its clean methods. Yet implicit in this rhetorical move is the assumption that we know when science was/is impure (mixed with power, used as a weapon) and when it is pure (as method, as official history). A critic might counter that by not respecting the distinction we move dangerously close to throwing the baby out with the bathwater. However, this already *presumes* the distinction: It is more analogous to say the difficulty lies in distinguishing the dirty from the clean water in the bath before throwing it out.

Gilbert then dissects what he calls "the most common source of the conspiracy theories circulating in New York State prisons," the work of William Campbell Douglass, MD (p. 59). I do not doubt his experiential claim of Douglass's prominence. However, it is important to highlight Gilbert's selection among the variety of AIDS conspiracy theories. I want to note that singling out Douglass for discussion makes possible generalizing statements that do not hold true for all AIDS conspiracy theories.

Before turning to Douglass, Gilbert establishes a political and activist frame for his interpretation. In this second phase of his two-tiered critique, in a section entitled "Dangerous to Your Health," Gilbert argues, as James did a decade earlier, that

> conspiracy theories divert energy from the work that must be done in the trenches if marginalized communities are to survive this epidemic: grassroots education, mobilization for AIDS prevention, and better care for people living with HIV. (p. 57)

These theories "distract from the urgent need to focus a spotlight on the life-and-death issue of AIDS prevention and on the crucial struggle against a racist and profit-driven public health system" (p. 57). In his experience as prison AIDS educator, the author has located "these conspiracy theories to be the main internal obstacle . . . to implementing risk reduction strategies" (p. 57).

Gilbert briefly notes research at the University of North Carolina that confirms his anecdotal experience (p. 57), though he provides no citation for this research. A similar study, carried out elsewhere by social psychologists Gregory M. Herek and John P. Capitanio (1994), correlates AIDS-related distrust to beliefs about casual-contact transmission and to personal risk reduction behaviors. It is worth mentioning and discussing the findings here.

Though the study found that "distrust is strongly associated with AIDS-related beliefs and attitudes," this distrust was limited to distrust of doctors and the perception that information about AIDS was being withheld (p. 372). It found that "[b]eliefs about casual contact were not related" to beliefs in the genocidal purpose of AIDS (p. 372). In addition, "distrust was unrelated to whether or not respondents reported behavior changes" (p. 372). Thus, suspicion of government could not be equated with suspicion of science, and in any case did not affect reported behavioral changes. The authors, however, still speculated that the lack of trust in health educators "springs from suspicions" about "malicious intent" on the part of the government (p. 373). This study may further anchor the notion of a "climate of distrust" and its ramifications for AIDS prevention, but its findings tell us little about specifics (p. 366).

Moreover, the study's exclusive focus on distrustful and alternative beliefs ultimately identifies those beliefs as the problem. This is not unusual, as concern over credibility and trust for health education appears in numerous problematizations of AIDS conspiracy accounts. It is especially directed at African Americans (see, for instance, Gehorsam, 1991). Focusing on "problem" skepticism ignores the historical relation between science and the state, a relation that itself could be considered a problem or obstacle. Recall that during this time period (1995 and 1996), the Ebola outbreak and other potential pandemics were also highly publicized health scares, and were accompanied by conspiracy accounts about the origin and purpose of these superviruses (Horowitz, 1996). In other words, biomedicine's relation to biowarfare was an object of public concern (especially in popular cultural texts like *Outbreak*, *Virus*, and the *X-Files*). While this fairly contained epidemic of signification was not the object of sustained empirical research, it was "in the air" at the time.

While it is important to understand behavior/belief correlations, Gilbert uses public reaction studies to make a causal articulation. He preserves portions of biomedical research from skepticism under the notion that this skepticism endangers health. Meanwhile, the reasons for skepticism are presumed to reside in the disbelievers rather than in the institutional/discursive history. Even if "good reasons" exist, the sociocultural approach finds mistrust as such unjustified (not just a particular narrative claim, but the skepticism that fuels it).

Research that focuses on "public reactions" to AIDS biomedical science often leaves the science/power articulation untouched. Rather than investigate how this history may produce a corollary mistrust of medical scientists, doctors, and health educators, public reaction research evaluates skeptical beliefs as obstacles (Shelton, 1997). This stance itself can further entrench the science/power alignment, and fuel further skepticism.[9] This seems to be an ongoing problematization: in January 2005 the Rand Corporation (in tandem with Oregon University) released the findings of a study demonstrating that almost half of the African American respondents believed AIDS to be man-made, with 12% believing it was created and spread by the CIA (Fears, 2005). Not as sensationalized was the finding that 75% believed that medical and public health agencies are working to stop the spread of AIDS in black communities. At least one half of those who believe AIDS was human-made also believe medical institutions were helping (showing a potential discrimination between biomedicine and biowarfare). Instead of actually demonstrating a link between belief and preventive behavior, the news accounts relied on health care practitioners' assertions like "It's a huge barrier to HIV prevention in black communities" (Fears, 2005).

One example that complicates problematizations of skepticism is the article by Stephen Thomas and Sandra Crouse Quinn (1991). Their work argues that "public health professionals must recognize that Blacks" belief in AIDS as a form of genocide is a legitimate attitudinal barrier ... with a legitimate basis in history" (p. 1503). The authors call for a dialogue in order "to develop and implement HIV education programs that are scientifically sound, culturally sensitive, and ethnically sensitive" (p. 1504). Now, while this employs a dietrological approach to conspiracy theories, it at least begins to recognize the dialogic necessities of education (though one wonders if this dialogue would still retain a fundamental faith in mainstream science—see Treichler, 1999, pp. 159–160). Despite these qualified and nuanced findings, Thomas and Quinn's work is cited in news briefs entitled "Conspiracy theories about HIV puts individuals at risk" (appearing on three different websites: Key, 1995a; Key, 1995b; and Clark, 1995). The researchers' careful claims are reduced to scare headlines about AIDS conspiracy theories in general. It is this kind of abstraction and generalization that informs Gilbert's citation of the uncited University of North Carolina study.[10]

To return now to Gilbert's political-activist critique: Gilbert makes three crucial links that will guide his reading of Douglass's conspiracy theory, as well as determine his perspective on conspiracy theories in general.

First, Gilbert finds that the mind-set of "denial" among prisoners is a result of their adherence to conspiracy theories. In doing so, he conflates HIV origin stories with HIV transmission stories (something he later takes Douglass to task for). He asks in the voice of the prisoners, "What's the point of all the hassles of safer sex, or all the inconvenience of not sharing needles if HIV can be spread, as many conspiracy theories claim, by casual contact such as sneezing or handling dishes?" (p. 57). While there *are* some conspiracy theories that do have a casual-contact version of transmission (Douglass being the premier example, as do many of the black genocide theories), it does not follow that *all* chemical-biological warfare AIDS origin stories or HIV splice theories contain them (again see appendix)

Based on this conflation, however, Gilbert makes a second link, between origin stories and behavioral practices. "People whose activities have put them at risk of HIV are often petrified and turn to conspiracy theories as a hip and seemingly militant rationale for not confronting their own dangerous practices" (p. 57). Origin stories, then, are rationalizations for risky behavior. While this may follow in some instances, Gilbert generalizes to the point of arguing that belief in conspiracy theories *as such* serves to evade "all the hard choices to avoid spreading or contracting the disease" (p. 57). In essence, belief in conspiracy theories leads to risky behavior, and resistance to AIDS education.

In his third link, Gilbert moves from preventative health education to preventative *political* education. Gilbert argues that "[conspiracy] theories provide an apparently simple and satisfying alternative to the complex challenge of dealing with the myriad of social . . . factors that propel the epidemic" (p. 57). Harkening back to his opening argument that conspiracy theories have "good reasons," Gilbert finds these origin stories to be overly simplified misrecognitions of the "real" conditions of oppression. Rather than locate origin stories as one possible factor within the "myriad" driving the epidemic, Gilbert chooses to describe them as a competing analytic framework, one that is too simplistic and ignorant of "real" conditions to have legitimacy as political analysis. Gilbert himself doubts the possibility of knowing the origin of AIDS any time soon, but is personally "convinced that humans did not design HIV" (p. 57). Origin stories about AIDS in this account are, at best, unknowable and thus unrelated to political and educational struggles, and, at worst, a deadly diversion from urgent prevention practices and real political analysis.

After articulating AIDS origin stories to transmission stories, unsafe behavioral practices, and political ignorance Gilbert now offers his principal assertion: "False conspiracy theories are themselves a contributing factor to the terrible toll of unnecessary AIDS deaths" (pp. 56, 57). It is this urgent proclamation that frames Gilbert's subsequent reading of Douglass's conspiracy theory and overall assessment of the political and educational effects of conspiracy accounts.[11]

The article proceeds with an elaborate and detailed explication of William Douglass's theory. Gilbert's description of Douglass is accurate, thorough, and coincides with the summary in the appendix. As mentioned earlier, Gilbert focuses on Douglass because he is the "most common source of the conspiracy theories circulating in New York State prisons" and his works "are prime sources for many black community militants and prisoners who embrace the conspiracy theory out of a sincere desire to fight genocide" (p. 59). But Douglass's theory also embodies all the problems about which Gilbert has already alarmed us. Douglass believes that AIDS is not a sexually transmitted disease, that it is an airborne virus and that it can be transmitted through eating utensils. Douglass's origin story (the splice theory), bound up as it is with casual-contact transmission, can clearly lead to severely destructive behavioral practices.

Douglass also has strong right-wing politics, believing AIDS to be part of a communist plot to destroy Western civilization (his view persists, despite the collapse of the Soviet Union). In addition, as Gilbert notes, Douglass's prescriptions for action primarily involve establishing and strengthening law-and-order policies (p. 61). These proposals include mandatory HIV testing, quarantining HIV-positive people, removal of HIV-positive children from school, and antiprostitution measures ranging from imprisonment to execution. Furthermore, Douglass issues a hodge-podge of reactionary calls to save Western civilization (through, for example, military action against Russia, the abolishment of the United Nations and the World Health Organization, and anti-Mexican immigration policies). Thus, Douglass perfectly embodies the worst of conspiracy theories, especially for the Left-leaning readership of the *Covert Action Quarterly* (CAQ). But in no way could he be said to adequately represent conspiracy theories in general.

Gilbert uses Douglass's reactionary theory as a springboard for a discussion of contemporary populist struggles. Linking Douglass to Lyndon Larouche through their mutual reliance on the work of prominent AIDS conspiracy theorist Robert Strecker, MD, Gilbert begins to articulate AIDS conspiracy theories monolithically to the then highly publicized right-wing movement in the United States. He trots out the familiar figure of Bo Gritz (a former Green Beret who was a prominent militia spokesperson in the mid-1990s), linking these theories to the militia movement and further entrenching the articulation to right-wing politics.[12]

There is a brief meditation on the danger of being seduced by the Right's populist, "attractive mantle of 'militant anti-government movement' " (a significant move that I will discuss in the next section). Gilbert then restates his main thesis:

> Whatever the right's motives, the practical consequences are clear: There is a definite correlation between believing these myths and a failure to take proven, life saving preventive measures. In the end, the lies promulgated by the likes of Douglass, Strecker, and Larouche kill. (p. 62)

The argument cements its articulation of AIDS conspiracy accounts to a particular political position by invoking the deadly effects that necessarily flow from these accounts.

The rest of the article elaborates what the "real" genocide is, providing a meticulous account of the numerous factors contributing to the horrific living conditions facing impoverished African Americans, and the criminally negligent role of the public health and political systems in furthering the AIDS epidemic. Gilbert concludes with a call for grassroots organizing and peer education, while decrying "the fundamentally right-wing conspiracy theories of Dr. Douglass and the like that lead us on a wild goose chase for the little men in white coats in a secret lab," which (once again) "divert people from identifying and fighting back against the real genocide" (p. 64). Gilbert thus concludes with ridicule (one is reminded of "little green men"), an urgent political warning, and a final appeal to the authority of the "real."

THE LEFT AND SOCIOCULTURAL APPROACHES

Gilbert's article demonstrates what I have called the sociocultural approach to conspiracy theories. This framework finds "good reasons" for these conspiratological beliefs (in the conditions of social/political oppression), giving them an understandable, rational basis. However, this approach still finds these narratives to be misguided in their *apprehension* of those conditions. That is, the conspiracy narratives cannot have a purchase on *explaining* those conditions of oppression, but they can be *explained by* an appeal to those contexts. Even at the discursive moment when the analysis invokes a shared historical context (of oppression), there is still a distancing effect produced between Gilbert and his objects. The analyst authorizes himself with a clearer, truer perspective that will explain how another set of claims has been misguided in their analysis of the "same" context.

Why focus on one article? For one thing, Gilbert's piece appears on the cover of a well-known radical periodical, recirculated as a pamphlet, and republished in a 2004 anthology of his work. The author is someone with respected Left credentials (former SDS and Weather Underground member). Most importantly, Gilbert, in my opinion, has provided the most cogent and serious treatment of the topic of AIDS conspiracy theories from the Left. Other leftist accounts are footnotes to his germinal piece (e.g., Hutchinson, 2005). It encapsulates in an impassioned and persuasive manner the assumptions and articulations made off-handedly by others in the sociocultural approach to conspiracy theories. Unlike the mainstream hatchet jobs performed on conspiracy theories, Gilbert's argument does not dismiss them out-of-hand as paranoid. He takes them on as a significant set of political claims, ones that develop from and respond to the same conditions as his own analysis (and by extension, the Left's).

The problem is that he too readily depicts them as a *competing* set of claims—in fact a competing *framework*—that simplistically assesses its own conditions. He attributes deadly effects to these mistaken beliefs, giving them the power of life and death in altering behavior. Finally, he locates these beliefs in a right-wing politics, turning the perceived competitor into an enemy. Two kinds of articulation, then, are performed by Gilbert: (1) conspiracy accounts are articulated to effects and behavior (origin to transmission to behavior) and (2) conspiracy accounts are articulated to a right-wing politics. Teasing out these linkages foregrounds the politics of articulation and elaborates the political stakes involved in Gilbert's analysis. His article crystallizes a more common process within conspiracy panics: Problematizations are formed as a result of selection and articulation.

Gilbert's discussion of the contemporary Right explicitly exhibits his selective process. The section entitled "Sign of the Times" is surprisingly tangential in an otherwise cogently structured argument. Like Lasswell's eruptive marginal section on the political paranoid seventy years earlier, its very "straying" offers insight into Gilbert's entire meditation on AIDS conspiracy theories. With logic reminiscent of Chip Berlet's account of Larouchite politics, Gilbert depicts the Right as a seductive force upon the terrain of radical politics.[13]

In his own best mimicry of a conspiratologist, Gilbert asserts, "the 'Populists' use anti-business rhetoric to try to recruit from the [L]eft" (p. 62). Wearing "the attractive mantle of 'militant anti-government movement,'" he continues, "the [R]ight has co-opted the critique of big government and big business" (p. 62). AIDS conspiracy theories, then, become merely one more instrument that the Right uses to appear radical and divert energies away from "real" problems (i.e., those that historically have come under the Left's domain).

The "Dangerous Diversion" that AIDS conspiracy theories present, then, is not primarily the distraction from AIDS activism or prevention, but from proper analysis and politics (i.e., Left politics). Concerned with a loss—of domain and of discursive authority—Gilbert articulates conspiracy theories to the Right as a preventative maneuver. He positions conspiracy theories in the opposition's camp to reduce their powers of seduction. Forgoing an exploration of a way to link AIDS conspiracy accounts to the concerns and strategies of a Left politics, Gilbert instead argues not only that conspiracy narratives are unlinkable to the Left, but that they are ultimately *antagonistic*. Rather than assessing if and how a conspiracy origin story might help define the contemporary social-political-economic context, Gilbert claims that a conspiracy theory conceptualizes an entirely different context, one that diverts attention from the real one. Such diversions need conceptual policing: They belong to the enemy; they are life threatening and Left threatening.

The political spectrum, anchored by Left and Right, is jeopardized by the emerging popularity of conspiracy theories (the threat of "fusion paranoia" explained in chapter 1). Gilbert responds to trouble on the spectrum via a conspiracy panic by placing conspiracy theories in the opposition's camp, where the threat is more intelligible and thus more manageable.

At stake in the CAQ article, then, are the very identity, stability, and legitimacy of the Left in the chaos of contemporary politics. How will the Left be oppositional yet viable? How will analytic frameworks articulate to conspiracy research? As explored in the following chapter, the 1990s was an era of identity crisis in leftist resistance. With the Democratic Party in charge of the executive branch, a fragmented Left (without the Reagan-Bush common enemy) sought to negotiate its relationship with the Clinton regime. When conspiracy theories arose they were primarily associated with the Right (often exacerbated by the actual production of numerous anti-Clinton conspiracy accounts—Whitewater, Vince Foster's death, Ron Brown's plane crash, Mena airport). In addition, researchers like Chip Berlet sounded warnings that conspiracy theories were a seductive weapon employed by the Right to woo Left dissenters. At the same time, the late 1980s and early 1990s saw the emergence of the sociocultural framework, a seeming nonpartisan approach to conspiracy theories (especially African American ones). Meanwhile, the legacy of JFK (the assassination and the film) continued to fracture oppositional dissent. Ultimately, this context informs Gilbert's article while also being articulated by it.

As Lawrence Grossberg argues (1992; 2000), without being aware of the articulatory practices informing its work, the Left project will hamper its own potentials. Gilbert's own articulations thus need to be foregrounded as a way of assessing these potentials. Eschewing a *politics* of articulation, Gilbert's article *performs* articulations through an identity politics, in which certain narratives have at their core a determined set of effects, and which are located in an identifiable and essential position in the political field.[14] Rather than open the Left up to critique and rearticulation with potentially valuable subjugated knowledges, Gilbert wishes to place the Left squarely within the dominant regime of truth where science and authority subdue competing subjugated claims. The article seeks to position the Left as the sanctioned bearer of correct analysis, as well as the legitimate judge of the truth of radical politics.

CULTURAL STUDIES, RACE, AND AIDS GENOCIDE ACCOUNTS

While Gilbert does represent a sophisticated position within broader leftist discourse, the academic transdiscipline of cultural studies offers further insight into the stakes of AIDS conspiracy theories, especially regarding race politics. John Fiske (1994) has explored the AIDS-as-black-genocide account without employing the standard sociocultural approach (pp. 191–216). He calls the account a "counterknowledge," which involves

> recovering facts, events, and bits of information the dominant knowledge has repressed or dismissed as insignificant. Other bits of information in a counterknowledge may once have been part of official knowledge, but have been disarticulated from it and rearticulated into a counter way of knowing, where their significance is quite different. (p. 191)

Above all, according to Fiske, a counterknowledge "must be socially and politically motivated" (p. 192). Fiske proceeds with a series of close readings of radio talk-show dialogues, primarily culled from Black Liberation Radio. In these accounts, AIDS is folded into a genocidal framework, itself an oppositional knowledge that

> depends upon a proliferation of "telling details" whose interconnections are not traced because the tellingness of each detail reverberates with the others and finally tells what is already known—in this case, genocide. These telling details are where more abstract knowledge is given flesh and blood and made part of lived experience. (p. 204)

It is this reverberation with history and lived experience that Fiske argues is lacking among mainstream whites, and thus produces an aversion to the concept of genocide. Even when mainstream news media address the AIDS-as-black-genocide account, the "taken for granted assumption is that the belief is mistaken: never once does it consider the possibility that it might be true . . . [it] implies that the problem for whites is Black belief in genocide, not the possibility that the strategy might really exist" (pp. 211, 213).

This is where Fiske provides a crucial contribution. He does not simply affirm the truth of the genocide account. As he states, we "will never know 'objectively' whether or not AIDS is part of a genocidal strategy, for any evidence that might establish such a truth will be 'lost' or, should it survive, be strenuously denied" (p. 215). However, since evaluation is still required, we need to select bits of information and make them resonate with each other to produce a truthful knowledge "as it meets the needs of the social position from which the process is undertaken and that provides the motivation to engage in it" (p. 215). In other words, Fiske is arguing that any knowledge claim ought to go through this simple filter: Who speaks it? From what position? What drives it? This perspectivism (which, unlike relativism, does not attach a value—even equivalence—to the claims) is thus a form of sociocultural analysis, but with one major difference: It is not exclusively applied to the "problem" knowledges or conspiracy theories. Fiske asks us to situate the positions taken from *within* conspiracy panics.

Later in his chapter Fiske offers an example of mainstream articulation and contrasts it to how a radical "might construct a quite differently articulated knowledge, and might link it to suspicions that segments within the CIA and the Pentagon are constantly formulating and executing covert policies" (p. 216). Ultimately, however, what matters for Fiske is that we examine our *strategies of disbelief*, since "one surety stands out: if AIDS is a genocidal strategy, widespread disbelief that this is so is necessary for its success" (p. 216). By shifting our attention from "reasons for belief" (the more common sociocultural dismissal within conspiracy panic) to "strategies of disbelief" Fiske invites us to reconsider our subjective relations to skepticism and faith.

When is something a target of suspicion, and when is it an object of affirmation? Rather than direct our own suspicion at a presumed excess of skepticism, after taking Fiske seriously we are left asking ourselves *where* this suspicion is directed, and which modes of belief it also presumes.

Mark Fenster (1999) has responded to Fiske's work critically. Fenster argues that the "implications of Fiske's argument are that all African American theories of genocide—including, perhaps, those positing Jewish control of the African slave trade—are presumptively populist and worthy of championing as practices of resistance" (p. 223). In doing so, Fenster reiterates a common criticism of Fiske's work, namely "his unexamined compulsion to champion certain beliefs and practices of the people as necessarily right or at least politically defensible (even if politically, historically, or scientifically inaccurate)" (p. 223). Ultimately, according to Fenster,

> Fiske's notion of "counterknowledge" is thus too abstract to explain the specificities of "resistance," failing both to explain the political and epistemological valences of black conspiracy theory and to provide a theoretical concept that can enable analysis of contemporary populist discourse. (p. 225)

For Fenster, Fiske fails insofar as he uncritically "champions" (the word is used twice in the same paragraph) the AIDS-as-black-genocide account and by doing so misses the nuances of counterpractices.

I am arguing, however, that Fiske is less concerned with affirming the account as heroic, truthful, or wholly articulatable than in analyzing the specific construction of a counterknowledge *and* the practices of subjugation directed at it. Because his main interest is in the counterknowledge and not the anticonspiracy discourse, the latter emerges in hints, aporias, and interstices. That is, Fiske, like many positions within conspiracy panics, analyzes how and why a knowledge is composed, seeking to understand conspiracy theories and their adherents. However, he has no interest in a priori disqualification of those accounts (the "why normal people believe weird things" model). In addition, he forces the reader to question *which* narratives get problematized, and *how* they get analyzed. This is what distinguishes him from conspiracy panic problematizers. Articulation is Fiske's overriding concern. In doing so, he highlights articulations by the "knowledge gangsters" as well as possible articulations to radical critiques. In sum, Fiske is more concerned with theorizing regimes of credibility and conditions of articulation, rather than using theory to provide programmatic judgments and practical guidance.

Fenster ignores the fact that Fiske is, precisely, examining one concrete account rather than seeking to explore all of the possible genocide accounts with their various reprehensible features. Instead, Fenster seeks a theoretical concept that could make a sweeping evaluation of genocide accounts *in general*. While Fiske emphasizes the bits and elements that compose a particular narrative, Fenster adds possible other bits (separatism, anti-Semitism) that would taint genocide accounts in general and prevent their articulatability. The issue is whether one locates the moments of openness or seeks to close down possible conjugations. If anything, Fiske may be too *specific* in offering little that could cut across accounts and articulations. But then again, if his point is to examine the "processes of counterknowledge production" along with the "strategies of disbelief" as a perspectival exercise, then criteria of evaluation may not be necessary to his analysis.

What Fenster is calling for, in his own words, is "a theoretical concept that can enable analysis of contemporary populist discourse" (p. 225). But his kind of analysis is a problematization of conspiracy theories *as such*. The discussion of Fenster's work in the introduction to this book makes this clear: While a more sympathetic and sophisticated account, he shares with many in the conspiracy panic discourse the desire to evaluate tout court an object that is synthesized in the analysis. Fiske, on the other hand, avoids the easy appellation of conspiracy theory to the AIDS-as-biowarfare account, examines the narrative in its constitution as a counterknowledge, and defers sweeping judgment on the account (much less on conspiracy theories in general). In fact, Fenster's assumption that Fiske's analysis of the genocide account and counterknowledge is an analysis of a conspiracy theory already begs the question of what kind of analytic object is being shared.

We can see what this means for Fenster. He follows his critique of Fiske with concluding remarks on conspiracy theories as a whole (they fail to be articulatable). Fenster makes a diagnostic judgment on an entire cultural practice, even while he himself has done much to tease out the nuances and variations in conspiracy theories. Fenster's multiplicity is still contained within a consistent, structured object. Once the object is positioned as coherent, his dietrological framework finds the characteristics that taint the object (as mistaken, as a misrecognition, as reactionary). Articulation is foreclosed, since the object itself is sealed with a fate that belongs to its composition. In contrast, Fiske locates the moments of multiplicity as moments of openness, stressing the possible articulatory lines rather than the cemented chains of equivalence.

Ultimately, I would also question whether providing a theoretical concept is adequate when it comes to articulation. Can the issues of articulation, counterknowledge, and political practice be resolved at the level of theoretical analysis? Fenster seems to think so, as his assessment of populism and conspiracy theories seeks to be the last word on the matter. But what is the role of political analysis and intellectual work?

Analysis is not a solution to the concrete articulations and practices circulating throughout culture. Instead, it reveals the specific possibilities an account (even the black genocide account) holds for political articulation. In its will to closure, its hermetically sealed assemblage of components, and its exclusionary form of identity politics, a genocide account may simply preclude any meaningful articulation to a progressive agenda. With this, I am in agreement with Fenster insofar as the black genocide account tends to define "its interpretation and narrative of the plight of its 'people' around certain core links that would preclude linkages to other movements of resistance" (p. 224). But this is debatable, as Fiske finds even in these identity-oriented narratives a possible articulatory project (for instance, finding common ground in critiques of the CIA and biowarfare history).

What is it that we are skeptical of in reading AIDS conspiracy narratives? Is it the way ChemiBioWarfare is articulated to a specific telos and action (political activism and preventive behavior)? Or is it something much more unsettling, something like the very *thinkability* of the CBW as a context for AIDS? This brings us back to the opening example of the UFO-AIDS narrative—which element in a subjugated knowledge ends up making the narrative unarticulatable? What other combinations are possible?

Take, for example, G. W. Krupey's (1993) conspiracy account that deploys the CBW context (see appendix). He, too, believes that the condition of AIDS is a result of human creation, planning, and introduction. The telos? To create a panic that would justify martial law. The effects on behavior? Krupey states that a radical cure is needed, one that is not just medical but political. A structural change in governing practices is required in which access and participation are opened up on a far more democratic scale. This double call does not necessarily preclude a cultural politics of science (much less prescribe hazardous preventative practices), it just argues that it can coexist with a cultural politics of power. It might have a higher degree of articulatability to Left politics, especially in the recent age of bioterror (where Avian Flu, Ebola, and Anthrax scares pose similar questions). But making this argument would require a more extensive evaluation of his account.

Also consider the Brotherly Lovers, an AIDS activist group based in Pittsburgh, who have attempted to spearhead a class-action petition for a government investigation into the possible artificial origin of HIV. Eric Taylor (presumably a member, since he directs requests for petitions to his address) described this effort in perhaps the most well-known conspiracy zine, *Paranoia: The Conspiracy Reader* (1994). His brief article lists numerous conspiracy theories and research as evidence (citing, among others, Cantwell, Strecker, Douglass). It also provides a context for organizing diverse bits of information (germ warfare, covert medical experimentation), and concludes "with all of these admitted precedents, why is the thought of AIDS biowarfare so unthinkable to most people?" (p. 54). A Federal lawsuit has been repeatedly filed by Dr. Boyd Graves, Director of AIDS Concerns for the international medical research foundation, Common Cause, which calls the president of the United States as a defendant.[15]

Finally, let's take Tetrahedron, Inc., a nonprofit educational corporation headed by Dr. Leonard Horowitz (1996), author of the conspiracy narrative *Emerging Viruses* (see appendix). In his book, Horowitz links the CBW context to black genocide, but the overall context is a history of U.S. political malfeasance (including the Nazi roots of the CIA, intimidation of domestic dissenters, population control programs, and foreign policy misconduct leading to global domination). In the book's opening, "To the Reader," Horowitz makes clear the intended effects of his conspiracy narrative:

> It is hoped this work will, therefore, help redirect AIDS science in search of a cure, free AIDS victims from the guilt and stigma attached to the disease, as well as prevent such "emerging viruses" from reemerging. I offer this investigation into the origin of AIDS and Ebola for critical review in the hope that it may also contribute to greater honesty in science, to political, military, and intelligence community reforms that are truly peace loving, and to self and social reflection as a preventative against inhumanity. (p. xi)

Tetrahedron was founded by Horowitz to, according to its press kit, provide employee assistance and education, professional development seminars, health education products and programs, and organize Horowitz's extensive lecture tours. According to the press statement, Horowitz's research into the origin of HIV and Ebola viruses is important for several reasons:

1. Scientific—new therapies might be developed from a better understanding of HIV's origin;
2. Ethical—the events precipitating such epidemics should never be allowed to happen again; and
3. Moral—those directly implicated in HIV's development and transmission are the same individuals and institutions capitalizing on the epidemic and humanity's suffering. (1997, press kit letter)

One could certainly raise objections to Horowitz's politics, but even from the brief sketch above we can note that the narrative's composition and practical effects are significantly more open to articulation than the generalized "AIDS conspiracy theory" that Gilbert and numerous others have problematized.

These examples begin to unravel the selectivity and articulations that Gilbert and others make of AIDS accounts. Furthermore, they highlight the issue of the Left's own participation in conspiracy panics. What kinds of articulation are possible, and which ones are anchored? From which perspective and motivation does the articulation emerge? These questions begin to formulate an approach that Fiske hints at: a critical problematization that does not share assumptions with the conspiracy panics.

This approach, based in a politics of articulation, needs to employ a different set of criteria. Even so, it cannot necessarily establish the validity or desirability of a given conspiracy theory; yet it would not adopt an agenda of political disqualification *at the outset* (for example, by assuming the need to differentiate it from Left politics). It would assume that there is *no* necessary relation between an AIDS origin story and its political effects, nor between the *desire* for an origin story and *its* political effects. A particular conspiracy theory could be a diversion from important political concerns, but it could also be a complement to them, even a catalyst for new forms of analysis and activism.[16]

CONCLUSION: HOW TO HAVE CONSPIRACY THEORY IN AN EPIDEMIC

It may be the case that many, if not most, narratives called "AIDS conspiracy theories" cannot readily be articulated to other struggles against AIDS or for social justice. Many conspiracy accounts essentially desire to be in the regime of truth, to anchor their authority within a dominant rationality (i.e., solely with the force of their evidence). This can prevent conspiracy accounts from representing themselves as a construction, as their own articulation. Fiske's analysis is important here again: Far from affirming the truth of counternarratives, it highlights the processes of signification and articulation that compose them. For many knowledge gangsters, the truthful authority of their narrative is assumed because it is based in science. Such AIDS conspiracy researchers as Cantwell, Strecker, Douglass, and Horowitz have drifted from mainstream medicine and science to the marginal status of renegade scientists, but their narratives retain scientific trappings. They seek authority through their own pedigrees, they conduct research, and their reports contain the language and styles of citation and evidence employed in mainstream AIDS science. Nor, indeed, is their scientific content likely to be theoretically dissonant. As Paula A. Treichler (1999) argues, "when all is said and done, few of these accounts, no matter how iconoclastic, are, in the end, fundamentally incompatible with the pervasive germ theory" (p. 323).

They believe, that is, in viruses. Ultimately they seek to plant themselves in the regime of truth, as better science, against the corrupting force of power.

Conspiratologists track AIDS as meaning, but do not always emphasize how certain meanings became definitions. Rather, they see AIDS as a sign to be decoded, demystified, and uncovered, revealing a truth of social and historical relations underneath it (e.g., genocide, New World Order, population control). However, the conspiratologists' recognition that theirs is a subjugated knowledge (not just a suppressed truth) opens up other, more flexible possibilities for the effects of knowledge. Some AIDS conspiracy theories fold the AIDS tragedy into other agendas (black genocide, communist global takeover, New World Order population control). Others have more specific goals and mandates: Open up classified information on biowarfare research to find a cure, seek alternative research and treatment regimens, transform the social and economic conditions that persist in fueling the epidemic, and finally end the suffering.

Evaluating these accounts has ramifications both for the AIDS crisis in particular and politics in general. Mainstream research, even if sociocultural, often focuses on "public reactions" to AIDS biomedical science and evaluates conspiracy accounts only as obstacles to health and education. As I have argued here, this type of conspiracy panic participates in the alignment between science and power that produces the skepticism in the first place. While the goal of this research may be to clear obstacles as way of ending the epidemic, the research ends up reiterating the problem (from the perspective of the conspiracy believers).

It is obvious that the authors of conspiracy accounts present themselves as contributors to efforts to end the AIDS epidemic. They, too, feel the urgency of the situation, and often claim that this urgency requires less, not more, reliance on authoritative knowledges. Given the periodic revival of the panics over AIDS conspiracy accounts, (e.g., the controversy over South African Health Minister's turn to AIDS conspiracy accounts for explanatory power [MacGregor, 2000], the debates over Edward Hooper's *The River* [Moore, 1999; Carlsen, 2001; and Weiss, 1999], the question of conspiratological narratives should be revisited more systematically and intellectually. Indeed, whenever alternative AIDS accounts become prominent, it is a moment of opportunity—opportunity to recognize that origin stories and alternative accounts matter, opportunity to take them seriously as articulatory projects rather than right-wing distractions or deadly diversions.

The evaluations of AIDS conspiracy accounts also bring to the foreground the practical stakes of politics and knowledge more generally. To continue Treichler's (1999) question, "What, in the midst of this terrible epidemic disease . . . is acceptable as 'good science'?" (p. 10) I would also ask, What is "good politics"? We can begin to ask different questions of conspiracy theories. We can move from demanding truth from them (enabling us to affirm or dismiss them, once and for all, based on their accuracy), or even asking for the truth *of* them (the sociocultural dismissal), and toward evaluating their possibilities and effects. What are they generating, how are they affecting others, how are they promoting or blocking certain activities? What do they offer as openings, and what do they foreclose? These are questions of articulation that can only be *raised* by analysis, not answered by it: the act of articulation is ultimately performed as a practical intervention, not conceptual practice.

In evaluating conspiracy panics, we ask, What can conspiracy theories (as an object of attention) tell us about our own articulatory commitments? What are the particular distributions of skepticism and faith employed? And when the Left engages in these problematizations, the question of what is oppositional becomes paramount. What does it mean to form a counterhegemony while still subscribing to a particular political rationality? An attention to strategies of disbelief, especially on the Left, can open up a politics of articulation. To pursue these questions in greater detail we need to leave the terrain of AIDS conspiracy panics for a wider sphere of conspiratological accounts, ones that can be said to "go global."

5

GOING GLOBAL

9/11, Popular Investigations, and the Sphere of Legitimate Dissensus

Among their other shared characteristics, both Bill Clinton and George W. Bush publicly denounced conspiracy theories.[1] Just as conspiracy theories were defined as part of a "fusion paranoia," conspiracy panics crossed party lines depending on who occupied the White House. But there was a twist. With Bush's reign, some of the Clinton-era conspiracy panickers found themselves the target of the same anticonspiracy discourse. This chapter traces some of that trajectory of the Left from its alignment with a dominant political rationality to having an ambivalent relationship with it. This chapter continues to assess the Left's participation in conspiracy panics but adds one crucial element: the way contemporary Left narratives about globalization (in the form of the war on terror/other U.S. imperialist policies) *themselves* become objects of conspiracy panics. Conspiracy panics around globalization and 9/11 end up highlighting the multiplicity and differences within the Left, as well as how some elements align with liberal political rationality.

Far from giving up its own conspiracy panic, elements of the Left continued their own, especially against globalization narratives represented by 9/11 conspiracy theories. At stake, thus, are how the forms of globalization contribute to the identity of Left as a counterhegemonic project. Post–9/11 conspiracy panics put into fresh relief the various competing and conflicting strands of what is called the Left. How has the Left become simultaneously a target *and* an agent of conspiracy panics? To answer this question, let's return briefly to the mid-1990s problematizations of conspiratological versions of globalization.

YOU SAY GLOBAL, I SAY CABAL

The conspiracy panics over the militias in the mid-1990s addressed a number of their conspiratological elements. One striking feature targeted was the belief in an imminent one-world government (aka the New World Order, with its institutional agent the United Nations and weapons like black helicopters, concentration camps, and jack-booted thugs). Much of the hostility from these populist rumblings was directed at Bill Clinton and the Democratic Party (often viewed as puppets for an international conspiracy involving communists, Luciferians, bankers, Jews, illuminati, or some combination thereof). Fear of a New World Order was seen as the prime motivator for conspiracy theorists, and, once linked to the Oklahoma City bombing, to be the most potentially dangerous.

It should come as no surprise that mainstream sources would protect the standing government, especially after the Oklahoma City bombing. But what was curious was the amount of problematization coming from more radical quarters. Various leftist sources also participated in the anticonspiracy theory discourse. Given the way conspiratologists were articulated to racist right-wing nationalist agendas (in some cases, accurately), it was easy enough for leftists to align against them.

In addition, the stage had been set for this articulation for a few years. The first years of the Clinton regime were marked by a widespread neglect of populist antigovernment motions. This was publicized by a number of watchdog groups soon after the Murrah bombing (in an "I told you so" style by people like Kenneth Stern and Chip Berlet). But this oversight was not just a lack of attention—there was an *active* silence about state violence against citizens at Ruby Ridge and Waco. The Left, faced with state murders, opted for relative quiet on the matters. Whether it was a case of "unworthy victims" or a need to defend the fledgling Clinton regime, the neglect of these acts of domestic state terrorism left a gap quickly filled in by rightists and nationalists. The diminished Left populist or antigovernment project at that moment set the stage for further retrenchment regarding globalization accounts.

The mid-90s populist imagining of globalization (the NWO) was thoroughly marginalized both in mainstream and Left discourse. Some less sophisticated analyses took on faith the mainstream representation of this populism as a purely right-wing phenomenon and easily dismissed its antiglobalization as anti-Semitic. These problematizations would make a boilerplate set of articulations (white supremacists, armed militias, gun protection groups, anti-immigrant associations, Christian Identity members, constitutionalists, tax resisters, Wise Use counterenvironmentalists). Other more complex treatments came from cultural analysts, especially within the academy. Taking their cue from Frederic Jameson's line about conspiracy theories being a "poor person's cognitive mapping," they found the NWO narrative a deformation, reduction, and oversimplification (Fenster, 1999; Melley, 1999; Mason, 2002; Willman, 2002). The enemies were too narrow, personalized, and misdirected. It was an excess populism, with a clear and distinct Us versus Them. The NWO focus on the UN as a puppet of shadowy international forces (against the United States) also contradicted the common leftist analysis of the UN as handmaiden to U.S. imperialism.

Others found the Patriot movement's nationalism repugnant. The U.S.-centric patriot resistance saw in the NWO an external corruption of an otherwise defensible and honorable nation-state. This was certainly at work among the more cold war–minded elements (which given how recently the Soviet Union had crumbled were numerous and prominent). When there was an economic or institutional analysis in the NWO account, it was downplayed in favor of the more sensationalistic examples. For instance, the populists themselves borrowed from and cited Left research (e.g., the Michigan Militia citing Chomsky and Herman's *Manufacturing Consent* on *Nightline*; Adam Parfrey's 1995 analysis of Oklahoma City).

But in addition to claiming that these antiglobalization conspiracy narratives were incorrect, racist, or nationalist, a number of Left analyses looked to explain the emergence of the narratives. Employing the sociocultural approach, they sought the context *behind* conspiracy theories, not ones conceptualized or produced *by* them. This context was at different moments defined as the "culture of hate," "climate of hate," "extremist culture," or "environment of extremism" (Stern, 1996; Dyer, 1997; Dees, 1996; *Washington Post* editorial, 1995).[2]

Militias, and the conspiracy theories that allegedly fuel them, were explained by a variety of historical conditions and social structures (e.g., a 1960s backlash, a *continuation* of the 1960s undermining of government, resentment against perceived disempowerment, the resurgence of the far Right in mainstream politics, a post–cold war need to find new enemies).[3] Conspiracy narratives in this formulation are considered an expression of frustration (the angry-white-male thesis): oversimplified and channeled in the wrong direction. Essentially they come from resentment—they are at best misguided, a misrecognition of political conditions whose genuine critical energy is manipulated and misdirected (Berlet & Lyons, 2000; Lee, 1997).

In this framework, the NWO accounts are rooted in right-wing culture; they are a continuation of white male domination (its armed wing), allied with hegemonic interests against "real" opposition and "authentic" minorities (African Americans, women, Jews, immigrants, etc.). It is true that dominant, conservative forces were at work within the militia movement and thus articulated NWO in racist and anti-Semitic ways (e.g., when narrative elements like Zionist Occupational Government, race mixing, anti-immigration, and Christian Identity were central). In addition, cold war logic did organize NWO globalization accounts, marking an oppositional identity to the political chain "Clinton/Left/internationalism/communism/globalism." While this context accounted for some paramilitary groups and theories, it primarily dealt with the armed units of already-established and self-proclaimed white-supremacist organizations (that is to say, nothing very new). At the very least, I would argue that the fixation on the right-wing elements of militias and NWO theories ignores the more pervasive anti-elitist, populist forces that comprised them and brackets the politics of articulation for a politics of fixed identities (more on this later)

But what are these other populist elements? Despite the dominant attempts to singularize them as "angry white men," militias were classed, raced, and gendered in numerous ways (Clark, 1997; Chermak, 2002).[4] Michigan Militia leaders cited *Manufacturing Consent* by Noam Chomsky and Edward Hermann (1988) as a key media analysis text, as well as declared themselves to be carrying on the American tradition of armed citizenship whose most recent example, according to them, was the Black Panthers. And, finally, how does one account for the fact that it was the Alabama Minutemen who infiltrated and exposed the "Good Ol' Boys Roundup" (the yearly backwoods gathering of Federal agents in which racist and anti-Semitic sentiments were openly displayed) in 1996, only to be ignored in the mainstream reportage of the scandal? Now, some may counter that these are just examples of tokenism, identification with the oppressor, or a manufacturing of an oppressed identity, but this would neglect the specific interests in each of these cases, and would, I argue, foreclose the counterhegemonic aspects of NWO conspiracy theories in general.

One can see this counterhegemonic possibility at work in the way conspiracy theories foreground social, political, and economic inequality in their research. While not always presented in a traditionally leftist framework, conspiratological research places inequities (and quite often explicitly classed ones) as a crucial component of its analysis. Distinctions between the powerful (at times omnipotent) and the powerless, the oppressors/oppressed, the elites and the people are presented as both the object of study and the very motivation for doing conspiratology in the first place.

The "othering" that takes place in much conspiracy narrativizing is thus not along a horizontal axis (the resentful exclusion and externalization of the enemy) but along a vertical one. The Other upon which hostility is directed is the elites; it is channeled *upward*.[5] Conspiracy theories often affirm the basic goodness of the "the people," which is depicted as having been exploited by elites. In a word, these forms of conspiracy thinking are populist (Fenster, 1999; Laclau, 2005). History is organized by a betrayal (by leaders), a turning away from citizens. Much conspiracy theorizing is done as an active effort to end the abuses of the oppressor, to overthrow oppressors and reestablish the right of the people to determine their own lives. Now, while there may be resentful elements in the tactics and/or future effects (e.g., a retributive morality, a vengeful reaction), it is not enough to say that these dissenting narratives are fundamentally conservative.

It follows then that the very context(s) produced/assumed in analysis is crucial, as well as contested. To position "conspiracy theories" *within* a politics of resentment (as an outgrowth or effect) is to draw and enforce their boundaries and contain them in a given context. For instance, articulating conspiracy theories to contexts like "anti-60s backlash," "cold war residual," "the rise of the new Right," "the paranoid style in American political history" would make a politics of resentment sensible as an explanatory tool. And, as I've stated above, these *are* contexts that inform the composition of conspiracy theories. They also end up being invoked by numerous conspiracy narratives (most obviously in the NWO narratives that target communism, a grand Zionist cabal, a secular humanist/Luciferian end times). However, if the target of NWO narratives is against elitist domination (an upward direction that is often called "the national security state," "corporate statism," "imminent fascism," or more often, the "elites," "those in power," "Them") then *there is no necessary relation* between conspiracy research and a politics of resentment. Now, of course, "the elites" or even "imminent global fascism" can be enfolded into resentful narratives (the elites merely being an ancient Jewish cabal, global fascism being an end product of communism) but this is not assured from the outset (i.e., from the "origins" of the conspiracy theories as such).

It is this latter context, globalization, which provides a good example of the conspiracy panic styles of articulating contexts at stake in this chapter. In this case it is not just a matter of asking, Which one? among competing contexts, but asking, Which one? among contested meanings of "one" context. Which globalization, which conception of a world is being put forth, and in which conspiracy accounts? Is it a globalization that is feared and resented because of the new mobility of labor forces/new flows of identities across and within geographical space (the fear of the other moving in—the anti-immigrant narrative)? Is it a New World Order, whose origins lay either in communist plots, in Zionist domination, or in a satanic end of history (or some combination of those)? Or is it a process of increasing capitalization of the world, one in which decisions about the future are being made by elites at the expense of the people? While the first two versions are commonsensical (in terms of what conspiracy panics expect from conspiratology), the latter is not, though it does permeate much of this kind of research.

It even turns up in surprising places. In 1996, I was listening to a conspiracy-oriented radio talk show broadcast out of Colorado. Having heard this program a few times before I was able to gather that it grounded much of its work in a Christian belief system (not the eschatological narrative of the satanic enemy, but more of the Christian patriot mix—"God's Country has been corrupted by power-hungry rulers"). Imagine my surprise when, during a show on NAFTA's aftereffects, the host and his guest were critical of NAFTA not because American jobs were being lost ("they—the Mexicans—are taking our jobs") but because both Americans and Mexicans were being exploited *as workers* ("they—the multinational corporations—are taking our dignity/our lives"). A populist alliance was being forged horizontally among the exploited over against the elites.

While anecdotal, this example at least highlights the importance of articulation to conspiracy narratives and to research *on* conspiracy narratives.

Recognizing that even something like "globalization" is a contested context *by* conspiratological research means that it cannot be assumed by research done *on* conspiracy theories. Rather than establishing it as a context that produces conspiracy theories (e.g., cold war), one needs to examine how globalization functions *within* the narratives. The context is not just the external condition of the phenomenon (an origin narrative produced by those who wish to understand conspiracy theories) but an element produced by that phenomenon as well. The question then becomes whether this context (as elaborated by CTs) differs (and to what degree) from the one defined by "other" researchers (academics, think tanks, Left criticism). And, finally, the question is whether it differs dramatically from the one espoused by the conspiracy panics. It is in this kind of comparative analysis that a politics of articulation begins to make sense.

Politics of articulation are engaged in by the conspiracy narratives themselves. They are enmeshed in the construction of a "people." Whatever one wants to say about the desirability or efficacy of articulating any popular counterhegemonic bloc, this is what is going on among conspiratological globalization narratives. In attempting to counter the prevailing common sense about globalization's benign and desirable effects, the NWO narratives are antagonistic. As part of a populist movement, they do not seek to create horizontal barriers but are concerned with building alliances in such a way as to create a frontier (between the people and the elites, between a vertical Us and Them). Now, whether, the formation of that bloc is one that appeals to elements on the Left is another story. Mark Fenster (1999), for one, recognizes the populism in conspiracy theories but ultimately finds them too self-enclosed and oversimplified to be articulable. Will the people have the familiar face of the white male, whose identity is grounded in Christian ideals that determine all others as inferior (in which the elites are then representatives of this inferiority)? Or will the people have a strong class (or other Left-oriented) component?[6] This, of course, is a matter of articulation.[7]

But rather than pursue a politics of articulation, antipopulist conspiracy panics joined in the chorus of denunciations of NWO globalization narratives. When extremism could easily be articulated as right-wing, elements of the Left jumped on the bandwagon. In a moment of political spectrum trouble (or fusion paranoia), the Left took great pains to distinguish itself from the political extremism and conspiratological knowledge that underpinned the disturbance. Not all of the Left was like this, of course, but publicly aired disagreements were few (Cockburn, 1995; Smith, 1995). In aligning with the political rationality of the Clinton era, the Left participated in antiextremism. This protection of the dominant middle and a will-to-moderation set the stage for a later scene. In this future act, the Left itself became positioned *as* this extremism, with its own antiglobalization and its suspicion over the increase in state powers of detainment and surveillance. By the time we get to the Republican administrative regime five years later, we begin to see the

Left reconfigure its relationship to political rationality. The Left's rifts will become starker when their own "legitimate conspiracy theories" (called institutional research or structural analysis) get problematized, and when antagonism increases against other globalization accounts, especially the ones surrounding the events of September 11, 2001.

TEN YEARS AFTER

A number of events changed the landscape of Left conspiracy panics in the ten years after the intense problematizations of populist antiglobalization conspiracy narratives. Due to spatial constraints I will merely mention them here. By the late 1990s the militias/Patriot movement subsided from public scrutiny (having been neutralized in representation and in material practice, if they ever were a serious threat to begin with). The late 1990s also saw a boom in "conspiracy culture" (Knight, 2001), where conspiratology became a popular cultural genre in film, television, radio programs, websites, zines, and books. The mainstreaming of fringe thought through entertainment and cultural production was an ambivalent activity, even for conspiratologists (Burden, 1995; Campbell, 1996). On a related note, the then-burgeoning cyberculture became a fuller communication infrastructure (Dean, 1998). Most significantly in this regard, we saw an increasing efficiency in duplication and distribution of video material on and offline. In November 1999, the eruptive protests against the World Trade Organization meetings in Seattle, Washington, brought a new antiglobalization movement to the public. This counterglobalization movement (expressed not only in demonstrations but in events like the World Social Forum) is a horizontal network of articulated (primarily leftist) interests (McNally, 2002; Katsiaficas, Yuen, & Burton-Rose, 2003; Seoane & Taddei, 2002; Olivers, 2004; Byrd, 2005). It was even noted as a populist movement (Kahn & Kellner, 2004; Luke, 2001; Plante & Niemi, 2004; Peoples Lenses Collective, 2003).

Finally, of great significance for leftist identity was the regime change at the executive level of the U.S. government. The ascendancy of George W. Bush to the presidency, and his administration's global and domestic actions post–9/11 reconfigured the Left in its relationship to the established institutions. There was much to provoke Left criticism. 9/11 became a rallying cry and a catalyst for a Bush-led terror/war and domestic repression. The Left found a renewed sense of oppositional identity—an alliance of numerous fragments. There were, to be sure, divisions around major issues (e.g., backing Kerry in the 2004 "anybody but Bush" campaign). But there was a sense at least of recognizing the profound corruption that was taking over Washington, DC.

These criticisms included the following: the invasion of Afghanistan and Iraq were done in order to secure oil supplies, neoconservative members of the Bush Administration used 9/11 as a pretext to invade these countries, that they deliberately withheld or misconstrued evidence of weapons of mass destruction (WMDs) to justify the invasions, and that they forged a nonexistent link between 9/11 and Iraq in the public's mind. In related matters, the leak of CIA operative Valerie Plame's name to the press, the circumvention of law regarding domestic surveillance, and the handling of Hurricane Katrina's aftermath all added to the dossier of Left criticism (and skepticism against Bush Administration accounts). As might be expected, these claims were dismissed as conspiracy theories (Hitchens, 2005; Lieber, 2003; Cohen 2004; Crouse, 2005).

9/11 altered the terrain of conspiracy panics. Now, the same people who were pooh-poohing conspiracy theories during the Clinton reign found themselves trafficking in them. The same experts and venues that aligned with dominant positions against extremism now found themselves the object of similar strategies of subjugation. The limits of dissent, problematized in the mid-1990s by left against right (in the name of democracy and the public) now were formulated in the other direction (in the name of democracy and the nation). Countersubversive discourses on each end revived populism, as the American people were invoked in each case as being protected against the threat of these subversive (even treasonous) knowledges (Coulter, 2003). But this was no simple reversal where the onetime "in-group" became marginalized when it was on the outs. As we'll see, some on the Left continued to play their roles as anticonspiracy theorists. Others changed their position from being a target to being a panicker (e.g., Normon Solomon, Christopher Hitchens).

Finally, take the convoluted trajectory of Mark Crispin Miller (mentioned in the previous chapter). In a 2003 interview about conspiracy theories, Miller promoted certain Left boilerplates about conspiracy theories, calling the film *JFK* "that crackpot-classic statement" and arguing that "we must distinguish between idle, lunatic conspiracy theorizing, and well-informed historical discussion." When it comes to standard leftist analyses of globalization like post–World War II U.S. imperialist policies (e.g., fomenting counterrevolutions), Miller asserts, "That's not conspiracy theory. That's fact" (as if these were mutually exclusive categories). During the course of the interview, Miller admits to believing that Flight 93 was shot down over Pennsylvania on 9/11/01 (because some people in the military told him). When asked if people consider him a conspiracy theorist Miller responds by saying it has happened, but not very much because "most people see that there's a lot of propaganda out there. I don't write as if people are sitting around with sly smiles plotting evil–they're just doing their jobs." When asked about how the term *conspiracy theorist* is used to delegitimize work and how researchers often have to act apologetic for being too deviant, Miller disagrees: "I wouldn't say that, because there *are* people who *are* conspiracy theorists."

Miller's emphatic assertions and distinctions between himself and conspiracy theories reaffirm the difficulties raised by the interviewer—Miller's
own ambivalent relationship to conspiracy panics. It is this ambivalence that
characterizes the post–9/11 Left, as this milieu becomes the target of subjugation, while elements of the Left continued their own conspiracy panic
from within. This new terrain is not just an aftereffect of that day—as we'll
see in the following section, leftist ambivalence hinges on the very interpretations of what happened on September 11.

THE 9/11 TRUTH MOVEMENT

9/11 alternative conspiracy accounts began to circulate soon after the attacks, as did the conspiracy panics and counterskeptical analyses (O'Leary,
2001; Tyrangiel, 2001; Parsons, 2001). Despite the seeming national consensus over the events, the skeptical narratives persisted. They quietly gained
momentum, making a public splash in mid-2002 with the high-profile media
appearances by 9/11 skeptic House of Representative member Cynthia
McKinney. Over the next couple of years numerous dedicated websites,
documentaries, and public presentations kept the accounts thriving. By 2004
an actual "movement" could be said to have formed (or at least began to
refer to itself that way), with major centers in Los Angeles, Toronto, San
Francisco, and New York City itself, which gained momentum (and news
coverage) through 2006.

A brief summary of some of the narratives is in order, with the caveat
that there is no unified agreed-upon set of evidentiary points in the 9/11
Truth Movement (9/11TM). Not only are there differences of opinion, there
are hostile accusations about certain accounts (especially regarding the
"no plane hit the Pentagon" theory and the "Jews were told to not go into
work that day" line) (http://www.oilempire.us/bogus.html; http://
www.whatreallyhappened.com/hunthoax.html; http://www.oilempire.us/
pentagon.html). There are two broad strains within this community, the Let
It Happen on Purpose (LIHOP) and the Made It Happen on Purpose
(MIHOP) groups. In either case, certain members of the Bush Administration (executive branch members of the Project for The New American
Century, Bush himself) knew in advance very clearly that the attacks were
to be made that day and deliberately did nothing to prevent them or deliberately assisted the project.

These theories reject the official account, especially as embodied in the
Kean Commission. It is considered an "incompetence theory," "coincidence
theory," or another kind of "conspiracy theory." For the 9/11TM the severe
failure of standard operating procedures on that day (by NORAD, FAA,
CIA, FBI) is the evidentiary fulcrum point. Will this breakdown be accounted for as massive ineptitude or via some degree of intent? Among the

different broad lines of inquiry for the actual attacks are the following: the way the Word Trade Center buildings collapsed, the lack of intercepting jet fighters, the quick production of a list of perpetrators, the lack of culpability admissions.[8] Upon this is added a context. Often it involves tracing the U.S. history of staging events as pretexts for war: for example, bombing of the USS Maine, Gulf of Tonkin, sinking of Lusitania, Iraqi incubator baby story, and Pearl Harbor itself.[9] The last is especially important, as conspiratologists cite the Project for a New Century claim that what would be needed to accelerate their globalization plans would be a "new Pearl Harbor." For the 9/11TM, oil is key for the global war on terror, as the West is in desperate need to secure new fuel resources (aka the "peak oil" thesis) (http://www.oilempire.us/).

In 2004 and 2005, the conspiratology community took a new leap in organizational form. Not since the mid-1990s militias/patriot movement had we seen such a fusion of conspiracy research and activist organizing. While nowhere near as national, secretive, long standing, and broad based as the patriots, the 9/11 conspiracy accounts began emerging into a loose movement. Public conferences and street actions were organized. Celebrities (Ed Begley, Ed Asner) and academics (Steve Jones, Professor of Physics at Brigham Young, David Ray Griffin, Professor Emeritus of Theology at Claremont, David Fetzer, Professor of Philosophy at University of Minnesota, spurring a "Scholars for 9/11 Truth" campaign) became outspoken adherents. The summer of 2004, deemed the "summer of truth," was kicked off with the International Citizens' Inquiry into 9/11. Held in Toronto, the conference saw forty speakers, numerous films and spanned six days.

In the spring of 2005, a few national commercials appeared (on such networks as CNN and ESPN) that asked questions about the official story. How could such a seemingly marginalized group afford such national exposure? James W. Walter, wealthy eco-utopian and philanthropist took an interest in 9/11 conspiracy research, founded reopen911.org and spent 4.5 million dollars promoting it (with 2000 commercial airings in New York City alone). Walter found himself the subject of media coverage from MSNBC, the New York Times, and on CNN's Anderson Cooper 360 facing off against the professional conspiracy problematizer Gerald Posner. He also organized and led a European conference tour.

The year 2006 saw the 9/11 Truth Movement take a leap into popular culture, even popularity. In March 2006 actor Charlie Sheen appeared on CNN as a result of his remarks to Alex Jones on the latter's radio show (devoted to 9/11, surveillance and martial law topics). This spurred a minor backlash via insults by other media outlets. An episode of the cartoon series South Park was devoted to conspiracy theories and featured a character who wore a 9/11truth.org t-shirt. Even while the character was ultimately ridiculed, it was done in such an ambivalent way that the effects of this representation are not known (for instance, it was obvious that the writers did their homework regarding what the conspiracy accounts were, as the character spoke in some detail about them).

Some of the main 9/11 conspiratologists, like Michael Ruppert, Alex Jones, and John Judge, had been active in 1990s conspiracy research.[10] Others were new to the field. The researchers appeared together at movement events as well as having their materials displayed. Meanwhile, starting in January 2003, members of NY 9/11 Truth (a New York City–based 9/11 action group) set up a vigil and eventually an information booth at Ground Zero on Saturday afternoons. This branch of the broader 9/11 Truth Movement was especially active, citing a Zogby poll that indicated almost half of New Yorkers believed officials "knew in advance that attacks were planned on or around September 11, 2001, and that they consciously failed to act," while 66% called for another investigation to probe the unanswered questions from the Kean Commission (*Zogby's*, 2004). The main goal of the movement seems to be amassing enough evidence to empanel a grand jury leading toward impeachment or even war crimes trials, while getting media attention to their cause.

TRUTH-IN-ACTION: THE MATERIAL AND THE TEXTUAL

In the New York area the movement seemed to have two major initiatives and methods during this time: education and action. Their activities included street protests (including a protest on 9/11/05 at the *New York Times* offices and a vocal presence at Ground Zero around the fifth anniversary), coordinated letter-writing campaigns, calling in to radio talk shows, passing out literature at events, and maintaining the mobile local infoshop (at Ground Zero). Beginning in summer 2005, a weekly public presentation/meeting was held at St. Mark's Church in the East Village.[11] I attended a number of these meetings, and some of the characteristics of these events are worth noting.

The first meeting was actually a prelude to the regular church gatherings. It was held in a small East Village cafe run by local progressives. The shop was filled with approximately 25 attendees piled onto the funky mismatched furniture, as well as standing. The event was comprised of a screening of Barry Zwicker's documentary *The Great Conspiracy: The 9/11 News Special You Never Saw* followed by discussion moderated by three men, including Frank Morales (long-standing anti-police-state researcher, activist, and pastor at St. Mark's Church). The discussion was lively, mostly geared toward elaborating Zwicker's claims.

The Sunday events were a similar mix of video and discussion, but were more sprawling, with sampler pieces of different documentaries (often a recording of a researcher's speech) and discussions. Meetings would last anywhere from two to three and a half hours, with heavy doses of video, expert talk, and heated audience participation. As the summer went on, the organizers sought to devote more time to organizational concerns (seeing a significant drop in attendance when the meeting would shift to organization).

The composition of the attendees is worth noting during this period (summer and fall 2005). The leaders were exclusively white males; there were approximately ten of them, primarily in their upper thirties and forties, with not all of them present at every meeting. The audience was more diverse. Its size ranged anywhere from 50 to 100; at some meetings they were up to 30% female, with a similar percentage of African Americans. The age range was not as broad: rarely were under-25 youth represented, and the vast majority of participants were comfortably older than 40. The age distribution changed drastically by 2006, when an estimated 50% of attendees of a 9/11 anniversary gathering were under 25, with a higher percentage at the Ground Zero site. At times the audience was quite docile, patiently watching videos (without being told how long or how many there were) and asking polite questions. A number in the audience were active believers (they tended to be more vocal) while some were inquisitive and receptive. No serious dissenters spoke up. Most of the meetings involved some degree of unruliness, in the form of audience members not waiting to be called on, soapboxing or hogging time (to the point of being cut off by moderators), or refusing to give up a line of interrogation of the leaders themselves. At least once, audience members tried to direct the meeting, protesting when moderators wanted to end discussion in order to show more video.[12]

Attending these meetings, I was struck by the mix of organizational models. While drawing from grassroots campaigns marking the networked counterglobalization movement, these meetings also operated with the classic top-down model of marxist organizing. At times there was an obvious cadre of administrators.[13] They set up and ran the meetings, selected the videos to be watched, and laid out the topics of discussion. They were quite open to audience participation, but often tried to gear it toward an education/information session. Questions, for instance, about the strategic rhetorical value of certain arguments (like the detailed dwelling on one thread of evidence) were turned into opportunities for minilectures. It was also obvious that the educational component was a prelude to getting people involved in more material actions.

Obviously, this movement is in process, signified by the tension between mass and network forms of organizing. Some desire to spread the counternarratives widely—seeking to influence mass-media organizations to broadcast their message (like those involved in the street protest against the *New York Times* http://summeroftruth.org/09-11-2005.html). Others seek to build a movement through a variety of grassroots activities, media, and spaces. In 2006, the newest phase of the movement was called a "citizen's countercoup" (http://3c.911truth.org/), embodying this ambivalence between bottom-up and vanguardist forms of organizing.[14]

Examining the 9/11 Truth Movement spatially, one could say that it exists as a conspiratology archipelago. It takes place in bookstores (Voxpop, owned by 9/11 researcher/activist Sander Hicks, which hosted a number of events), church halls, streets, websites, conference centers, community fairs, coffeeshops, and the World Trade Center site. The movement is also a multimedia affair, using websites, TV commercials, print magazines, public speeches, organizational meetings, stickers, radio programs, documentaries, and books. It even recognizes its own efforts as "viral" in form (Jamieson, 2005). The New York branch, and perhaps the broader movement, is emerging as an aggregate of different researchers and sites, relying on the decentralized (and often free) distribution of media, especially documentary films such as *Loose Change*. It is to one of these media outlets, its "official" magazine, that I now turn to assess the articulatory practices of the movement.

Global Outlook is based in Oro, Ontario, Canada, and published by *Monetary Reform Magazine*. It bills itself as *the* magazine of the 9/11 Truth Movement. While it had run 9/11 conspiracy research before amid other articles, its spring/summer 2005 double issue (#9) firmly anchored its role as the official organ. On the cover, the subtitle announces, "A *Much* Better World Is Possible." With this tagline (also the title of the opening editorial), the 9/11TM signifies its relationship to another counterglobalization movement (a variation of the Seattle war cry "Another World Is Possible"). The 9/11TM very deliberately aligns itself with that sentiment, even adding to it (with the word *much*). The cover also displays its primary target with the screaming headline: "9/11 Report: Rejected, What They Are Not Telling Us!" The contents includes articles, a transcript of Barry Zwicker's film (the one shown in the initial East Village cafe meeting), reprints of letters to the editor, a multipage centerfold of political cartoons, a sidebar request for people to distribute the magazine, a letter from Lawyers Against the War to Canadian Prime Minister Paul Martin requesting a declaration of Bush as persona non grata, one non–9/11 article (on 2004 election fraud), and ads for the videos and books mentioned in the articles,

Publisher/editor Ian Woods's article "We Reject the Official 9/11 Report" lays out the major case for the 9/11 Truth Movement. More than just asserting an account or picking apart the official account, Woods questions the very integrity of the official investigation. He challenges the notion of the Kean Commission's independence (investigators were "hand-picked by White House and riddled with conflicts-of-interest" p. 3). In other essays, the timing of the commission (441 days after the attacks), the initial proposal of Henry Kissinger as its head, and the refusal by Bush and Cheney to testify publicly were all cited as reasons to doubt the commission's report.

Like much of the conspiratology community (going back at least to the Warren Commission), what is at stake is not which narrative is true but which body is authorized to make statements within the regime of truth. In other words, the authority of official investigations is questioned. Woods counterposes the Kean Commission to "hundreds of grassroots activists from around the world [who] were busy conducting their own investigations into 9/11" (p. 3). This parallel is continued in other articles, which note that "an emergent '9/11 Truth Movement'" empanelled its own 9/11 Citizens' Commission to answer the questions the official commission ignored.

In addition to questioning the 9/11 Commission's investigation, the magazine challenges the investigatory powers of mainstream journalism. Much like the wider movement, the magazine targets the gaps in mainstream coverage. One common theme is raised by Paul Thompson 2004/2005 (p. 27): "it's about connecting the dots." We will explore this persistent metaphor of dots and connections as an articulatory project later. For now, it is interesting to note that for Thompson, connecting dots means using information found in mainstream journalism. In his formulation, mass media produces good facts but they are buried, marginalized, or not made to resonate with others. The lack Thompson sees is not missing information but a dearth of putting that information into a "greater pattern." Thompson provides one pattern via a timeline of that day's events.

In other words, Thompson is calling for more *contextual* analysis. The lack of contextual analysis within mainstream media has been an ongoing critique by journalism scholars and was even part of the public journalism movement (see chapter 2). When does context matter, and how is it composed? Even when assembled into a linear timeline, what gets put in and what is left out? For the 9/11 Truth Movement, for instance, the history of war pretexts is necessary in the timeline.

Paul Thompson goes one step further. His timeline is drawn purely by connecting the dots provided by mainstream news sources. He does so not because he only has access to those resources or because he thinks they provide the best possible research. Rather, he deliberately uses official sources to appeal to a wider audience, "the kind of people who normally would be turned away by the very mention of the word *conspiracy theory*" (p. 28). In other words, his choice reflects a meta-awareness of the context of reception. Justification of his narrative comes not in the veracity of the information but in the sources that would be deemed acceptable by a wider swath of society.[15]

The self-aware use of the term *conspiracy theory* continues throughout the magazine (and in other movement texts). Barry Zwicker (in his documentary as well as the reprinted transcripts in the magazine) argues that the term *conspiracy theory* is a "thought stopper." The letter to the editor is titled "No Outrageous Conspiracy Theories, Please" (Raymond, 2004/2005). The piece essentially takes George W. Bush's conspiracy panic line, "Let us not tolerate outrageous conspiracy theories about September 11th" and applies it sardonically to the official account.[16]

On one level, the magazine's narrative building operates much like John Fiske's (1994) concept of counterknowledge (examined in the previous chapter). They take bits of information suppressed or marginalized (but often produced) by dominant investigative sources. They then "connect the dots," making information resonate within a broader context. Often, these connections take place due to the gaps in public accounts (e.g., "what they didn't tell you"). Sometimes even when other investigations find gaps, it is not enough. In December 2005, the *Village Voice*'s cover story was on "10 Unanswered Questions" from the 9/11 Commission. Some of the questions overlapped slightly with the 9/11 Truth Movement's own inquiries. However, as the following week's letters to the editor, the *Voice*'s online forum, and nonaffiliated websites demonstrated, there were even more omissions, even by the ostensibly culturally leftist magazine.

But unlike Fiske's "knowledge gangsters," the 9/11TM writers are not African Americans sharing a history of oppression. Like many activist organizations, theirs is a mixed composition. At least extrapolated from the Sunday meetings at St. Mark's Church, the diversity of the rank and file is not matched by the relative homogeneity of the organizers. But maybe in this case the identity-position of the storytellers isn't the prime determinant in the composition. The 9/11 Truth Movement begins to complicate Fiske's own emphasis on the social identities of the conspiratologists,[17] displacing the importance of the sources by highlighting the importance of effects. What are the openings and closures a conspiracy account produces? Are there elements that prevent certain connections from being worthy of pursuit? From which position, social or otherwise, do we judge investigative, articulatory projects?

In addition to acting as a counterknowledge, the 9/11 conspiracy accounts recognize their subjugated status and acknowledge the conditions of their potential reception. The 9/11 Truth Movement is a metadiscourse: It not only promotes alternative accounts of September 11th, it explicitly engages the context of producing accounts. In other words, it addresses *conspiracy panics*. The stated goal of amassing enough evidence to take the case to court (via grand jury) is only one level of engagement. The court of public opinion is also at work here, and the conspiratologists do not just participate in it as one party but as commentators on the judgment process itself. In other words, through this self-reflexivity the conspiratologists both act within a context and seek to modify that context at the same time. This discursive context is what will be examined next, especially both the mainstream and left responses to the 9/11 Truth Movement.

OFFICIAL DISMISSALS OF 9/11 TRUTH MOVEMENT

The 9/11 Truth Movement found a lack of truly independent official investigations by mainstream media. Official account adherents attributed a different kind of lack to the conspiratologists: lack of reason, of certainty

(Barkun quoted in Voboril, 2005), lack of faith in randomness, incompleteness, and human error (Cockburn, Berlet) and, finally, lack of power (Fenster, Berlet, Pipes).

In more official statements, the White House and the Kean Commission have "dismissed these questions as conspiracy theories" (Kemper, 2005). George W. Bush himself declared: "Let us never tolerate outrageous conspiracy theories concerning the attacks of September the 11th; malicious lies that attempt to shift the blame away from the terrorists themselves, away from the guilty. To inflame ethnic hatred is to advance the cause of terror." The cover story for the March 2005 issue of *Popular Mechanics* became a well-cited conspiracy panic piece, and its book-length version (Dunbar & Reagan, 2006) was even lauded by elements of the usually critical Left. The editors frame their evidence with a series of rhetorical dismissals at the "poisonous claims" being "increasingly accepted abroad and among extremists here": "Healthy skepticism, it seems, has curdled into paranoia. Wild conspiracy tales are peddled daily on the Internet, talk radio and in other media" (Chertoff et al., 2005). Of course, there were many retorts to this attempt to refute the skeptics (*OilEmpire.us*, 2005; 911review.com). *Newsday* published an article that opened with a line whose spatial metaphors could have been drawn directly from mid-1960s panics over extremism: "Sept. 11 conspiracy theories have edged into the mainstream" (Voboril, 2005). Some coverage was more generous, like the *Village Voice*'s three-part series in late February 2006 (Murphy, 2006a/b/c). Even in unexpected places like *New York Magazine* (Jacobsen, 2006) and the *Washington Post* (Powell, 2006), one could find nuanced reports. Others considered the accounts as part of the booming "conspiracy industry" (Horrie, 2002). *Vanity Fair* featured an article dedicated to debunking 9/11 conspiracy accounts, written by longtime conspiracy panic expert Richard Cohen (2004a). The rise of the blogosphere included sites "devoted to smashing conspiracy theories and humiliating their purveyors!" (WhatDIDN'Treallyhappen.com).

9/11 conspiracy theories were not just the exclusive domain of Americans. In what seems like a precursor to the anti-French delirium in the United States near the beginning of the Iraq invasion, one of the early 9/11 conspiracy panics was directed at a Frenchman. Thierry Meyssan was, to be fair, one of the earliest prominent promoters of a 9/11 conspiracy theory. His bestselling book *L'Effroyable Imposture*, or *The Horrifying Fraud*, claimed among other things that the Pentagon was hit by a missile not a plane. In a *New York Times* frontpage story, the correspondent wonders if the popularity of the book is a "symptom of latent anti-Americanism" (Riding, 2002).[18]

In this global war on terror, however, French beliefs were not that significant. As might be expected, "conspiracist" beliefs by Arabs constituted the biggest problem. Even before 9/11, Arabs had been identified as having a peculiar affinity for political paranoia (Pipes, 1996; editorial, *Economist*, 1995). It became an acute issue during the terror/war, especially in Iraq.

According to an Associated Press item, belief in these conspiracy theories by Iraqis "may have dire consequences for U.S. efforts to build a stable Iraqi government" (El-Tablawy, 2005). They can be "offensive and dangerous" even "bolster the evil cause of Islamic fanaticism" (editorial, the *Post and Courier*, 2005). In 2005, a man hired to be the Muslim chaplain for the New York City Fire Department had to withdraw from the position. He became a target of ire for expressing doubt that the official suspects (the 19 hijackers) were behind 9/11.

Why would Arabs be more predisposed to conspiracism? Robert Robins, the familiar expert from 1990s conspiracy panics over political paranoia, has an answer. He finds Arab paranoia understandable since Arab governments have a history of conspiracies, and this can get projected onto other societies. For Robins, where "government is less institutionalized and personal relationships play a larger role, suspicion may be more common" (in Goode, 2002). In other words, we see here the sociocultural approach "go global." Globalizing the condescending framework contains a strong whiff of American exceptionalism. The United States, having modernized into institutions, is immune from the primitive governmental forms based on despotic personal relationships. "They have no idea of what a complex society the U.S. is," says Robins. Given the rampant "civilization vs. barbarism" rhetoric, as well as more sophisticated versions via Samuel Huntingdon devotees, Robins's comments fit in well with the dominant common sense.

Problematizations of the paranoid worldview of "Arab Street" and media like Al-Jazeera proliferated after 9/11 (Johnson, 2001; Ghitis, 2004; Verneire, 2004; Foster, 2003; Ross, 2005; Weiner, 2005). But the street-level knowledge was not the exclusive residence for Arab propensities. We saw denunciations of an African head of state (Muammar Khaddafi) as well as a global businessman (Dodi al-Fayed) as conspiracy theorists (Dickey, 2003; MacGregor, 2000; Pipes & Khashan, 1997).[19] Together, these civilized conspiracy panics over the Other comprised what might be called the beginnings of a "globalization of conspiracy panics."

Perhaps the most vitriolic anticonspiracy diatribes were directed at then-U.S. House Representative Cynthia McKinney. In spring 2002 McKinney made a number of public appearances and statements where she called the official account lacking and demanded a fuller investigation. She was quickly denounced by her political peers and journalistic watchdogs. Zell Miller, a conservative Democratic Senator from her state (who spoke at the 2004 *Republican* National Convention), called her comments "loony." White House Press Secretary Ari Fleischer told the press corps, "The congresswoman must be running for the Hall of Fame of the Grassy Knoll Society." Some news outlets deemed her a "nut" (the *Atlanta Journal-Constitution*) while others called her an "idiot" (Goldberg, http://www.nationalreview.com/goldberg/goldberg051702.asp). Even ostensibly Left commentators piled on the attack (Corn, 2002a, 2000b). According to mainstream news sources, this issue contributed to her ouster from Congress (Kemper 2005). The 9/11 Truth Movement claims she was a deliberate target for removal by a coordinated Republican scheme (known to focus on a number of key Democrats in recent elections).

The most official of anticonspiracy theory statements comes from the U.S. State Department. In a kind of cybercool version of McCarthyite suspicion, its Bureau of International Information Programs launched a website in July 2005 called *How to Identify Misinformation* (http://usinfo.state.gov/media/Archive/2005/Jul/27595713.html). It opens with the following statement: "How can a journalist or a news consumer tell if a story is true or false? There are no exact rules, but the following clues can help indicate if a story or allegation is true." The top section asks, "Does the story fit the pattern of a conspiracy theory?" and provides a number of elements to look for. In January 2006, the top misinformation story that needed attention was September 11 conspiracy theories (http://usinfo.state.gov/media/Archive/2006/Jan/20-672210.html). Later in the year, the State Department updated the project with a list of the top 10 conspiracy theories (2006).

No one could expect a government to provide journalists with tips on how to identify state-sponsored disinformation, or give the public a guide for critically reading news reports. But it is important to note the state's preferred orientation of detection techniques: of the people by the people. Peer-to-peer suspicion, however, could not fully exhaust popular detective work. One conspiratology blog (in another ironic reversal) applied the State Department's discernment techniques against the official 9/11 account (Watson, 2005).

FROM RIGHT-WING TO WINGNUTS: EXTREME GLOBALIZATION STORIES

Mainstream denunciations of 9/11 conspiracy research are to be expected when preservation of the contemporary regime, especially in a time of terror/war, is paramount.[20] But even Madeline Albright, not known for her leftist tendencies nor conspiracy musings, was accused of trafficking in conspiracy theories (Lakely, 2003). Criticism of the Bush Administration after 9/11, conspiratological or not, was met with condemnation, even being called treasonous, and a threat to homeland security. But the same Left outlets that were being called conspiracy theories performed their own admonitions, sometimes on the same targets as mainstream news outlets. Thus began the self-policing, or self-governing, by what the 9/11 Truth Movement calls the "gatekeeper Left."[21]

The "gatekeeper Left," according to Barrie Zwicker, Mark Robinowitz, and August West and the site leftgatekeepers.com, is represented by people like Noam Chomsky, Howard Zinn, Amy Goodman, Chip Berlet, Michael Albert, as well as various progressive media outlets like the *Nation,* the

Progressive, Z, In These Times, Pacifica News, and *Democracy Now.* Even within the antiwar movement (the natural home for the circulation of 9/11 conspiracy narratives), 9/11TM found themselves shut out.

We could define this self-policing or "regulated resistance" (Shaw, 2005a, 2005b) as a reconfiguration of skepticism: It finds its limits, even against Bush. For instance, the belief that the Bush Administration used 9/11 as a pretext for invading Afghanistan and Iraq was common parlance for Left criticism. However, to argue that 9/11 happened *because* of this desire is beyond the pale. Whether in the LIHOP (let it happen on purpose) or MIHOP (made it happen on purpose) accounts, the notion that 9/11 was deliberately allowed to take place exceeds the sphere of acceptable skepticism. To put it bluntly, while the Left could engage in promiscuous comparisons of the Bush Administration with Nazis, these similarities end at the steps of the Reichstag.[22]

The usual canards were trotted out in the Left gatekeeping. Chomsky, Zinn, and Albert led the charge for anticonspiracy discourse from Left. For Zinn (2003) conspiracy theories are a "diversion from real issues. They are attractive because they simplify problems and enable people to focus on a handful of people instead of on complex causes." Zinn is an ambivalent figure, however, as he wrote a supportive blurb for David Ray Griffin's book (2004).

Chomsky recognizes that the term is one of disqualification, and thus regularly distinguishes his own work from it (institutional analysis vs. conspiracy analysis). According to Stephen Shalom and Michael Albert (2002) in a lengthy problematization of 9/11 conspiracy theories, they ignore "society's underlying institutions," and are essentially a moral outlet for anger and outrage. They produce convenient scapegoats: rejecting "some vile manipulators, but not society's basic institutions."[23]

There are moments when the gatekeeping Left even borrow from the 1990s problematizations of the *medium* of conspiracy theories (discussed in regard to Gary Webb): Norman Solomon describes 9/11 conspiracy theory as "much ballyhooed via the Internet" (2002), and Chomsky once called it an "internet theory" (http://www.oilempire.us/chomsky.html). Essentially, the Left conspiracy panics argue, conspiracy research focuses too much on individuals, on the explicit actions of small groups, and on a moral discourse of evil that treat symptoms and aberrations, not structures. In other words, conspiracy narratives lack or misread *context.*

These are classic conspiracy panic charges: Conspiracy theories are oversimplifying, distracting, uncontrollably spreading. At times (especially in the concentrated attention to conspiracy theories on the fifth anniversary of 9/11/01), mainstream and culturally liberal print outlets (*New York, Village Voice, Time, Washington Post*) carried less hostile accounts of the 9/11TM than the more strident leftist outlets (like *Counterpunch*).Yet there is one major and telling difference between mainstream and oppositional conspiracy panics. For consensus-based denunciations, the problem with conspiracy theories is that they do not just see rogue individuals and corrupt agents, they cast suspicion on society's basic institutions. For the Left, just the opposite is true: conspiracy theories focus on individuals, while leaving the structures intact!

At times, the conspiracy panickers make their own fusion of institutional analysis with conspiracy research by posing, as Chip Berlet does, questions such as "How could there be a conspiracy involving the military, the executive branch, Congress and the media in which somebody didn't rat it out and get a Pulitzer Prize?" In his rhetorical stretch to absurdity, Berlet makes a big leap, one that few 9/11 skeptics do. He aligns all of these major institutions into a cabal structure only in order to dismiss the very claim.

The 9/11 Truth Movement researchers are well aware of their marginalized status within the Left. In 2005, 9/11TM lobbied United for Peace and Justice (an umbrella, antiwar organization responsible for amassing numerous demonstrations and actions) to get a 9/11TM speaker on the slate at an assembly. They were denied, adding to their marginalization in the antiwar movement, according to Charles Shaw the publisher of *Newtopia*, a member of United for Peace and Justice. Sander Hicks, 9/11TM author, bookstore owner, and briefly candidate for senator of New York, encountered this standard division between institutional and conspiracy research on his book tour (more on this later).

9/11 became a divisive issue for Left in ways that NWO populist antiglobalization narratives of the mid-1990s did not. The politics of 9/11TM were less articulated to right-wing agendas (though some 9/11 conspiracy accounts certainly did, even growing out of the same milieu as the NWO narratives). The "Right Woos Left" narrative from Chip Berlet and others from the previous decade's conspiracy panics continued to inform the basic anxiety over diversion and distraction. There was no easily available concrete image of the seducers, unlike with the militias and Patriot movement. The 9/11 Truth Movement was precisely discomforting to the Left because of its indiscernible political possibilities.

The 9/11TM's splintering effect raises an important conceptual note.[24] When Chomsky says that JFK/CIA conspiracy theories have torn the California Left to shreds, he makes a significant linguistic shift that favors his own cause (in Parenti, 1996). The mere existence and circulation of conspiracy accounts cannot inherently have these effects. It is more accurate to say the "issue" or "question" of conspiracy theories has created divisions. Blaming conspiracy theories themselves is akin to saying *violence* splinters the Left, rather than that the *strategic question of violence* causes rifts. In fact, I would argue it is more accurate to say that conspiracy *panics* divide leftists. The reason for this is the *reactive* character of conspiracy panics: they necessarily involve turning on other (even potential) Left positions. Conspiracy accounts don't inherently require antagonizing potential peers—conspiracy panics do.

9/11 Truth Movement adherents claim that the gatekeeper Left/foundation-funded Left refuses to deal at the level of evidence, preferring ad hominem, ideological objections and tangential issues (Zwicker, 2006). Also, the most public members of the Left typically do not reply to 9/11TM responses, eschewing dialogue for panic and problematizations. Occasionally this means telling conspiracy researchers to "shut up" (Weinberg, 2006). Sometimes this translates to direct action. In 2002, Normon Solomon (one of the more prominent Gary Webb supporters in the 1990s) tried to get radio station KFCA to ban Michael Ruppert from getting coverage on the *Pacifica* network affiliate.

The articulation performed by most Left analyses is thus not dialogue but a specific kind of polemical representation. Michel Foucault, in "Polemics, Politics, and Problematizations," differentiates polemics from dialogue:

> The polemicist . . . proceeds encased in privileges that he possesses in advance and will never agree to question. On principle, he possesses rights authorizing him to wage war and making that struggle a just undertaking; the person he confronts is not a partner in the search for the truth, but an adversary, an enemy who is wrong, who is harmful and whose very existence constitutes a threat. For him, then, the game does not consist of recognizing this person as a subject having the right to speak, but of abolishing him, as interlocutor, from any possible dialogue; and his final objective will be, not to come as close as possible to a difficult truth, but to bring about the triumph of the just cause he has been manifestly upholding from the beginning. (1997b, p. 382)

Responding to the "danger" of the 9/11TM is a maneuver in this polemical game. Instead of a debate, conspiracy panic purveyors prefer the safe distance of the sociocultural approach. The gatekeeper Left's attachment to a particular kind of rationality entails addressing the claims not at the level of the evidence but at the level of the legitimacy to make the claims at all. Some on the Left (Weinberg, Cockburn) were more knowledgeable about the accounts they were dismissing than others (in other words, they read something). But attempting to *end* discussion via researched and detailed evaluations was fruitless, as counterresponses quickly emerged (Doraemi, 2004; Kane, 2006; Nimmo, 2006). The panics overall are more interested in threat detection and pattern recognition (a la Daniel Pipes), at times even resembling, prefiguratively, the State Department's guide to identifying conspiracy theories in our midst (Staudenmaier, 2004).[25]

9/11 Truth Movement's critique of this gatekeeper Left is not just that it suppressed their accounts. They argued, for instance, that the antiwar movement was too single-issue focused. While correctly seeking to withdraw troops from Iraq, the antiwar movements did not have a thorough analysis of the context of the war on terror (Shaw, 2005a; MalcontentX, 2002; Schiffler, 2002). In other words, 9/11TM had a *better* contextual analysis. Once again we are faced with a seeming intractable problem: The differences between the gatekeeper Left and the 9/11 Truth Movement are drawn via their articulation of contexts. It is to this discursive knot that we now turn.

CONTEXT AND ARTICULATIONS

9/11 is an event that opens up a context which itself is composed in the analysis. Pundits from the mainstream and the Left refer to the problematic way the 9/11 conspiracy accounts "connect the dots" (Goode, 2002; Voboril, 2005; Corn, 2002b; Goldberg, 2002). This metaphor for articulation is one drawn both from childhood puzzle games (where the image is preprogramed) and investigation discourse (much like piecing a puzzle together). These game metaphors acknowledge the necessity for interpretive work but constrain its possibilities to a known truth hiding among the deliberately organized bits.

In addition, for a number of problematizers conspiracy narratives can have a "kernel of truth" (Goode, 2002; Voboril, 2005). This brings up Hegel's famous spatial metaphor of the rational kernel within the mystical shell. What are we to make of a practice of articulation that claims to be able to tell the difference? The shell/kernel model also resonates with conspiratologists' own approach to mainstream sources: While mostly polluted, one can find telling facts buried within. Paul Ferguson did it with his alternative timeline drawn solely from mainstream sources. Even deliberate disinformation gets the shell/kernel treatment: As Peter Dale Scott (UC Berkeley professor and longtime chronicler of U.S. Drug malfeasance) puts it, "disinformation in order to be effective has to be 95% accurate" (in Hecht, 2004).[26]

When it comes to selecting sources for their articulations, the 9/11TM does not seem to have a preordained method. At times, the summer 2005 meetings would use video clips of talks and documentaries from the more acceptable Left: John Stockwell, Bill Moyers, *The Power of Nightmares*. Much of the time, they used nonconspiracy theories (or "institutional analyses") as evidence of a long-standing context of secrecy, security, foreign interventions, and corporate malfeasance. At the same time, some conspiratologists were not afraid to criticize certain Left-embraced sources, like Richard Clarke. Webster Griffith Tarpley (2006, p. 26) asserts that Clarke's commission testimony was a piece of histrionics designed to win over victim families' sentiment while shoring up the official version. Clarke's challenge to the Bush Administration has more to do with arguing against the Iraq War than it is about challenging the official version of 9/11. His quasi-heroic status among anti-Bushites ends up containing critique and entrenching the sphere of legitimate controversy.

Also, take the example of the movie *Fahrenheit 9/11*. It too was called a conspiracy theory by mainstream and right-wing sources (Cohen, 2004b; Kopel, 2004; Hitchens, 2004; GOP.com, *Nine Lies*, 2004; Isikoff, 2004; Goodman, 2004). It too was critiqued by a few elements of the Left, sometimes for being a conspiracy theory (Furuhashi, 2004), more often for oversimplification and incomplete analysis (Jensen, 2004, Davis, 2004). The 9/11TM rarely relies on or draws from Michael Moore's film. Occasionally, they make reference to Moore's depiction of Bush's reading of *My Pet Goat* after being told the country was under attack. But *Fahrenheit 9/11* was primarily an anti-Bush, antiwar film. Moore himself acknowledged that the scope and timing of the film was designed to influence the 2004 election. Yet this narrative, at one point a very *popular* one, was rarely pilloried by the gatekeeper Left for its fixation on individuals, on its moralizing, or on its distracting character (Walsh, 2004). Panics are selectively applied.

At other times, right-wing sources have been cited by 9/11 skeptics. Most contentious has been the use of anti-Semitic and/or anti-Zionist narratives.[27] Far from being seduced by right-wing narratives (as if belief in a 9/11 inside job is a "gateway theory" to anti-Semitism) the quarrelsome character of the 9/11 skeptics' milieu forces the source's perspective to be foregrounded. However, the sources aren't considered poisoned just because their articulations presume a different, even repellant, context. A disagreeable source does not prevent the facts from being usable (undergoing similar filtering processes as agreeable ones). Articulation here is a practice involving parsing out bits, thus it refrains from a wholesale dismissal of an account because of its teller.

We can ask then, What kinds of allergens and poisons are presumed by Left articulatory projects? How are these allergens distributed when the Left encounters the 9/11 Truth Movement's articulations (rather than their data)? According to Normon Solomon, they are "narrowly factual yet presented in a misleading way" (MalcontentX, 2002). In response to Michael Ruppert's timeline model, Solomon states that it does "not 'establish' any such foreknowledge. Instead, he has hammered together fragments of reports from various sources and used them as a springboard for a gigantic leap—to conclusions that aren't supported by what he cites." Solomon likens Ruppert's approach to that of a "selective vacuum cleaner—pulling in whatever supports a thesis and excluding context and perspectives that undermine it." But 9/11TM proponent and Left observer MalcontentX responds in Ruppert's defense: "There is considerable food for thought here. It's not airtight. There are fragments; yet there's also an intelligence behind the fragments which is unique and noteworthy—for its capacity to organize them into a meaningful picture of what may be happening." In each case, what counts as context is at stake. When are articulations preordained by an already-given context (connecting dots of a given image), and when do they open up to modify that context (as pattern recognition)?

To reiterate, many on the Left claim that the 9/11 conspiratologists misread the context (through oversimplification, demonization, personalization). Sometimes, these claims overestimate the scope of the 9/11 conspiracy research. While some accounts do focus on Bush and his cronies, many accounts do not limit themselves to the ouster of "those responsible" (in fact this issue has been a source of much debate). 9/11 conspiracy accounts address broader questions of consent, of the legitimacy of government, and of historical corruption. For some, removal of the Bush Administration is one immediate aim; akin to the broader impeachment movement (not via elections whose legitimacy has been called into question due to 2000/2004 electoral fraud). These are modest and specific political aims and not global gestures that seek to supplant an entire mode of analysis (e.g., Marxism) or a political project (the counterglobalization movement). Indeed, the 9/11 conspiracy accounts rarely challenge the legitimacy of the U.S. or international court system.[28] In other words, the immediate actions called for are within the bounds of already existing legal institutions and based on the U.S. constitution (even as a bulwark *against* revolution). However, for many adherents the 9/11 event is a "gateway issue" that allows for a broader-based inquiry and action into state/corporate malfeasance (often called the military-industrial complex or shadow/invisible/parallel/secret government, and involving issues of oil dependence, war, surveillance, police-state emergence, and globalization).

INSTITUTIONAL ANALYSES: ON OVERSIMPLIFICATION AND INVESTIGATORY POWERS

According to the Left conspiracy panics, conspiracy theories oversimplify individual motives to "evil." Yet this moralism by no means prevails in all conspiracy accounts, nor is it limited to them. Many conspiracy accounts operate with very mundane assessments of motivation (greed, lust for power, self-interest, cronyism, advancement of class interests). Others do impute more arcane agendas (e.g., secret societies or Luciferianism) but even those are not necessarily due to some mystical quality but to an older, premodern set of allegiances. On the other hand, the moralism that attributes evil to elites' intentions infuses the most mundane of critical discourse. Anti-Bush (yet anticonspiracy theory) critics often employ this moral rhetoric, casually calling Bush and his associates evil, or visually depicting them as devils or pop culture villains (e.g., Darth Vader, a zombie, Sauron and Gollum from the *Lord of the Rings*).

The claim that 9/11 conspiracy accounts oversimplify the intricate workings of capitalism also needs situating. One can hear in this charge nonleftist Robert Robins's claim about Arab paranoia: "They have no idea how complex the U.S. is" (Goode, 2002). Robins's statements shade into American exceptionalism. The kind of modernist progressivism that shapes Robins's colonialist sentiment (about premodern political orders) infuses Left criticisms as well. Only now "we moderns" refers not to the nation-state (and civilization) but to the mode of production (and its political institutions). When we hear the mantra that capitalism and U.S. governmental structures are too complex and messy (even inept) to warrant a conspiracy analysis even of a single event, we know that this modernist exceptionalism is at work.

Nationalism seeps into leftist discourse in another way. A rarely articulated assumption in Left analysis is the notion that the U.S. government would never resort to killing its own citizens as a matter of deliberate action. This goes for presidents (JFK assassination) as well as civilians (9/11, Oklahoma City bombing, Waco, Jim Jones's People's Temple, Ruby Ridge). This presumes that the nation is the basic unit of allegiance for elites as well as for the rest of "us" (the populace). It also leaves unchallenged the civilian/military distinction (at least within U.S. borders while often noting that the two are becoming blurred in other spheres). More importantly, this nationalism presumes American exceptionalism and progress in contrast to "savage warlords" and barbarian governments that butcher their own. Even with certain kinds of denial and forgetfulness when it comes to events like Waco and Operation MOVE in 1980s, exceptionalism also ignores recent Western cases of official "self-mutilation" as technique (the 1970s Italian strategy of tension, for example).[29]

Ultimately, the notion that we need to work within an institutional analysis (that excludes conspiracy analysis) presupposes either: (1) conspiracies have never been a part of governance, or (2) they once were, but the West has left that behind with modernization. The first ignores history; the second presupposes a progressivist (even ethnocentric) historiography. Either way, institutional analysis seeks to account for the entire context ("everything is structure"). 9/11 conspiracy researchers are less inclined to assume the totality of articulations within a context ("everything is conspiracy"). This flies in the face of panics over conspiracy theories, which often cite the theories' totalizing tendencies as a reason to disqualify their misrecognitions. Turning a conspiracy claim about 9/11 (a conspiracy linked to U.S. political history and governing structure) into a conspiracy worldview (U.S. political history and governing structure is best described as a conspiracy) is a rhetorical operation that says more about the Left's adherence to totality than it does about the conspiracy claims.

In addition to its latent ethnocentrism, the "incompetence thesis" has another potential effect. Many on the Left (Corn, Albert, Cockburn, Johnstone, Frank) follow the official commission's findings of government negligence and ineptitude. This was not only the case with 9/11, it also took front stage during the post–Hurricane Katrina criticisms. The incompetence theory essentially explains a catastrophic event by positing a lack of foresight, communication, ability, qualification, or readiness within the state. With all of these lacks, it is a short step to call for a proper corrective; namely, filling in the lack with *more* (centralization, state intervention, suspension of normal procedures, resources for security, executive powers). The "magic lack theory" creates gaps so they can be filled, bolstering sagging processes and augmenting strength (especially regarding state security power). It also acts magically as a *preventive* theory: It wards off questions of intent and action. The incompetence argument, unless it takes care to distinguish its articulations, feeds into the hegemonic solution, whereby competence best comes from a strong state.[30]

We can also address the Left conspiracy panic's claim that conspiracy theories are distractions from real politics. 9/11TM adherent MalcontentX has already addressed it, with a rhetorical maneuver. S/he turns the tables on the Left after examining the Solomon/Ruppert exchange:

> A very good case could be made here that the tide of verbiage we are presently having to wade through (in order to set the record straight on Ruppert, Corn, Solomon, etc.) is a far greater distraction than one Ruppert may be creating; and for this, Solomon and Corn must be held responsible.

What is more distracting, the effort put into conspiracy research or the gatekeepers' turn *against* it? Of course, that depends on the stakes involved in calling something a "distraction." For the above analyst, the marginal effects of the subjugated knowledge are not considered a resource drain, it is the excessive discourse subjugating it (whether Left or mainstream) that demands our skepticism. To put it simply, it's the conspiracy panics that matter more.

What elements of the 9/11TM are unarticulatable?[31] Like the NWO narratives of the mid-1990s, the 9/11 skeptics are invested in articulating a context of globalization.[32] And once again the question emerges—What makes this populist articulation proximate to a more common leftist one, or not? Is the 9/11TM's context unfailingly discordant with more traditionally recognizable Left projects? The above discussion would make it seem that this is an intractable difference. Filled with polemics and problematizations, the war context seems to translate into a discursive war *over* contexts. But not all articulations find this dissonance to be elemental and intractable. The following section tracks a few examples where articulations across discourses are made possible.

Articulation Potentials from Left

In 2004, Alternet carried an article titled "Top 10 Conspiracy Theories of 2003–2004" (May 18, 2004). At first glance this seems like a standard conspiracy panic title, listing the biggest threats to political reason. However, author Mike Ward thwarts expectations when he wonders, in response to Tony Blair's dismissal of oil-based explanations of the Iraq War as "conspiracy theory," if there may be something to these subjugated narratives. Perhaps the Left and 9/11 conspiracy theories have something in common?

Sander Hicks certainly thinks so. The previously mentioned owner of VoxPop bookstore and brief New York senatorial candidate recounts the following anecdote while on his book tour promoting *The Big Wedding: 9/11, the Whistleblowers, and the Cover-Up*:

The events coordinator at the Rainbow in Madison was a combative and somewhat cranky Marxist who hadn't read my book, but in the middle of my talk launched into a broadside critique of conspiracy theory. One thing he said, I took with me: History demands hard work. And it's ahistorical to scapegoat individuals when power is expressed through oppression of class against class. To that I say yes, and that my own work corroborates this theory. (Hicks, "9/11 Truth Movement")

Hicks sees an obvious common ground between the gatekeeper Left and the 9/11 Truth Movement, an overlap that is recognized by Robert Guffey when he notes a distinction between *legitimate* conspiracy research ("Chomsky ... prefers to call it 'Institutional Analysis' ") and *illegitimate* conspiracy research. The subjugation of one is replicated internally on the Left. The similarities are also a point of discussion on a couple of North American Independent Media Centers (Hamilton [Ontario, Canada] Independent Media Center, Portland Independent Media Center). In the heat of the firestorm surrounding Cynthia McKinney, *In These Times* published a fair-minded piece on the difficulties in sorting information, as well as the potentials for working with McKinney's suspicion (Muwakkil, 2002). On the anti-authoritarian Left, Lawrence Jarach (2005–2006) notes that the term *conspiracy theory* acts as a "derisive dismissal," equating counter-narratives with fantasy or falsehood (he prefers the term *conspiratology*) (p. 34). Jarach ultimately finds conspiracy to be a normal mode of functioning for governments and hierarchies, while at the same time arguing that a focus on the details of the culprits is a distraction.

Danny Schechter (2005), renowned media critic and filmmaker, also presents a nuanced assessment of the Left's relationship with 9/11 conspiracy accounts and highlights how this articulation is fraught with difficulty. Schechter attended and spoke at the Washington DC 9/11 inquiry conference in July 2005. He too calls the 9/11 Commission Report an "official conspiracy theory" and heaps praise and respect on Cynthia McKinney for her courageous solitary stance in Congress. Schechter's own openness towards the "sprawling decentralized band of activists that calls itself the 9/11 Truth Movement" ran up against its limits during his talk at the press club. After urging the movement to be more aware of how journalists operate and to participate in the media reform movement, "the reaction of some in the room shocked" him. He was allegedly denounced for being naïve, even a war criminal. For Schechter, the event was a shining example of "why the 9/11 Truth Movement has to do better to get its issues before the people, a public that might agree with them if they were better able to articulate their concerns" (2005). While Schechter is not exactly using the term *articulate* in the sense we have been here, it does refer to being able to speak across differences, not just to being clearer speakers. Schechter's experience well defines the difficulties inherent in a left articulation project, as well as what counts as the people or the public (given the growing popularity of 9/11TM).

Perhaps the most thorough treatment of this shared ground comes from Anu Bonobo in an article titled "Plan Wellstone: Conspiracy, Complicity, and the Left," from the storied anarchist magazine *Fifth Estate*. Bonobo recognizes the subjugated status of conspiracy research within the Left project: "Most radicals, leftists, and some anarchists join the sober, centrist mainstream in marginalizing and rejecting the dialogue out of hand" (p. 36). This is an understandable allergy, since many of the right-wing conspiracy theories over the course of decades have targeted the Left (under various names like socialism, communism, Democratic Party, liberal elites). But, according to Bonobo, conspiracy theories "have a potent radical tendency that traces all evil to a power-obsessed elite of corporate and government criminals hellbent on global, imperial domination" (p. 37). Because of this trait, "the lines between radical conspiracy theory and radical journalism blur" (p. 37).

Bonobo, like Michael Parenti and others, does not see a paradox or antagonism between conspiracy and institutional research. "Conspiracy itself is a necessary norm for the state and capital," says Bonobo, therefore "[s]houldn't we hold despotic perpetrators accountable at the same time we dismantle the institutional underpinnings that prop them up?" (p. 38). To the standard Left criticism that conspiracy narratives seek to merely eliminate individuals as the poisoned roots of society, Bonobo counters: "Why do leftists assume that avid conspiracy theorists would simply remove a despot and leave the despotic system in place?" Bonobo's statement complicates Albert and Chomsky's (1993) claim that conspiracy theory is fixated on concentrations of power that operate *outside* normal structures. Rather, there is no single set of allegiances that comprise social and political structures—numerous agendas and loyalties (not just, or even primarily, class) can be operational.[33]

Bonobo is not content just to defend conspiracy narratives against Left conspiracy panics. He argues that anarchism, due to its "hearty suspicion, healthy fascination, and critical thinking" may have something to offer the controversy over conspiracy theories in the Left milieu: "Radicals and anarchists might reject the common kneejerk allergy to conspiracy theory" (p. 36). Indeed, anarchists may be able to challenge the state-oriented leftists about the dangers of reducing political institutions to an instrument of class.

But more than just being in dialogue with other leftists, Bonobo suggests that the conversation be extended to the conspiratology community itself. He does believe that conspiracy researchers have something to gain from radical perspectives: "Conspiracists should abandon their thick, detailed research long enough to ponder the revolutionary implications of what they discover" (p. 36). For Bonobo, conspiracy research without a radical perspective ends up sweating the small things, mired in a "marsh of legalistic detail" spending "endless hours dedicated to dredging up more detail" (p. 38). To revive the "connect the dots" metaphor of articulation, the dots being connected remain at a local level, driven by a desire to find and connect more dots at that level. Bonobo suggests that a radical perspective would provide a more expansive set of connections, producing a metalevel awareness of revolutionary work and a more mobilizing pattern-recognition process.

In other words, Bonobo suggests an articulatory project that reworks the context of the conspiracy accounts. Like Parenti, Zwicker, Jarach, and others, Bonobo sees conspiracy and institutional analyses not as antagonistic, but as complementary methods. Both are working on contexts—the issue is *which* context is to be fought for and against. This struggle is not unique to conspiracy versus institutional analyses—it permeates oppositional political cultures in general (e.g., competing views of globalization, the role of the state in revolutionary movements, the importance of race and gender to class analyses). Conspiracy research versus institutional research, rather than being two fundamentally opposed practices, contend over a definable context in an articulatory project. It is through this recognized struggle that the "shared alienation" between structural and conspiracy narratives can turn into a strength in activism (p. 38).

POPULAR INVESTIGATIONS AND REGIMES OF TRUTH

In a cafe bar on the Lower East Side of Manhattan, an unlikely couple is engaged in conversation. A forty-something male with five-day-old stubble and disheveled stringy gray hair is explaining to a stylish woman in her early twenties the architectural impossibility of the collapse of the twin towers due to burning jet fuel. They just happen to be sitting at the same table, and she "began" the conversation by asking him about the bumper sticker on his laptop. It reads "9-11, The Truth Will Set U.S. Free." He is all too happy to elaborate the details of the 9/11 conspiracy account. We have moved far away from the classic figure of the man with the sandwich board or the conspiracy buff in the basement. He does not proselytize on a soapbox but is confident that, with the correctly placed signal (the sticker), the truth will begin to spread in a networked manner. Conscious or not, his presence in a public place with a provocative beacon itself signals a new development in the spatial distribution of skepticism and subjugated knowledges. Is he a "leading" 9/11 skeptic? Or part of a legion, whose dispersal in mundane spaces is producing a kind of viral skepticism? The savvy use of new media techniques of production and distribution, the leaderless network of researcher/activists, and the swarming around new published findings and hit pieces (e.g., *Popular Mechanics*) give an emergent and distributed character to this movement.

Perhaps what we are beginning to see is a *popularization* of investigative practices.[34] The wake of 9/11 has produced a very public investigation, but like the Warren Commission it seeks to be the *last* word on investigations.

We are thus not only dealing with subjugated *accounts* in discussing the 9/11 Truth Movement, but subjugated *investigations*. The knowledge/power relations under scrutiny here aren't embedded in official accounts but in *official investigations*, or what might be called the "sphere of legitimate investigations" (to update Dan Hallin's term). Who counts as a researcher or investigator? What body is invested with the powers of articulation? How does a noninstitutional or amateur investigation accrue cultural authority?

Conspiracy panics, as a means of constraining the range of investigations, continue the notion that conspiracy accounts represent an *exaggeration* of liberal skepticism. Liberal political rationality, as we explored in chapter 1, operates as the sphere of acceptable criticism, of properly moderate self-reflection. The 9/11 Truth Movement is yet another example of taking this suspicion too far. It does not even respect the proper protocols of investigation! Rather than invest faith into the institutional integrity of self-policing and liberal self-correction (represented by the "independent" Kean-Hamilton commission), 9/11TM sees corruption and motivation in the very heart of institutional self-correction.

But what happens outside of the neoliberal consensus perspective? What about the investigations from the more radical Left? Normon Solomon articulates one form of dissent management when he asks, "Aren't the well-documented crimes of the U.S. government and huge corporations enough to merit our ongoing outrage, focused attention and activism?" (in MalcontentX, 2002). Alexander Cockburn (2006) claims that, like the Warren Commission, the evidentiary chain on the part of the government is persuasive, and that investigations should focus on cronyism and corruption under Giuliani's then-mayoral reign. Joshua Frank (2006) says "we don't need conspiracy theories to make the case," echoing a common sentiment that the Left already possesses all of the arguments it needs. No need for further investigations: We have assembled our portfolio! Apparently not, however, as JoAnn Wypijewski (2006) melancholically notes. She writes about her visit to Ground Zero on the fifth anniversary, where she is overwhelmed by the popularity and enthusiasm of 9/11 skeptics (whom she baitingly calls "black t-shirts") versus the frail remnants of peace activists.

The sphere of legitimate dissensus emerges also when leftist commentators rely on a split between professional expertise and amateur investigations. Numerous analysts turn to the *Popular Mechanics* special issue and the subsequent book to ground their dismissal of 9/11 skeptics (Weinberg, 2006; Hayes, 2006; Monbiot, 2007; Rothschild, 2006). Reliance on this apparently nonideological, scientifically neutral arbiter dovetails with, in some cases, a revival of Hofstadter's ghost (Hayes, 2006; Lemann, 2006; Weinberg, 2006). Counterposed to this professional expertise is the amateurish quality of the 9/11TM, whose investigations are referred to as "hobbies" (Hayes, 2006) and "a bunch of kids with laptops" (Monbiot, 2007). These disqualifications accompany the more familiar attacks on conspiracy accounts as "fantasies" and "rants" (Rothschild, 2006), fear-based myths (Garcia, 2006), a "cult" (Monbiot, 2007) with its own "guru" (Rothschild, 2006), and a set of "esoteric interests" leading to a "rabbit hole of delusion" (Hayes, 2006).

More importantly, expert mediation is called upon to *settle* the matter of 9/11 once and for all. Like an update of Gerald Posner's *Case Closed*, contemporary leftist problematizers tell the 9/11 skeptics to "get over it," that it is "enough, already" and to "shut up, already" (Hayes, 2006; Weinberg, 2006). And no wonder these polemics are acceptable. As George Monbiot (2007) notes (perhaps channeling David Gilbert from a decade earlier): "this crazy distraction presents a mortal danger to popular oppositional movements." The swarm of collective investigation is rhetorically transmuted into a deadly pandemic, one that, like its biological counterpart, can be stopped by turning to the professionals.

The gatekeeper Left doesn't claim to have all the answers, only all of the problematizations. As Jodi Dean argues, conspiracy thinkers seek "a space of action beyond the limited terrain they have before them" (2000a, p. 304). While her claim justly targets pluralist political culture, we could extend the "terrain" to the gatekeeper Left. Proper spaces of action are not just determined by a consensus center. They depend on the kinds of alternative spaces offered, spaces that often regulate *themselves*. This is where the sphere of legitimate dissent has a different logic than Hallin's sphere of legitimate controversy: It is formed not primarily via a relationship to the mainstream but within dissent itself. In other words it is formed as a component of liberal political rationality, as both a spatial distribution of self-governance, and dissent management through a responsible reason.

We can, however, question this limited range of investigation. For instance, much leftist ink has been spilled (actual and virtual) on the lies, cover-ups, and misinformation that led up to and continued after the Iraq invasion. Why has there been so much attention to those deeds and so little to 9/11? One might counter that this is a question of investigatory powers. While 9/11 has received an institutional investigation, at the time of this writing there has been no independent commission on Iraq War misdeeds (while a number of institutional logistical assessments have been made). The state's investigative slack, according to this argument, has been taken up by journalists and citizen critics. But is this all it takes? What if an ostensibly "independent" commission on Iraq was established—would other investigations be displaced? Would leftist curiosities be satisfied?

The place and form of investigations matters. How is a sphere of legitimate investigation produced, not just by a consensus center but by a well-tempered dissensus? While many investigations may be taking place around an event, only some are recognized (even by radical researchers) as the proper venues for them. What would articulation across those investigations look like?

For MalcontentX, the answer seems simple enough:

> In the early days after Sept. 11th, credible, significant evidence was hard to come by (swimming in the midst of shock, confusion, then some wild accusations, fuzzy logic, etc.); yet this is often the case with investigative reporting: a "case" for review literally does not exist, (in most people's eyes) until a few instinctive, enterprising reporters follow a hunch and gather evidence together. Critics of government policy should understand this, support the process of inquiry; and it is instructive to note when and why otherwise intelligent, progressive people choose to rule out certain questions before they/we have taken the time to ask them.

This appeal to the broader Left makes sense as an opening move, allowing for an extensive, popular inquiry to take place without policing from within and without.

At the same time, the 9/11 Truth Movement has its own articulatory blockages. Schechter notes the baseline hostility and hypersuspicion directed even at potential allies. Eschewing the dominant language of "excessive" skepticism, we could point out how skepticism, when haphazardly directed can create barriers to articulation. But this skepticism does not exist in a vacuum—it is predicated on a truth zealously possessed and defended by adherents as a component of their identity (Weinberg, 2006). There is, in other words, an overriding faith in the righteousness of one's position. As Jodi Dean (2000a) remarks about American conspiracy theories generally, they are "far from radical in their assumption that the truth is out there and can be revealed according to the norms of publicity" (p. 293).

Faith in truth does create a tension regarding popular investigations, especially for the 9/11TM. Many in the movement claim to *want* truth, and seek better investigations to reach it. Others claim to *have* truth, and want to spread it and create a movement around it. At times the call for an inquiry is a masquerade for a confirmation hearing. Even the request for a grand jury is shot through with these conflated processes: *wanting* truth to come out (whatever it might be) versus *having* truth and wanting it to be released. And this goes for both courts here: the juridical forum and the court of public opinion. Furthermore, reliance on information or exposure as an organizing tool is not necessarily empirically practicable. And thinking of the movement as progressive or libertarian because of its decentralized form does not take into account the various types of subversion and deterrence that infiltrates networks (see my Bratich, 2006a). 9/11 conspiracy research can thus cut off potential articulations with its dead-ends and black holes.

While the full implications of popular investigative powers cannot be fully explored here, the issues surrounding them come into clarity around the 9/11 Truth Movement. Reaching back into journalism history, we can see the issue of investigative powers embodied in the struggle between what Gretchen Soderlund (2002) calls "street-based information" and "institution-based sources" (p. 442). With the recent rise in bloggers, grassroots activists, citizen journalists, and independent media we can see that amateur investigations are increasing in scope and intensity. Even while on the rise, these amateurs have been disqualified as unreliable sources for their very nonprofessional status. Amateurism versus professionalism was a key issue in the Gary Webb case (the popular uses of technology) and has been used to further subjugate conspiratologists (Pipes, 1997, p. 33). While the lone conspiracy researcher in the Manhattan coffeeshop may be working in tandem with other amateur investigators in the conspiratology archipelago, their proliferation doesn't assure success. More amateurs, more problematizations. This swarm intelligence is not just characterizable as "more" skepticism (a quantification that resonates with the liberal conspiracy panics over excess). It begs the question of how to organize around popular suspicion, even when those articulations are blocked from within.

CONCLUSION: THE LEFT AND DISSENT MANAGEMENT

The post–cold war era of conspiracy panics has been particularly convoluted for the Left. The trajectory of conspiracy panics maps nicely onto the recent history of the Left's fraught relationship to (neo)liberal regimes of governance. Little attention has been paid to this trajectory (see Brown, 2006; for an analysis of the "communitarian" tendency see Rose, 1999; Hay, 2005). Left criticisms of Bush wrongdoing often draw a direct line from Bush I to Bush II, as though the reign of the latter has produced amnesia about the Clinton years (or worse yet, a nostalgia for them). But this "great leap over (Clinton)" ignores the complexity of the Left's own composition as well as the precursors to the current predicament.

The relatively common project of the Left against the Reagan-Bush Administrations quickly devolved into a divide between moderate liberals and the radical Left when Clinton came to power. Within the Democratic Party, the centrist Democratic Leadership Council (DLC) fought for control of the party against traditional liberals. Meanwhile outside the party, other struggles took place around the role of reasonable dissent and proper radical analysis.

While fusion paranoia was used to describe conspiracy theories, a type of fusion *panic* was also taking place, one where the Left met Right in conspiracy problematizations (Purnick, 1995; Applebome, 1995). The fusion panic was so troubling that, in the middle of the decade, antiauthoritarian leftists saw it as yet another reason to dole out "scathing critiques" to both Left and Right insofar as they have ultimately colluded in their support for the two "opposing" sides of capitalist development (Jason McQuinn, 1996, p. 2). What we saw then was a revival of the political spectrum's categories: not just Left/Right, but center/margins.

As Clinton moved further to the center, the split in the Left was organized around the classic distinction between moderate and extreme.[35]

Early events like Waco and Ruby Ridge set the tone: Who among Leftists was about to defend ostensibly right-wing religious nuts against the recently elected liberal administration (complete with a female head of the FBI)? With a new will-to-moderation permeating political culture, elements of the Left identified with the Clinton Administration and the mainstream media around the problem of conspiracy theories (especially post–Oklahoma City bombing). Defenders of the Clinton White House dismissed AIDS conspiracy accounts, even the Gary Webb series, as a way of shoring up consent to the beleaguered regime. The Clinton Administration itself was a target of conspiracy accounts and, according to Hillary Clinton, of "a vast right-wing conspiracy." Some of these defensive conspiracy panics found their way into consent-management programs like public journalism and other pro-civil society enterprises.

The will-to-moderation comprising conspiracy panics was a symptom of the split within the Left over its relationship to governing institutions and practices. Characterizing this split was a mobilization of suspicion against dissent. On the institutional liberal end, this involved a proposal of techniques to regulate thought and action via political rationality (as in public journalism). More informally (and effectively), we witnessed a growth of watchdogs against forms of populist discourse (such as Political Research Associates, Center on Hate and Extremism, FAIR, Southern Poverty Law Center, Anti-Defamation League, Center for Democratic Renewal). The preferred leftist modes of engagement involved detection, investigation, and monitoring (via nonprofit watchdogs, research institutes, and private intelligence agencies; http://eyeonhate.com/eyeonhate.html).

This fractured relationship to neoliberal governance didn't just play out as a conspiracy panic, but conspiracy panics were a contributing factor to the composition of the political rationality. The ambivalent relationship to state power is an ongoing dialogue within radical movements and expresses itself still around conspiracy panics, as is evidenced in the 9/11 Truth Movement case. Ambivalence also appears within the conspiracy community, such as when the 9/11 Truth Movement finds itself divided over the radical quality of its project, as well as its form of inquiry and truth telling.

How do conspiracy polemics and panics thus hamper the capacities for an active Left movement? While the problematizers argue that conspiracy theories splinter the Left, I have argued above that it is the panic discourse itself that provokes difference and antagonism. As the network of popular investigatory powers grows, what are the costs of blocking and rerouting it? In a moment where counterglobalization might still be a significant component of a Left project, at what cost are populist 9/11 accounts excluded?

The Left's fractured and hazardous trajectory regarding modes of governance, political rationality, and conspiracy panics has effects on the reorganization of dissent and consent. If the Left polices itself conceptually through reason, it will have functionally enacted liberal self-governance. And this is what I believe the stakes in a politics of articulation are: What are the possible forms of dissent in the current conjuncture? What kinds of critical activity are allowable, and which are increasingly being constrained? What new possibilities are emerging with amateur investigative powers, and how are those potentials being redirected and blocked by conspiracy panics? By analyzing the 9/11 Truth Movement both in its rhetorical range and in its ongoing friction with the gatekeeper Left, we can see how the Left operated simultaneously as a target and an agent of conspiracy panics. This split is not a healthy debate within an opposition movement, but a new dissensus whereby activity is split from its own powers in order to self-regulate dissent within a sphere of legitimate investigation. The Left is left diminished at the very moment when its activist components are/were beginning to be effectual.

CONCLUSION

What is it? I cried out with curiosity—which one is it? you ought to ask!

—Friedrich Nietzsche

Why conspiracy theories? This question is often translated as Why do people believe in conspiracy theories? In this form, the question typically provokes speculations about innate human traits of suspicion, the "American character," an age of uncertainty or relativism, or the failure in recent decades of political leadership. But the question itself is anchored in an a priori disqualification of conspiracy narratives, akin to Why do people believe in ghosts? I therefore prefer beginning with the question, Why not? As I have been arguing, this question does not entail affirming the veracity of any of the narratives; rather, it interrogates the regimes of truth and reason that compose political life and examines the conditions under which alternative narratives are disqualified.

We might also ask, Why do conspiracy theories persist? or as *Time* magazine's September 2006 cover story put it, why they "won't go away" (Grossman, 2006). One common answer refers to their form: They are compelling and unassailable narratives. They persist because they ceaselessly incorporate new scandals into an already-formed metaconspiracy machine, because they inexhaustibly generate more conspiracy theories, and because, by definition, they must fail (thus regenerating).

A more generous reading finds their persistence in an ongoing struggle over forms and limits of dissent, and the kinds of knowledge that can circulate with authority. Conspiracy theories, as objects of conspiracy panics, are sites where citizenship and political rationality converge. What are the games of truth by which individuals come to recognize themselves as rational political beings and seek to regulate the conduct of self and others accordingly? How do games of truth participate in the self-reflection that constitutes the citizen-subject, and how can they organize political possibilities (Miller, 1998)? If conspiracy theories are primarily composed by the problematizations that take them as objects of concern, then we can answer the above question thusly: The continuous *crisis* over conspiracy theories makes them persist.

The question that opened this project, What is a conspiracy theory? is obviously not a neutral one. Others have asked it in order to determine its characteristics and have come to many, often contradictory, conclusions. Conspiracy theories are too complex (refusing to apply Occam's razor) or too simple (ignoring the complexity of modern political structures). They either impute secrecy into public institutions or misrecognize the obscure mechanisms of politics by attributing blame to visible causal agents (Robins in Goode, 2002).[1] They refuse the easy explanation (a lone gunman) or take the easy explanation (a cabal). They are irrational or hyperrational. Like other unspecified enemies, conspiracy theories are considered numerous enough to constitute a threat but too few to be considered truly popular.

Conspiracy panics are rife with contradictions, and as Freud has alerted us, contradiction expresses the force of a desire. What is this desire? To pursue this line of thinking, we no longer direct our attention to conspiracy theories but to the discourses that produce them, to their contexts. But this context is not the dietrological one that seeks to understand conspiracy theories by going *behind* them to find their grounds of emergence (in a culture of hate, roots of resentment, histories of oppression, etc.). Rather, we look to the same plane of statements that comprises the discursive object "conspiracy theory." In other words, we examine the problematizations of them.

Conspiracy theories come to exist as objects when they come to exist as objects of concern. How conceptual practices come to constitute conspiracy research as a *problem* is of utmost importance. Under what circumstances are we compelled to detect and identify conspiracy theories? The question, What is conspiracy theory? as I have argued throughout this book, is usually asked by those who wish to disqualify the claims.

We do not, therefore, need to trace the rise in popularity of *beliefs* about conspiracy but, instead, to map a heightened intensity in the *panics* over the beliefs. Certainly we might say that the narratives have been on the rise, with an increased visibility and circulation via new technologies (fax machines, Internet) and popular culture representations. Even a conspiracy researcher in the early 1990s called it the "conspiracy decade" (Vankin & Whalen, 2001). But, more importantly, the recent resurgence of conspiracy theories can be attributed to the *crisis* surrounding them. In this crisis, we see an increasing fervor surrounding issues of dissent, reason, governance, activism, populism, globalization, new technologies, consent, and truth converging on the problem of conspiracy theories. How were conspiracy theories made visible in this crisis?

Here is where we shift perspective. These real issues only become part of public discourse via a set of ruminations *on* conspiracy theories. Problematization of conspiracy theories becomes a means by which official, rational views on these issues can be grounded. Public anxiety over new developments (technology) and resurging problems (professional authority, popular culture, race, extremism, populism) get managed through conspiracy panics.

My project touches on some of the discourses that came to define conspiracy theories (medical fields, professional journalism, scholars, alternative criticism, and political punditry). But I also define problematization as a practice of thought, a practice irreducible to discourse (Foucault, 1988b, pp. 154–155). Whether by liberal experts, professional journalists, or Left activists, problematizations of conspiracy theories help constitute contemporary political rationality, enabling liberal governing at a distance to continue to take place through thought at work upon itself.

CONTEXT: CONSPIRACY PANICS IN PANIC CULTURE

The post–9/11 world has been marked by what some have called a "culture of fear" or "panic culture." The proliferation of modulated terror alerts, threat level warnings, and detection of unspecified enemies has been part of the New Normal (Bratich, 2006b). An "omnicrisis" (Hardt & Negri, 2000) or virtual terror (since it can appear anywhere/anytime) produces a number of preventive measures in the name of homeland security (see the special issue of *Cultural Studies* edited by James Hay and Mark Andrejevic). In the case of quasi pandemics, like SARS and the Avian Flu, the health of a population is invoked. We have moved from a cold war national security state to a terror/war homeland security mode of governance (Hay, 2006). Of course, there is increasing concentration and acceleration of security functions within executive branch departments (as well as military, local law enforcement, and the judicial branch). But the "homeland" also depends greatly on cultural practices, everyday life, and civic institutions (Hay, 2006). From citizen-oriented readiness programs (Andrejevic, 2006) to militarized media outlets, war is immanent to everyday life. As James Hay and Mark Andrejevic (2006) have argued, even this seeming revival of the centralized state is predicated on a number of decentralized programs that depend on mutual suspicion among citizens. We could even say that homeland security is an acceleration and intensification of neoliberal techniques that were forged over the previous decade (Bratich, Packer, McCarthy, 2003, pp. 17–18).

Conspiracy panics play a role in this new war and its panic culture, specifically as a means of monitoring dissent. This role is not new—the stage was set in a bipartisan way for ten years prior. Knowledge threats had been problematized in an acute manner for over half a decade. In the mid-1990s, panic culture was mixed with the sentiment of lamentation. A crisis was located in civil society. On one hand, we saw a bemoaning over the lack of participation in it (the *Bowling Alone* critiques, journalism's waning audience and role, sagging electoral turnouts). On the other hand, we saw a low intensity panic over extreme action (e.g., excessive uses of emerging technologies, populist suspicion of mass media, sensationalist popular culture, armed struggle). Conspiracy research was caught in this double-headed problematization, the twin scourges of apathy and hyperpathy.

The problem at that earlier moment was alienation from the dominant institutions and consensus discourses, be it via a passive withdrawal or an active exodus. Whether lack (loss of community, waning public participation) or excess (extremism), the center fears its own dissolution, its ability to have gravity. As Jodi Dean puts it: "When pundits and pluralists attack conspiracy thinking, they are not aiming for more political involvement or increased political activity. They want action within the parameters defined by elites, action that legitimizes the status quo, that confirms the party system, pays lobbyists, and provides daily soundbites" (2000a, p. 299).

Conspiracy panics are deployed within a renewal project of civil society and political culture. Different solutions were proposed, usually either absorption or marginalization. When something was identified as reviving sluggish discourses they could be incorporated. For instance, the clamor for more interaction was met with public journalism, and popular uses of the Internet were taken as an opportunity to increase journalism's mission. When hyperpathy was not assimilable it was expelled as Other, as scapegoat (e.g., the sacrifice of Gary Webb, the extremist uses of talk radio). Moreover, the crisis specifically focused on existing institutions' ability to *resolve* crises.

As a number of Foucault-inspired political theorists have argued, the response to the ongoing crisis of the welfare state was a recalculation of government along neoliberal lines (Rose, 1999; Barry, Osborne, & Rose, 1996; Dean, 1999). While many have made a similar argument about the reinvention of government in response to a cumbersome welfare state, the question of scale and of what constitutes liberalism differs. Neoliberalism, often equated with privatization, is usually counterposed to welfare statism. Yet within the governmentality studies literature, the reinvention was a technical adjustment *within* the liberal arts of governing (Barry, Osborne, & Rose, 1996). Liberalism itself is defined as a meditation on governing, on moving its limits. Thus, the turn to neoliberalism represented not a withdrawal of governing as such, but a management and adjustment of its boundaries. Not to govern less, but to govern better: the tension between administrative centralization and decentralization is thus a moment within this broader trajectory.

The 1990s saw a shift, even a return to older forms of liberalism. The burden of governing now fell on the self-management of populations. Civil society, filled with private foundations, civic associations, public life renewal projects, volunteerism, nonprofit organizations, and other cultural practices could complement the more traditional governmental practices like voting, lobbying, and party building. Popular culture, in the form of news, entertainment, and new communication technologies, could also be a site for neoliberal governance (Miller, 1998; Packer, 2002; Simons, 2002; Bennett, 2003;

Miklaucic, 2003; Palmer, 2003; Ouellette, 2004; Hay & Ouellette, 2006). Disruptions that cannot be channeled through normal political means get handled culturally.

These are not just randomly aggregated techniques—they compose a political rationality. And in this case this political rationality harkens back to liberalism's genesis in Enlightenment reason. In a nutshell, 1990s neoliberalism depended in part on problematizing a fusion of irrational thought and extremist action, in other words on conspiracy panics.

LEFT AND POLITICAL RATIONALITY

There was a parallel crisis over thought and action on the Left, at least with a particular segment of it. The Clinton era, for many the pinnacle of neoliberal reinvention, created an ambivalent relation to the state that strained any provisional alliance between liberals and the Left. Many constituents aligned with Clinton explicitly throughout, some got queasy when he moved to the center, others refused from the beginning. We could view this as the political expression of a broader trend whereby alternative sectors became mainstream (e.g., indie film, grunge music, microbrews).

To make this a more explicitly political analysis, I refer to Wendy Brown's discussion of ressentiment (drawn from Friedrich Nietzsche) in *States of Injury*. She defines ressentiment as a "project of antifreedom; it takes the form of recrimination against action and power, and against those who affirm or embody the possibilities of action and power" (p. 26). It is a "tendency to moralize in the place of political argument," a moralizing that "emerges from the powerless to avenge their incapacity for action" and that maintains itself by denying "that it has an involvement with power, that it contains a will to power or seeks to (pre)dominate" (pp. 27, 44, 46). Insofar as it draws from moral panic discourse, leftist conspiracy panics approximate this resentful politics.

Conspiracy panics run the risk of infusing the Left with a divisive tendency, the splitting of active forces, forcing them to turn against each other. To characterize conspiracy theories as being opposed to Left concerns (even aligned with the dominant) is to already defuse active dissent (investigative powers, organizational efforts) that could potentially be linked to leftist politics.

Articulation within conspiracy panics is thus a resentful one that leaves a dominant consensus intact. Dissent is reterritorialized in the domain of the state, within the sphere of legitimate investigations, or in a reasonable dissensus. This can take the explicit form of the Left's call for more law and order to stop the militia "threat" in the mid-1990s or the more subtle ways of feeding into a problematization that frames conspiracy theories within an antiterrorism security state.

The crisis on the Left, then, was over the ability to control forms of opposition. The Left regulated itself, moderating dissent by turning to watchdogs and turning into gatekeepers. Whether in the liberal form of public journalism against populist media excesses or the more radical leftist protection of proper research and real institutional politics against conspiracy theories, the Left crisis meant establishing the forms of articulation for a sphere of legitimate dissensus. In this way self-governance via reason was carried out.

The ramifications of this Left conspiracy panic carries over into a contemporary paralysis in the terror/war. When George W. Bush declared that the war on terror had turned into a war on "hateful ideology," he was not problematizing something new. While the content may have changed (Islamic fundamentalism for conspiracist hate speech) the form of the problematization is older. He is borrowing from a conceptual context, one that the Left substantially contributed to with the articulation of irrational thought/violent action in its conspiracy panic. The Clinton-era clamoring for a rational-based politics didn't just render the political space vulnerable to future machinations of the Right. It contributed to a self-divisive tendency, one that in turning dissent against dissent made the Left reactive and weakened its ability to understand and expand via new popular movements.

9/11 AND THE "SUBCULTURES OF CONSPIRACY THEORIES"

The events of September 11, 2001, reorganized dissent and activism. The liberal "turn to thought" took on more authoritarian overtones even while operating via similar subjective techniques. A few days after 9/11, George W. Bush called for a National Day of Reflection. While this day took on a mournful tone, it was also intertwined with the statements by White House Press Secretary Ari Fleischer to "watch what you say" and with various cultural repercussions for illegitimate forms of speech.[3] Homeland security and patriotism now became the operative principles that directed citizen-subjects and political thought.

Bush and other panic experts eventually problematized conspiracy theories as part of the dangerous knowledges afoot. The State Department's "How to Spot a Conspiracy Theory" guide gave an official stamp to dissent detection. Daniel Pipes's 1997 call for a perpetual struggle to form a subject capable of withstanding the lure of conspiracism now had explicit governmental support. The State Department guide operates as a democratization of a sci-fi precrime unit: detecting nascent violence and extremism within forms of thought. This *preventive* intervention into styles of thought has its roots in 20th-century dissent management, from the modern social psychology of Harold Lasswell's personality types through the 1960s fascination with the paranoid style and political extremism to the 1990s explosion of attention in numerous sectors to the popularization of conspiracy theories.

And knowledge detection is no parlor game. It is now part of an effort to combat terrorism, which finds nourishment in subcultures of conspiracies and misinformation. At the time of this writing, one of the emerging effects of this repression was the increasing public scrutiny paid to academics teaching or discussing "conspiracy theories" in the classroom (e.g., William Woodward and Kevin Barrett, see Jaschik, 2006) resulting in the eventual dismissal of leading 9/11 conspiracy scholar David Ray Griffin (Sullivan, 2006).

Conspiracy panics, like the moral panics they resemble, have concrete effects: legislation on hate speech, material constraints on Internet usage, investigations into academics and others who "traffic in" conspiracy accounts, a proposed reconfiguration of professional journalism (public journalism) as well as its actual reconfiguration as it went digital. As part of the broader movement to revitalize civil society, conspiracy panics inform the material constitution of the "We" that underpins institutional practices done in the name of a "community" or "public" (Dean, 2000a). Conspiracy panics also inform foreign policy, as a component of the global war on extremist ideology, as well as justification for surveillance and dissent management in the homeland. They contribute to the promotion of certain kinds of investigative practices over others, distinguishing professional from amateur inquiries. Conspiracy panics anchor the proliferation of civilian watchdog groups, think tanks, and private intelligence agencies. Finally, they contribute to the formation of oppositional forces, organizing the range of acceptable forms of counterglobalization dissent.

Conspiracy panics are not causal, nor the most significant influence on the contemporary state of politics. But as a fusion of thought and action into a problem, they set the conceptual stage. These various conspiracy panics contribute to a political rationality that is one context for the current terror/war, especially its thought theater.

POLITICAL RATIONALITY

What I argue is that this political rationality, among other things, formed around an emergent *will-to-moderation* determining the field of possible thought/action. The post–cold war era ushered in an array of governing techniques defined around "being against" extremism. New means of consent securing via governmental techniques were needed. Mobilizing citizenry to engage with particular forms of existing civil society entailed managing forms of dissent. Conspiracy panics contributed to this will and to this political rationality, whose dispositif depended on "reason" itself. Conspiracy panics were first turned inward nationally (the demonization of domestic dissent) and then went global (international extremist ideology). By fusing thought to action, marginalizing certain forms of it as extremist, and making this extremism an unspecified threat, conspiracy panics anchored this moderate political rationality via *cultural* means.

Yet this moderate political rationality can only be characterized as a particular set of techniques, an *attempt* at cohesion. There is a danger in treating a political rationality as a totalizing system, a full positivity. It can ascribe too much power to it, attributing a systematicity and unity to it that it doesn't have. Foucault himself worked to undermine this notion of a "dominant project." As Foucault argued, it is not about reason in general but a specific set of rationalities. We too can draw from Nietzsche as Foucault does, by asking of political rationality, Which one? Which will-to-power infuses conspiracy panics and produces conspiracy theories as a problem for thought?

In this way, my project has attempted a minor genealogy of the present, focusing on the composition of rationality via popular culture. Rather than identify with the conspiracy panic and its will, we can ask what are its conditions of existence? Conspiracy theories are usually diagnosed as a symptom of something else (the pathological mindset of their adherents, of untrustworthy technologies, an irrational populace, loss of civility, lax moral leadership, institutional erosion, misguided interpretations, history of identity oppression). But what is this diagnosing discourse's own will—what is *it* a symptom of?

Conspiracy panics operate only via a series of contradictory analyses, self-delusional claims, even its own paranoid projections. They ultimately operate in similar ways to the objects they problematize, especially scapegoating (seeking a figure for incrimination). Moreover, the noid style is obsessed with its own borders, with its own proximity to its presumed Other, and with the exaggeration and mimicry of its own processes. These are symptoms not of a clinical condition, but of a political culture and a type of rationality.

In Spinozan terms, conspiracy panics and the noid style are expressions of an *inadequate* rationality, one whose capacities are predicated on a need to destroy its viral pretender. Conspiracy panics are ultimately reactive: They depend on dividing forces against themselves and depriving active forces of their power. The result is neither a healthy political body nor an effective rationality. The fixation on scapegoating rituals and rooting out unjust pretenders renders the will to conspiracy panic a feeble one.

Constituent Skepticism and New Populisms

Beyond evaluating this will, however, we need to acknowledge that it is merely one will among many. A conspiracy panic analysis allows us to ask, What other conceptualizations are possible? Once the contingency of the problematizations is demarcated, a clearing emerges for alternative concepts. Conceptual politics of this sort allows us to examine the ways our creativity is regulated and to consider modes of escape (Todd May, 1994, p. 106).

Thought, because it has been made governmental under liberalism, can be made a point of contestation. By analyzing the ways thought has been governmentalized, we make the exercise of reason contingent, thus opening up a thinking-otherwise.

Anticonspiracy theory discourse may have achieved temporary ascendancy (though even this is debatable depending on how one measures the popularity of conspiracy accounts). But we cannot assume it is the *active* force: formulating problems, creating objects of concern, and fusing thought to action. Conspiracy panics are one set of forces in a broader milieu. We thus need to examine the *heterological*, the antagonisms that prevent a political rationality from suturing itself into a totality.

Therefore, I would add to the governmentality studies approach the following perspective: These governmental techniques are a *response* to antagonisms and struggles.[2] The shift in governing techniques did not simply occur in a vacuum of institutional imperatives or in the hermeticism of policy makers. This is where a robust notion of the popular can reenter the analysis: Popular culture is not just a site for the extension of governing techniques; it is a terrain on which a populace is formed. To shift terminology for a moment toward what has been called "autonomist social theory": Conspiracy panics incorporate and defuse antagonisms by turning a "multitude" into a "public" or a "people" (Hardt & Negri 2000, 2004)—a national citizenry defined by a social democratic relation to the state.

Neoliberal citizens manage themselves, monitor others, and ceaselessly struggle against the lures of irrationality. This governing at a distance takes place partially through popular culture, be it through journalism, new technologies, political magazines, or peer-to-peer suspicion. But is popular culture the realm of purely autonomized self-governance in accordance with neoliberal political rationality? Or is it a terrain of antagonism, where a *struggle* over the popular takes place? We see attempts at managing populism through culture, for instance in creating a public We as opposed to a populist Us.

Conspiracy panics are reactive. Faced with unruly forces (populism, amateurism, hyperpathy, immanent associationalism, thought/action outside normal bounds) this discourse responds to them as if a threat, "prohibiting connections and relationships that could profoundly modify the structure of the field of knowledge" (Jean Marie Vincent, quoted in Dyer-Witheford, 1999, p. 223). The center holds only insofar as it is criss-crossed by the shadows of exclusion, by the repository of scapegoats. Conspiratology circulates in this shadow and in the interstices. Whether via demonization, incorporation (as civic or public), or capture (by the official Left), anticonspiracy theory discourse *responds to* autonomous scattered knowledges. The reactive structures of exclusion can become a basis for new social conflicts.

What can be said about these scattered practices? Without ascribing a unity to these popular powers (and certainly not a political valence), we can point to their existence and composition as noteworthy. It seems like an appropriate way to conclude: At the end of a treatise on conspiracy panics, we can acknowledge the forces that spur the panic reactions, without calling them "conspiracy theories."

We could call these practices, using Antonio Negri's language (1999), a "constituent power" of skepticism. The immanent associations belong to what he and Michael Hardt (2000/2004) call "the multitude," and are the subjective dynamics that comprise radical democracy. Perhaps it is here that we can locate popular skepticism, even its populist dimension. The constituent power of skepticism challenges not just the legitimacy of a particular order but the ground of the order's being, the capacity of the order *to control the degrees of suspicion*. It unfounds the ability of an order to rein in skepticism within proper limits, to absorb it as a form of authorized self-reflection. Constituent skepticism is more than liberalism's exaggeration and mimicry— like the simulacrum it is *prior to* any founding of order. What would happen if we did not fixate on the "constituted power" of conspiracy panics, the ones that divide suspicion into proper and improper categories? What if we refused the conspiracy panic?

Imagine a world that accentuated the virtual components of this popular constituent power, one that sought to link radical skepticism with the capacities and wills to create new political possibilities. This constituent power is not accessible as narrative form, sociocultural background, or psychological pleasure. It is glimpsed in the composition of the collective: a general intellect and collaborative effort at creating a web of research as well as a political community. Mark Fenster (1999) finds in these efforts at constructing a conspiracy community a failed project. Yet his premature judgment seeks in conspiratology a conformity to a model of consensus that belongs elsewhere. Instead, we can look to Jodi Dean's work on conspiratology's relationship to cyberia and action (2000b, p. 103). We can also look to the nascent network subculture, or experimental social meshwork, of the 9/11 Truth Movement to see openings and blockages.

Are folk devils fighting back? Or are they creating a networked intelligence that cannot easily be defined as target group? Perhaps they are a "whatever subculture," an unspecified thought-action hybrid. In these emergent practices we ask the question, What *type* of subject is being composed? Reformulating conspiracy panic questions around constituent skepticism leads us to ask, What kinds of subjects are possible with conspiracy research? Conversely, what subjects are produced via conspiracy panics? While this project has primarily examined the links between knowledge and power, here we end by noting Michel Foucault's third concept, the processes of subjectification.

With Michel De Certeau's (1986) concepts we can consider constituent conspiratological skepticism as the anonymous murmurings of creative power, a realm of popular tactics located in the "interstices" of structured power (pp. 187–189). Conspiracy panics, then, only operate "in a world bewitched by the invisible powers of the Other" (DeCerteau, 1984, p. 36). What ways are there to live with these proximities, these para-zones, other than expulsion or absorption? What new mutant bodies are possible? Conspiracy panics encounter the simulation, and seek to either partially incorporate it or to scapegoat it. At the same time as they expel the mimic, they find themselves repeating many of the same actions (scapegoating, dietrological explanations, projection). As the 9/11 Truth Movement claims, we all choose our conspiracy theory, it is just that some are given institutional support and investigative authority. As Jodi Dean (2000a) so clearly puts it, "Maybe the most significant difference between conspiracy thinking and legitimate reason is who's calling the shots" (p. 303). We are opened up to a new dynamic here, one of mimicry and countermimicry (Taussig, 2002). And this puts us on a terrain different from the liberal reflections on dissent, one that De Certeau sees as the realm of popular culture and guerrilla tactics. This "ageless art" calls for a new methodology, what De Certeau calls a "polemological analysis" (p. 40).

Formed around a dissensus, the conspiratology collaborative intelligence is a fabulation that brings parties together to produce collective utterances. Some conspiracy accounts represent a people in the reactionary image of a past unity (a lost tribe). Others preserve liberalism in their libertarian fetish of the individual as a model for action. Still others, as an insurgent minority, are "contributing to the invention of a people who are *missing*" (Smith, 1997, p. xlii).

Conspiracy panics also invent a people, but in an effort to disarticulate conspiracy theories from popular support and recruit a people against the scapegoat. This is no less a fabulation, no less a making-popular. But it has to be evaluated: Which people? We are brought back to the process of articulation, as these networked localized experiments can be brought together in "a new common language that facilitates communication" across different forms of dissent (Hardt & Negri, 2000, p. 57). As conspiratologist John Judge (1995) elegantly states, "even paranoids have enemies . . . but that doesn't mean that the paranoids know who their enemies are" (p. 8). A crucial political task thus becomes "[c]larifying the nature of the common enemy" (Hardt & Negri, 2000, p. 57).

Assessing the milieu in which conspiracy panics circulate, we can borrow from De Certeau when he states:

> When one examines this fleeting and permanent reality carefully, one has the impression of exploring the nightside of societies, a night longer than their day, a dark sea from which successive institutions emerge, a maritime immensity on which socioeconomic and political structures appear as ephemeral islands. (1984, p. 41)

Consensus politics, pluralist values, and liberal public spheres can be understood as these ephemeral islands. While seeking to maintain their border integrity from the lapping waves, they fail to recognize that in these para-zones they *overlap*. Ultimately these captured positions and techniques fail to acknowledge that they are surrounded, or if they do, their response is to futilely beat back the sea. But it is into this immense nightside that we can look for a constituent skepticism, a virtuality embedded in "conspiracy theories" but whose radical democratic potential is persistently thwarted and captured by conspiracy panics. Is there a political body, a popular will, a *people to come* that can bear this intolerable simulation?

APPENDIX

AIDS Conspiracy Theory Chart

Author/ Key Text	Origin/Source	Spread	Historical Context/ Purpose	Prescription
Dr. William C. Douglass, AIDS: The End of Civilization	Artificial splice between Visna virus and HTLV-1 at Ft. Detrick, MD. Deliberate introduction into populace.	WHO in Africa/CDC in United States. Both via vaccine programs. Casual contact	CBW. Communist plot to destroy Western civilization.	Boost law and order; dismantle WHO/UN; fight communism.
Drs. Jakob & Lilli Segal, "AIDS: USA Home-Made Evil" (self-published pamphlet, 1986)	Artificial splice between Visna virus and HTLV-1 at Ft. Detrick, MD. Accidental introduction into populace.	Tested on U.S. prison inmates, who accidentally spread it to New York's gay community. Not casual contact	CBW. General U.S. malfeasance (accused of being KGB disinformation).	More scientific research.
Dr. Alan Cantwell, Jr., AIDS: The Mystery and The Solution; AIDS and The Doctors of Death; Queer Blood: The Secret AIDS Genocide Plot	Human-made, probably artificial splice, but could be old virus. Deliberate introduction into populace.	WHO in Africa/CDC in United States. Both via vaccine programs. Not casual contact	CBW, military-medical-industrial complex. Genocide, especially against gays, and then "blame the victims." Possible introduction of New World Order.	Become better health practitioners and healers; educate selves; fight back against power.
Jon Rappaport, AIDS Incorporated: The Scandal of the Century	Multifactorial: source is anything that suppresses immune system, including malnutrition, poverty, pharmaceutical and street drugs, pesticides, African Swine Fever, deliberate introduction.	Poor environmental conditions and behavioral practices. Some treatments (AZT) contribute to problem. Not necessarily viral.	Collusion between pharmaceutical corporations and medical establishment; unaccountable institutions; sloppy and unethical research; possible CBW. Potential martial law.	Take better care of immune system (including safer sex); open up new lines of AIDS research (nonviral); activism: revolution in health care.
The Strecker Group (Dr. Robert Strecker, et al.) The Strecker Memorandum	Artificial splice between Visna virus and Bovine virus. Deliberate introduction into populace.	WHO in Africa/CDC in United States. Both via vaccine programs. Can be carried by mosquitoes; condoms will not prevent spread. A viral cancer—contagious.	CBW, history of unethical experimentation on populace. Trial experiment; communist plot to exterminate U.S.	Research into electromagnetic cures; no intravenous drugs; reduce sexual promiscuity; no blood products; and start questioning official reports.

Source	Origin of Virus	Transmission	Underlying Forces	Solution / Action
Dr. Peter Duesberg, *Why We Will Never Win The War On AIDS; Inventing The AIDS Virus*	Nonviral: social factors, lifestyle, drug use.	Poor behavioral practices and continued unethical scientific practice. Some treatments (AZT) contribute to problem.	Collusion between pharmaceutical corporations and medical establishment; power of "virus hunters" (research establishment elite). Greed.	Change behavioral practices (especially stop drug use); open up new lines of AIDS research (nonviral).
Dr. Leonard Horowitz, *Emerging Viruses: AIDS and Ebola—Nature, Accident, or Intentional?*	Artificial splice. Possibly accidental, but probably deliberate introduction into populace.	Vaccine Programs, with CIA & military-medical-industrial complex backing.	CBW; military-medical-industrial complex; CIA human experiments and foreign subversion; postwar Nazi International. Genocide, against gays in U.S., blacks in Africa. Population control/New World Order.	Broaden social, political, and scientific perspective; heads Tetrahedron, Inc., an educational/activist organization.
Haki R. Madhubuti, "AIDS: The Purposeful Destruction of the Black World?" in *Black Men: Obsolete, Single, Dangerous?*	Human-made, synthesized from smallpox and hepatitis B vaccines. Deliberate introduction into populace.	WHO in Africa, via vaccine programs. Also can be carried by mosquitoes. Virus can live outside body.	CBW; history of unethical experimentation on black populace, including Jonestown massacre. Genocide against "the black world."	Educate selves; be understanding of those that are ill; be activists; seek preventive health; fight for that which is good, just, and right.
G. J. Krupey, "AIDS: Act of God or the Pentagon?" in *Secret and Suppressed*	Artificial splice by U.S. military and civilian research nexus. Deliberate, but possibly accidental introduction into populace.	WHO in Africa/CDC and NIH in United States. Both via vaccine programs. Not casual contact	CBW, military-medical-industrial complex; cold war politics; militarization of health research. Justification for suspension of civil liberties and imposition of martial law.	Cause is secondary: need to prevent & cure AIDS; fight bigotry and reactionary panic; need radical cure—not just medical, but political (make government accountable).

NOTES

Introduction. Grassy Knolledges

1. To put it another way, this project is one of articulation, an analytic strategy that "involves drawing lines or connections which are the productive links between points, events, or practices within a multidimensional and multidirectional field" (Grossberg, 1992, p. 50). And this exteriority is not simply a given structure of determinations. The "practice of articulation reworks the context into which practices are inserted. The context is never a stable object of study" (Grossberg, 1992, pp. 54–55). In this way, articulating a context for an object is already a conceptual politics. Conspiracy theories are examined as both produced and a productive force.

2. This overabstraction is similar to the ones found in repeated journalistic efforts to locate the Oklahoma City bombing in a "culture of hatred and violence." In this case, we can see a shift from a focus on the individual (Timothy McVeigh is no lone gunman) to a climate that produces such activities (including conspiracy theories).

3. A brief note on risk society and governmentality studies is warranted here, as neoliberal political rationality has been assessed through Ulrich Beck's work. Robert Castel, in his contribution to an early governmentality studies collection, links governance with risk. Mitchell Dean states it clearly: "The individualization of risk is linked to new forms of liberal government" (1999, p. 191). Pat O'Malley (1996) complicates the linkage by arguing that rather than assume a notion of a "risk society" that displaces disciplinary society, researchers need to examine specific social technologies as they get deployed in particular political rationalities. Similarly, Hay and Andrejevic (2006) ask us to move beyond the risk-society thesis, which can be too "epochalist." As they note, the National Strategy for Homeland Security fuses risk management and neoliberal governmentality. However, these governing strategies are a series of programs and techniques that use prudentialist and deterrence measures. These governing techniques may form a dispositif, but it appears under certain conditions, and those specific circumstances need to be foregrounded, not lost in a totalizing notion like "risk society." Some of the differences in hybridizing risk-society and governmentality studies may be due to disciplinary exigencies, where sociology and criminology often retain an attachment to a notion of social totality, whereas the cultural studies inflected work of Hay, Andrejevic, and Packer highlight the dispersed and antagonistic field of governing practices.

Chapter 1. Political Science Fiction

1. What constitutes "hate" is not clarified in the text. This translation of dissatisfaction and protest into hate carries over into such material practices as the formation of a Center for Hate and Extremism.

2. Interestingly enough, Lasswell recognizes that "society depends on a certain amount of pathology, in the sense that society encourages the free criticism of social life, but establishes taboos upon reflective thinking about its presuppositions" (p. 200). This limit to dissent (and its excesses) will become crucial to the later problematizations.

3. For the Overstreets, the problem is primarily that it is "hard to draw the line between Radical Rightism and the farthest right of legitimate conservatism" (p. 20). While the authors do think their analysis will be useful for liberals in keeping the extreme Left (aka communism) away, their book is written for right-wingers who are in danger of "becoming extreme," and giving anticommunism a bad name (like the John Birch Society). The book seeks to resecure the Right's consent to the legitimate spectrum, and reading the book is already practice of reintegration.

4. Pipes, for instance, makes it clear that the Left is perhaps even more insidiously promoting conspiracism, because of the overattention to the Right and because the Left is more sophisticated, subtle, and convincing (pp. 159–165).

5. The line that Hitchens quotes is "not even wrong," but the sentiment is similar.

6. We can also take the "corrupt" politician as an example of the just pretender. The corrupt figure is one marked by a *failure* to subsume personal interests (greed, wish for fame, lust) to public ideals. S/he betrays a lack of commitment to the standards of governance; his/her performance is inadequate to the prescribed tasks of a leader. This deviance can be countered with a description and reinstantiation of those political ideals and a judgment upon the actor's failure to conform to them.

7. Pipes extends this mistrust, however, to other nations. In fact, Pipes feels that some regimes, like Soviet communism and Nazi Germany, were *founded* on conspiracism (primarily because their respective leaders were paranoids).

8. It seems that when political paranoia takes an activist, organized form people appeal to direct state intervention. In much of the concern over militias there is a call for stronger laws and enforcement of them (most notably the letter from Morris Dees, head of the Southern Poverty Law Center, to Janet Reno pleading for increased surveillance powers for the FBI). In addition, the conflation of extremism with hate speech led some watchdog groups (especially the Anti-Defamation League) to draft proposed laws and petition for harsher penalties for extremist behavior. In both these cases, however, it's the armed and violent character of the activities that is highlighted, not the political positions of the actors. When it comes to the more recent problematization of "subcultures of conspiracy and misinformation" the material repressive effects are yet to be determined.

9. There are moments when these problematizers want to turn extremism into "error" as a way of taming the threat. Error is manageable within reason, within

a regime of truth as merely one opinion within it (a false one). The authors run up against a blockage though, because (1) by definition conspiracism is not about falsifiable content but about style; (2) the exaggerated qualities of liberal values make conspiracism too close to the norm to be error; and (3) they do not allow dissent over the procedures of dissent. But this metadissent is precisely what defines extremism and political paranoia. They are unreasonable precisely because they take reason as an object. Even when attempts are made to define extremism as an integral component of Americanness (Schlesinger, 1962; Archer, 1969; Sargent, 1995; George & Wilcox, 1996) it is only done so in order to render it provisionally sensible (as an oppositional force, as necessary dissent). Very quickly, the problematizers find themselves needing to expel conspiracism as intolerable.

10. And how can we think of this attachment as a *general* mechanism? Is this subjective process of sorting out political excesses and simulations solely a local technology of political subjectivation (i.e., only when presented with "extremist" or dangerous dissent)? Or is it a more general condition of *technologizability* (the ability for a technology to stick)? The regime of truth can be thought of thus as a consent mechanism.

Chapter 2. Pop Goes the Profession

1. The channel empanelled three historians to review the evidence. In April 2004 based on the panel's findings the channel apologized to the Johnson family and withdrew the documentary. The principal conspiracy researcher cited in the documentary, Barr McClellan (father of G. W. Bush Press Secretary Scott McClellan), requested equal time to present a rebuttal to the panel, and proposed that a third party arbitration panel be set up. As of this writing, these requests have been refused.

2. During the same month the documentary aired, CBS pulled its miniseries on the Reagans after public pressure about the "accuracy" of the project. For more on the History Channel and conspiracy narratives, see Popp (2006).

3. As Michael Parenti (1993) argues, "reporters and editors who say they are guided by professional integrity and journalistic standards of autonomy and objectivity have rarely, if ever, defined what they mean by these terms. 'Professional integrity' remains largely unexplained and somewhat contradictory" (p. 59).

4. Among scholarly analyses, Fenster (1999) and Knight (2001) devote significant attention to the film.

5. Of course, there are the tabloid stories that promote the view that Kennedy staged his own death to avoid really getting killed, and is now in hiding (or at least his brain is) in Argentina.

6. The official version of the assassination is a well-worn account. A lone gunman (Lee Harvey Oswald) fired three shots from the Texas Book Depository to kill Kennedy and wound Texas Governor John Connally; Oswald was later captured by Dallas Police. Originally constructed by AP and UPI news services within an hour after the assassination, this version dominated contemporary news reports. It was officially

stamped by the Warren Commission the following year and has subsequently been retold in TV movies, news reports, and documentaries (CBS has broadcast at least one in each decade), and nonfiction books (such as Gerald Posner's 1993 *Case Closed*).

At the same time the official story was being pieced together, alternative accounts of the assassination were already beginning to circulate. Dozens of witnesses gave accounts of multiple shooters, of four to seven shots, and of another site from where shots seemed to originate—a grassy knoll alongside the parade route. While the lone gunman account was the most visible, speculations and hypotheses posited other figures involved in the assassination. The trajectory of the bullets and angle of the gunshot wounds, for example, seemed incompatible with the notion of a single gunman stationed at the Texas Book Depository. Even before the Warren Commission's report was released (less than a year after the assassination) some of these speculations became book-length published theories (e.g., Joachim Joesten's *Oswald: Assassin or Fall Guy?* and Thomas Buchanan's *Who Killed Kennedy?*; see Simon, 1996, for a comprehensive inventory). The Warren Commission report was met with incredulity among the community that would become known as "assassination buffs" (Simon, p. 11). David Lifton, for example, was dissatisfied with one detail in the Warren Commission account—the physics of the "magic bullet," and spent the rest of his life trying to unravel the mystery of Kennedy's assassination. Other well-known books from the mid-1960s in this vast literature include Sylvia Meagher's (1967) *Accessories After the Fact*, Josiah Thompson's (1967) *Six Seconds in Dallas*, and perhaps most notably Mark Lane's (1966) *Rush to Judgment*, which stayed on the *New York Times* bestseller list for six consecutive months.

7. For a thorough chronology of the various texts and actors (both critical of and sympathetic to the official account), see Art Simon (1996) as well as Anthony Frewin's (1993) annotated film, TV, and videography.

8. This is not to say that the state exerts no influence on journalistic practices, especially during wartime military management (some might argue we are now in a state of permanent war). However, this is primarily done through journalism's *own* professional protocols (e.g., the reliance on official sources). This way, state dependence can be enacted and justified as an internal rule, rather than as an external imposition.

9. The closest thing to a link was the fact that McVeigh visited Elohim City, an explicitly fundamentalist Christian compound. Even though they stored arms in their compound, the Christian identity–oriented militants of Elohim City were not technically a militia, who were defined as nationalists and constitutionalists but essentially did not articulate their mission as a religious one.

10. This linking of terrorism to new technologies did not end domestically. After 9/11, they were closely linked to Al-Qaeda. See Brush, 2002.

11. This strategy (at least on the part of the liberal Left) changes a decade later to one of mimicry, with the launch of Air America.

12. Popular culture also finds ways of articulating hyperpathy. In addition to *Arlington Road* analyzed above, examples like *Broken Arrow* and *The Rock* involve disgruntled citizens becoming extremists.

Chapter 3. Trust No One (on the Internet)

1. In 1985, Associated Press reporters Robert Parry and Brian Barger broke the story in an AP dispatch (Kornbluh, 1997). A year later, the Christic Institute conducted investigations into the relationship between the agency, the Nicaraguan anticommunists, and cocaine's infusion into the United States as a component of the Iran-Contra affair. Christic's legal brief and video documentary *Coverup* set the template for future research into CIA/Contra/crack research. The link between the CIA, drug smuggling, and support of anticommunist insurgent groups is even older. As the Christic Institute's findings point out, many of the major players in Iran-Contra were involved in running heroin from the "Golden Triangle" (Laos, Cambodia, and Vietnam) to the United States in the early to mid-1970s and using the profits to support anticommunist fighters in the region. For an earlier version of this research, see Alfred McCoy's (1972) *The Politics of Heroin in Southeast Asia.* The Senate Committee Report headed by John Kerry in 1989 indicated that CIA agents had knowledge of Contra cocaine smuggling. *Cocaine Politics* (1991) by Peter Dale Scott & Jonathan Marshall elaborated Christic's findings, as did numerous articles in such progressive magazines as *Covert Action Quarterly, The Nation,* and *In These Times.* For an overview of some of this progressive literature, see Vankin, 1996, especially pp. 186–201; see also http://www.copvcia.com/ for an archive of this literature. Celerino Castillo, former DEA agent, wrote of his firsthand experience in *Powderburns: Cocaine, Contras and the Drug War* (1994). Bill Clinton's potential role, both as governor of Arkansas, where the city of Mena was allegedly a major stopover for Contra cocaine smugglers, and as president, was investigated by Terry Reed and John Cummings in *Compromised* (1995) as well as in an ongoing series in the *Arkansas Gazette* from 1988–1991. And the narrative circulated outside of published works, informally among African Americans on what Patricia Turner (1993) calls the "black grapevine" (see especially pp. 180–201) and in visual culture (like the movie *Panther*).

2. A similar approach can be found in Michael Warner's *Letters of the Republic,* in which the history of print technology is bound up with, and given meaning by, the political and symbolic contexts in which the technology comes to be what it is. John Tagg's (1988) work on photographies also provides a useful framework that avoids technological determinism. Bringing Warner's historical account of print's symbolic contexts together with Tagg's genealogy of the discursive and institutional conditions of a medium's emergence works against the grain of technological determinism.

3. For a more detailed account of this counterattack see Cockburn and St. Clair, 1998 (especially chapter 2); Solomon, 1997, and the various articles published by Robert and Sam Parry in *The Consortium* (www.consortiumnews.com).

4. The effects of this attack became very clear. For example, *Dateline NBC* cancelled its follow-up segment on Webb's series after the counterattack began.

5. These internal investigations validated most of Webb's claims and produced even more admissions. In May 2000 CIA Inspector General Frederick Hitz released the third volume of a report from a four-year in-house investigation on the

relationship between the agency, the Contras, and crack cocaine. According to Peter Dale Scott (2000), the reports acknowledge that the "CIA made conscious use of major traffickers as agents, contractors, and assets. It maintained good relations with Contras it knew to be working with drug traffickers. It protected traffickers which the Justice Department was trying to prosecute, sometimes by suppressing or denying the existence of information" (p. 19). This report followed two previous reports acknowledging that, indeed, Contras financed themselves through cocaine sales in the United States and listing about fifty participating Contras. The CIA, in these reports, worked with over half of them even after becoming aware of their drug trafficking. The reports also revealed that the Reagan Administration (specifically the Department of Justice) protected these activities by giving the CIA clearance not to report any knowledge of them. Taken together, the reports, even with their heavy redactions, present more charges than Webb's relatively tame series. Not surprisingly, the major daily newspapers generally ignored the reports' release. When they *were* reported, the findings were sanitized and downplayed; the *New York Times*, for example, cast the CIA in a passive role (as "ignoring or "failing" to investigate the drug-trafficking allegations) (Parry, 1998c, www.consortiumnews.com/consor31.html). In addition, the *New York Times*, even though it knew the basic findings of the reports, chose to publish an unfavorable review of two books (*Dark Alliance* by Gary Webb, and *Whiteout* by Alexander Cockburn and Jeffery St. Clair) that reached many of the same conclusions as the official report. The reviewer, James Adams, deemed the two books "unsatisfactory" and their claims of a CIA cover-up "laughable" (Adams, 1998, p. 28).

    6. Lack of follow-up prevented substantiation or verification of some of Webb's claims, and ultimately *Mercury News* publisher Jerry Ceppos printed a correction apologizing for the story's lack of safeguards against misinterpretation. In a display of buckling to pressure from the more established newspapers, Ceppos's correction (which was not a retraction) eventually led to Webb's reassignment and eventual resignation. Not surprisingly, Ceppos's correction garnered frontpage coverage. When Ceppos became upset at how his statement had been interpreted as a retraction by the mainstream news organs (especially the *Washington Post*), he wrote a letter of response and clarification. The *Post* refused to print it.

    7. This kind of attack followed almost inevitably from mainstream journalism's consensus on earlier claims of a CIA/Contra/cocaine nexus. When John Kerry's congressional report on Contra drug links was released in 1989, *Newsweek*'s "Conventional Wisdom Watch" captured the media's reaction in its labeling of Kerry as a "randy conspiracy buff" (Parry, 1998a, www.consortiumnews.com/ consor12.html).

    8. In the Webb case, press-state relations are important, both in the propaganda model offered by Chomsky and Herman (1988) and in more explicit forms. For Cockburn and St. Clair, the presence of former CIA operatives on the staff of the major news organs may have contributed to the vociferous defense of the agency and the vitriolic attacks on Webb. In addition, the disclosure (in the *New York Times* no less) that "the Agency has 'owned or subsidized' more than 50 newspapers, news services, radio stations, periodicals, book publishers, and other communication entities, most of which were overseas" has solidified this government-media connection (Lee & Solomon, 1990, p. 117).

9. For an elaborate treatment of the friendly fire account, see James Sanders (1997).

10. This critique of conspiracy narratives as overload of data is *itself* a standard technique of disqualification. Here, the glut is seen as a dangerous swarming multiplicity that begs for filters, standards, and techniques of discrimination, best provided by professionals.

11. "Integrity" here refers to its two definitional components: (1) soundness, wholeness, structural consistency, and (2) moral uprightness, honesty, truthfulness, and trustworthiness.

12. Across the Atlantic, the coding of the Web as anarchic in order to be governed is made more explicit. Jim McClellan (1995) argues that while the "Net is clogged with paranoia" and "bona fide daft ideas," "if it could just get beyond moral panic and conspiracy paranoia, the Internet could play a crucial role in doing something about this sense of 'disaffiliation' and actually involve people in some sort of 'process of governing' " (p. 63).

13. Of course, this movement of crisis as opportunity never closed. The rise of blogs, citizen journalists, indymedia, and other information-dissemination vehicles have arisen subsequently to provoke more reflection and reorganization. Since my focus here is on conspiracy panics, I cannot fully explore these developments but can note that each eruption poses a similar kind of threat (citizens turning to nonofficial sources) and promise (more interactivity with readers).

14. This link is strongest in the "social responsibility" theory of the press, which promotes "a liberal hostility to government, a liberal faith in reason, [and] a liberal belief in private property. Social responsibility is clearly a species of liberalism, as the label 'neoliberal' implies" (Nerone, 1995, p. 99). Journalists define their social role as "gatekeepers," as having the power "to regulate the marketplace of ideas on behalf of the public" (p. 52).

15. Other versions of freedom involved in journalism, such as wider participation in the production of news, or increased access to information about state practices and to decision making, is left unaddressed at best or explicitly subjugated.

16. Gary Webb's own trajectory deserves more attention here than space allows. A few months after the controversy raged over his series, the *San Jose Mercury News* demoted him to work in the classifieds bureau in the Sacramento office. His book garnered favorable attention among leftist critics and he briefly traveled on a lecture circuit. Despite being vindicated for his initial series' findings, Webb never fully returned to the profession. Tragically, in 2004 he died of self-inflicted gunshot wounds to the head, according to the coroner's report. Like the subject of his life's work, his death was surrounded by controversy and speculation, as commentators used the fact that he had two headwounds to make the case that he was "suicided."

Chapter 4. Left Behind

1. On *Nightline* (1996) that evening, Ted Koppel ended the program by saying that Deutch "deserves his full measure of credit for trying anyway." Koppel's introduction to the program likened the story and its response to a kind of out-of-control

brushfire: "What began quietly as a newspaper series caught fire on the Internet. . . . Fueled by suspicion, it raged on talk radio. . . . The fury sparked hearings."

2. For example, CBS *Evening News* (1996) foregrounded the emotional responses of the crowd, relying on images of the crowd in an uproar and studiously avoiding showing individual questioners. In addition, *Washington Post* writer James Glassman felt that Deutch failed by "listening passively as paranoids and lunatics shouted epithets at him" (quoted in Cockburn & St. Clair, 1998. p. 90).

3. For an extended account of the construction of "black paranoia" see Knight, 2001, pp. 147–155.

4. These two approaches aren't always very distinct from each other. Even Lasswell was seeking the social conditions that contribute to the development of certain political types. Hofstadter, as well, looked to social and political contexts (namely an alienating political system) to help define the paranoid style. More recent problematizations, including Robins and Post's *Political Paranoia* (1997) and Daniel Pipes's *Conspiracy* (1997), draw mostly from Hofstadter's analysis, while supplementing it with a more thorough investigation into social, economic, historical, and political conditions of "political paranoia" and "conspiracism." Even given this mutuality, however, I am arguing here that the sociocultural contexts of "conspiracy theories" have been given more prominence recently, as the authority of the political-psychological apparatus has waned in its efforts at bolstering the regime of truth. It is no longer sufficient to dismiss a theory because it is irrational or a crackpot—more sophisticated techniques of disqualification are at work now.

5. While the appendix lists both viral and nonviral alternative theories, I am concentrating on viral theories. While not all viral theories are conspiratorial in the same way (some posit that accidental release of the virus might have occurred and that now a clean-up and cover-up program is in effect), their reliance on HIV gives them some degree of comparability. To put it another way, I am interested in AIDS conspiracy theories that concern the origins of HIV and not in the nonviral theories that concern the origins of AIDS. Nonviral theories (such as Duesberg's) often posit multifactorial causes of AIDS (combination of drugs, behavioral practices, social factors—malnutrition, pollution) and even multidiseases (that AIDS is often a misdiagnosis of various other conditions). Purposeful targeting of groups is not usually a major component of nonviral theories. Rather than conspiracy, they emphasize collusion (medical, pharmaceutical, and governmental institutions) and cover-up (countervailing evidence is ignored and suppressed because it might threaten research funding and careers of mainstream scientists). These nonviral theories and their struggles with mainstream science have a story to be told, but I do not have the space here to pursue it.

6. I cite this in order to locate the author's political affiliations squarely with the Left, in case that wasn't apparent from the source. As if that's not enough, an earlier version of this chapter (Bratich, 2002a) was reviewed harshly by leading radical academic Ward Churchill, partially based on the credentials of Gilbert.

7. Duesberg has received this kind of criticism many times. In a review of Duesberg's book *Inventing the AIDS Virus*, David Perlman (1996) claims that "this book, however passionate, can only confuse an already confusing global tragedy" (p. 3).

8. In essence, the splice theory argues that HIV is a result of the scientifically engineered, artificial splicing of two or more already-existing viruses (usually a visna or bovine virus with a human one).

9. The belief that conspiracy theories are an obstacle to health is not limited to AIDS-related accounts (see Desantis & Morgan, 2004, for an analysis of conspiracy logic in a smoker's magazine).

10. Some health educators are attempting to transform their knee-jerk dismissals of AIDS biowarfare accounts (Scanlon, 1998). Others are devoting websites to debunking these accounts in the name of health (*Healthwatcher*, http://www.healthwatcher.net/Quackerywatch/Horowitz/).

11. The use of the phrase "false conspiracy theories" appears to be a redundancy in this argument. But read another way, it could signify the possibility of *true* conspiracy theories. Perhaps in this reading we need better, truer conspiracy narratives?

12. This article appeared during a time when much media attention (from both the mainstream press and Left-leaning journalism) was focused on the American militia movement (of which Bo Gritz was a key member/metonym).

13. For this "Right Woos Left" logic, see Berlet, 1994, 1995; and Berlet & Bellman, 1989. This view has been taken up by a number of other leftists, including Noam Chomsky who feels that conspiracy theories have "just wiped out a large part of the Left" (quoted in Parenti, 1996, p. 188). Mark Fenster (1999) provides a thoroughly critical analysis of Berlet's perspective, arguing that it conceptualizes conspiracy theory as something "that becomes increasingly popular as a result of the pressure of external forces" (p. 60). Berlet's framework "depends on seeing the belief in conspiracy as singular . . . pathological, and unwarranted, and as a wholly political product of largely marginal demagogues" (p. 61). Doing so prevents Berlet from recognizing both the complexity and populist impulse in conspiracy narratives (p. 61).

14. Interestingly enough, Gilbert's article even demonstrates the various political positions espoused by conspiracy theories. At one point, when Gilbert discusses Jakob and Lilli Segal, early proponents of the HIV splice theory, he places them in a communist context, even hinting that this theory was promoted as Soviet disinformation. Later, however, Douglass's appropriation of this splice theory is firmly rooted in an anticommunist framework. As Gilbert unintentionally demonstrates, even in the starkly divided political context of the cold war, there is no necessary relation between an AIDS origin story and a political position.

15. "Dr. Graves submitted this flowchart as evidence to the Sixth Circuit Federal Court in a case that named the president of the United States as a defendant to answer a petition acknowledging the authenticity of the flowchart. On January 12, 2001, the case was dismissed as "frivolous," and then referred to the district's Appellate Court, which ruled in favor of the lower court. Eventually, it went to the Supreme Court, which refused to hear it without giving comment as to why" (*FinalCall.com*, 2004).

16. In a similar way, we would not want to equate all *dismissals* of origin stories' importance. When Simon Watney or John James call origin stories unimportant, they are doing it for different reasons than when David Heymann, then head

of WHO's Global Programme on AIDS, announces "The origin of the AIDS virus is of no importance to science today.... Any speculation on how it arose is of no importance" (quoted in Fiske, 1996).

Chapter 5. Going Global

1. A week after the Oklahoma City bombing, Clinton urged Americans to resist "the purveyors of hatred and division, the promoters of paranoia."

2. A Lexis Nexis search of the terms "culture of hate" or "climate of hate" in full text of major newspapers finds 46 hits from 1992 to 1994, jumping to 132 during the period 1995 to 1997. In a book-length study, Joshua D. Freilich (2003) argues that the major factor contributing to the rise of militias is cultural, not economic.

3. There are differences between mainstream problematizations of African American conspiracy theories and those of white theories, however. White conspiracy theories tend to get a variety of depictions, ranging from the harmless obsession of Kennedy assassination buffs to the dangerous theories of militias and Timothy McVeigh (still defined as baseless). African American accounts (also depicted as baseless) tend to garner a more sympathetic response, one that assesses the danger to African Americans themselves and to reason more generally. Each kind is "understandable" from a detached perspective, but one receives the added sentiment of condescension.

4. At the simple empirical level, the makeup of militias is not uniform. How does one account for Ohio Militia former leader James Johnson (an African American), or the predominantly African American Detroit Constitutional Militia, or the Jews for the Preservation of Firearms? In addition, Linda Thompson, lawyer and general adjutant of the Indiana Militia, has declared her strength as a woman via her leadership role in this organization.

5. Let us take as an example the question of race. Some of the most widespread conspiracy theories are not suspicious of other races, but of a state that seeks to gain from pitting races against each other (a reactive divisiveness). In numerous conspiracy accounts, a race war is not desired but is feared as a move in a larger strategy—the implementation of martial law by the state. To participate, then, in a politics of resentment (creating barriers, desiring annihilation, keeping the other contained) is to be a pawn in the state's strategy.

6. Similar questions were on the table regarding the more prima facie progressive counterglobalization movement that came to public notice during the Seattle protests.

7. An example of this contingent politics of articulation was the struggle over the term antigovernment. How is it that "antigovernment" came to be associated with white supremacists, the neo—and not so neo—Nazis, the Christian Identity movement and synonymous with "anti-black, anti-immigrant, anti-Semitic?" The elision equates government with these identities and, as such, sets up the state as the proper authority for adjudicating issues of race, class, and gender and not as contrib-

uting factor to those oppressions. These articulations, I would argue, are what made it so difficult for a leftist "antigovernment" stance back then. Even more, they allowed for an alignment with the state, as evidenced in the calls for an *increase* in state powers to stop the threat of these critiques.

8. These are only a few of the broadest threads. For a more thorough list of questions as well as websites and groups pursuing them, see. http://www.911truth.org/links.php; http://www.oilempire.us/; http://www.whatreallyhappened.com/9-11BasicQuestions.

9. The recent exposure of the Kennedy-era project Operation Northwoods has fueled these "prewar provocations" theses.

10. Ruppert was a leading researcher into the CIA/crack link, even asking Deutch a question during his historic visit to South Central after Gary Webb's series.

11. This church has a long and storied tradition of housing and supporting countercultural events and radical actions. Less than a year before the 9/11 Truth Movement meetings, the church was a crucial space for housing and organization during the protests against the Republican National Convention.

12. The majority of the audience that expressed itself in that instance wanted to continue talking, but to no avail: The moderators (themselves somewhat conflicted on the matter) decided to go ahead with the preplanned order of events.

13. A number of essays on the main website are produced by something called "The 911truth.org Steering Committee."

14. The New York City chapter of the 9/11 Truth Movement has seen its share of articulated tensions here, from an attempted senatorial campaign by Sander Hicks, to public accusations that organizers were working for Lyndon Larouche, to other sectarian splits and purges.

15. This is a tricky strategic move, especially if one believes that mainstream outlets are unreliable not because they are biased, but because they can be instruments of disinformation. For instance, how would the outlandish story (repeated on numerous occasions by media outlets) that Atta's passport was found in the rubble of the Twin Towers fit into a timeline? How could one distinguish among these bits?

16. The claim that the official account is itself a brand of conspiracy theory complicates the historical argument that conspiracy thinking *was* once central, even rational (in the foundation of the United States), while now it is relegated to the margins and irrationality (see Dean, 2000). Instead of this linear account, we are witnessing a simultaneity of competing conspiracy theories, official and popular.

17. This overreliance on identity opened Fiske up to Mark Fenster's charges of an uncritical populism that would not prevent the *Turner Diaries* being considered a populist resistance text.

18. Meyssan is a controversial figure even within the 9/11TM: His research has not only been consistently rebuked, it has been accused of being disinformation that poisons the well.

19. Mbeki was accused of trafficking in conspiracy theories along with his minister of health after the 2000 global conference on AIDS (held in Durbin), where they questioned the HIV hypothesis and cited prominent conspiratologist William

Cooper. Khaddafi was skewered for his belief that the Pan Am Flight 103 that crashed over Lockerbie Scotland was a CIA operation, as well as supporting fellow Arab Dodi al-Fayed, who believes elements of British Secret Services (on behalf of the Royal Family) killed his son along with Princess Diana.

20. If the mid-90s conspiracy panics defined their problems as "right-wing," the 9/11 conspiracy researchers found themselves with a different label, though sharing similar political "space." The term *wingnut* retains a sense of extremism as an epithet (of course adding to it the classic psychological dismissal with the nut metaphor).

21. Even the choice of whether to use the term *Left gatekeepers* makes a difference.

22. The Reichstag was the name of the building torched in 1933 that paved the way for Hitler's declaration of emergency state powers. While a lone communist was blamed for it, subsequent investigations and historians have concluded that the arson was an inside job.

23. At the same time, Albert's ambivalent (yet ultimately direct) support of John Kerry in the 2004 election (part of what many called the "Anybody But Bush" reformist Left) indicates that "vile manipulators" are indeed the primary targets of politics.

24. One could also argue that the question of the 2004 election (namely whether to concentrate activist energies to oust Bush with Kerry) was as divisive, reviving the long-standing debates around the effectiveness of participating in elec-toral politics. The acute and periodic (rather than acute and ongoing) nature of the voting question puts it in a different category.

25. "This analysis will concentrate on the logical structure of conspiracy theory as such, and attempt to illuminate its psychological, political, philosophical, and historical roots" (abstract http://www.homemadejam.org/renew/archive/2004/2004–2.html#anarchism-of-fools).

26. When it comes to articulatory practices, we may have entered a phase of what I call "vortextuality," where the key distinction is no longer truth from falsity, nor even truth from deliberate disinformation, but disinformation from the claim to have revealed it.

27. This generated a heated discussion during the speaker series/rally after the September 11, 2005, march on the *New York Times*. Mimi Rosenberg (host of a radio show on WBAI Pacifica station) denounced the use of materials from her colleague Ralph Schoenman. Schoenman is an extremely controversial figure within the 9/11 TM (and in other activist quarters) for his placement of Israel at the center of 9/11 narratives.

28. The same faith in international tribunals are present in Albert and Chomsky, given their calls for war crimes trials, sometimes for the same characters.

29. What is a body capable of? For conspiratologists, this is the lesson for the Left: In order to produce an effective movement we need to know what the current institutionalized body is capable of (e.g., killing its own).

30. There were conspiracy accounts of Katrina, from weather modification narratives to witness accounts of explosions before the levee broke. Of course,

anticonspiracy theory articles quickly appeared, both in mainstream news accounts and on leftist media (Garcia, 2005).

31. Perhaps the most damning element that makes a narrative unarticulatable is anti-Semitism (whether or not the charge is justified). The case of Ralph Schoenman is telling. His radio show *Taking Aim* on the Left-leaning New York City station WBAI has caused a significant stir. While his analyses are quite systematic and institutional, they are centered around a strong anti-Zionism, which has made him a target of criticism on the Left. This raises a significant articulation issue: Should the taint of anti-Semitism destroy the credibility of a narrative? What does it take to undermine *any* narrative?

32. Not only is the main 9/11 print outlet called Global Outlook, but a key website comes from the Centre for Research on Globalization (http://www.global research.ca/).

33. As Mark Andrejevic (2006a) argues, reality television programs are one popular cultural form whereby detection and investigative processes are rendered entertaining and informational.

34. Of course, for mainstream and marginal rightwingers there was no distinction regarding Clinton, as even his centrism was considered leftist.

Conclusion

1. "The world is obscure and what is happening is often obscure," Dr. Robins said. "Conspiracy theories make the world seem a lot more rational" (Goode, 2002).

2. New Left historians, among others, argue that the 1930s New Deal operated to thwart populist, even socialist, aspirations.

3. One is reminded of Clinton's post–Oklahoma City exclamation about improper speech: "When they say things that are irresponsible, that may have egregious consequences, we must call them on it."

REFERENCES

ABC News presents the Kennedy assassination—Beyond conspiracy. (2003).

Abbott, Andrew Delano. (1988). *The system of professions: An essay on the division of expert labor.* Chicago: University of Chicago Press.

Achenbach, Joel. (1996, December 4). Reality check. *The Washington Post*, p. C01.

Achenbach, Joel. (2004, July 27). They're out to get you, into a multiplex; Alas, paranoia isn't what it used to be. *The Washington Post*, p. C01.

Adams, James. (1998, September 27). Moonlighting? *The New York Times*, p. 28.

Albert, Michael, & Chomsky, Noam. (1993). The Chomsky tapes: Conversations with Michael Albert. Retrieved December 17, 2005, from http://www.zmag.org/ ZMag/articles/chomalb.htm

Alberts, Sheldon. (2005, September 7). On I-10's "Trail of Tears," conspiracy theories swirl. *The Gazette* (Montreal), p. A1.

Albrecht, Brian. (1995a, June 11). Hate speech; Across Ohio and throughout the nation, the venom is spreading faster than ever before. *Plain Dealer* (Cleveland, Ohio), p. 1A.

Albrecht, Brian. (1995b, June 18). Some talk radio now the hate spot on your dial. *Times-Picayune* (New Orleans, LA), p. A8.

Alexander, A.B.H. (1997). 60 Minutes exposed. *Probe*, 3(3), 13–19.

Alter, Jonathan. (1997, March 24). The age of conspiracism. *Newsweek*, 47.

Anderson, Benedict. (1991). *Imagined communities: Reflections on the origin and spread of nationalism.* New York: Verso.

Andrejevic, Mark. (2006a). The discipline of watching: Detection, risk, and lateral surveillance. *Critical Studies in Media Communication*, 23(5), 391–407.

Andrejevic, Mark. (2006b). Interactive (in)security. *Cultural Studies*, 20(4–5), 441–458.

Applebome, Peter. (1995, May 7). Terror in Oklahoma: Violence, anger of the 60s takes root in the violent Right. *The New York Times*, p. 1.

Arab media show no sign of being objective. (2004, April 19). *The Atlanta Journal-Constitution*, p. 11A.

Archer, Jules. (1969). *The Extremists: Gadflies of American Society.* New York: Hawthorn.

Asim, Jabari. (1993, February 23). Black paranoia far fetched? Maybe, but understandable. *The Phoenix Gazette*, p. A13.

August, Oliver. (1997, December 31). America looks to "John Wayne" to halt Microsoft's stampede. *The Times* (UK). Business section.

Baker, Peter, & Chandrasekaren, Rajiv. (1997, July 2). Clinton calls a summit on internet smut. *The Washington Post*, p. A06.

Barkun, Michael. (2003). *A culture of conspiracy: Apocalyptic visions in contemporary America*. University of California Press.

Barrs, Rick. (1996, October 31). A barracuda tries to eat the messenger. *New Times Los Angeles*. Retrieved July 27, 1997, from http://cgi.sjmercury.com/drugs/postscript/controversy/controversy1031.htm

Barry, Andrew, Osborne, Thomas, & Rose, Nikolas (Eds.). (1996). *Foucault and political reason*. Chicago: University of Chicago Press.

Baudrillard, Jean. (1988). Simulacra and simulations. In M. Poster (Ed.), *Jean Baudrillard: Selected writings*. Stanford: Stanford University Press.

BBC News. (2001, May 13). Libyan HIV trial adjourned—Again. http://news.bbc.co.uk/2/hi/middle_east/1328300.stm

Beato, G. (1996, November 26). Beta journalism: G. Beato on the Web's "Dark Alliance" with tabloid TV. Retrieved July 27, 1997, from, http://www.feedmag.com/96.11beato/96.11beato.html

Belsie, Laurent. (1997, October 7). UFOs? Secret agents? On the Net, conspiracy theories abound. *The Christian Science Monitor*, p. 12.

Bennett, Tony. (2003). Culture and governing. In J. Z. Bratich, J. Packer, & C. McCarthy (Eds.), *Foucault, cultural studies, and governmentality* (pp. 47–63). Albany: State University of New York Press.

Berg, Steve. (1997, April 24). Information everywhere, but not a drop of knowledge. *Minneapolis Star Tribune*, p. 21A.

Berlet, Chip. (1994). *Right woos Left: Populist Party, Larouchian, and other new-fascist overtures to progressives, and why they must be rejected*. Cambridge, MA: Political Research Associates.

Berlet, Chip. (1995, June). Friendly fascists. *The Progressive*, 56(6), 16–20.

Berlet, Chip, & Bellman, Joel. (1989, March 10). Lyndon Larouche: Fascism wrapped in an American flag. A Political Research Associates Briefing Paper. Retrieved September 15, 2003, from http://www.publiceye.org/larouche/ncic1.html

Berlet, Chip, & Lyons, Matthew N. (1995, June). Militia nation. *The Progressive*, 22–25.

Berlet, Chip, & Lyons, Matthew N. (2000). *Right-Wing populism in America: Too close for comfort*. New York: Guilford Publications.

Birchall, Clare. (2004). Just because you're paranoid, doesn't mean they're not out to get you: Cultural studies on/as conspiracy theory. *Culture Machine*, 6. http://culturemachine.tees.ac.uk/Cmach/Backissues/j006/Articles/birchall.htm

Birchall, Clare. (2006). *Knowledge goes pop: From conspiracy theory to gossip*. Oxford, UK: Berg Publishers.

Birkhead, Douglas. (1984). The power in the image: Professionalism and the "communications revolution." *American Journalism*, 1(Winter), 1–13.

Black, Bob. (1994). *Beneath the underground*. Portland, OR: Feral House.

Blumenthal, Robin Goldwyn. (1997, September/October). Woolly times on the Web. *Columbia Journalism Review*, 36(3), 34.

Bock, James. (1994, March 27). Farrakhan aide charges plot by whites to wipe out blacks. *The Sun* (Baltimore), p. 6B.

Bonobo, Anu. (2004, Spring). Plan Wellstone: Conspiracy, complicity, and the Left. *Fifth Estate*, 39(1).

Bracken, Len. (1999). *The arch conspirator*. Kempton, IL: Adventures Unlimited Press.

Brandt, Daniel. (1995a). Big brother covets the Internet. *Flatland*, *12*, 44–46.

Brandt, Daniel. (1995b, October–December). Infowar and disinformation: From the Pentagon to the Net. *NameBase NewsLine*, *11*.

Bratich, Jack Z. (2002a). Injections and truth serums: AIDS conspiracy theories and the politics of articulation. In P. Knight (Ed.), *Conspiracy Nation: The Politics of Paranoia in Postwar America* (pp. 133–156). New York: New York University Press.

Bratich, Jack Z. (2002b). The knowledge gangsters: African American conspiracy theories, political rationality, and the governance of dissent. *Information, Theory, and Society*, *1*(1), 91–108.

Bratich, Jack Z. (2005). Amassing the multitude: Revisiting early audience studies. *Communication Theory*, *15*(3), 242–265.

Bratich, Jack Z. (2006a). Public secrecy and immanent security: A strategic analysis, *Cultural Studies*, *20*(4–5), 493–511.

Bratich, Jack Z. (2006b). Apocryphal now redux. In M. Giardina & N. Denzin (Eds.), *Contesting empire/globalizing dissent: Cultural studies after 9/11* (pp. 264–279). Providence, RI: Paradigm Press.

Bratich, Jack Z., Packer, Jeremy, & McCarthy, Cameron (Eds.). (2003). *Foucault, cultural studies, and governmentality*. Albany: State University of New York Press.

Breton, Albert, Galeotti, Gianluigi, Salmon, Pierre, & Wintrobe, Ronald (Eds.) (2002). *Political extremism and rationality*. New York: Cambridge University Press.

Bridges, Tyler. (1995, April 26). Bombing agents seek man with tie to local talk show. *Times-Picayune* (New Orleans, LA), p. A8.

Britt, Donna. (1996, October 4). Finding the truest truth. *The Washington Post*, p. B1.

Brown, Joseph. (2001, January 14). Get busy—Or sulk over election? *The Tampa Tribune* (Florida), p. 6.

Brown, Wendy. (1995). *States of injury: Power and freedom in late modernity*. Princeton, NJ: Princeton University Press.

Brown, Wendy. (1998). Genealogical politics. In J. Moss (Ed.), *The later Foucault: Politics and philosophy* (pp. 33–49). London: Sage Publications.

Brown, Wendy. (2006). American nightmare: Neoliberalism, neoconservatism, and de-democratization. *Political Theory*, *34*(6), 690–714.

Brush, Heidi Marie. (2002). Policing the porous: Electronic civil disobedience after 9/11. *Cultural Studies ↔ Critical Methodologies*, *2*(2), 163–165.

Buckley, Christopher. (1997, November). Kooks around the corner. *Washington Monthly*, *29*(11), 42–44.

Burchell, Graham. (1991). Peculiar interests: Civil society and governing the system of natural liberty. In G. Burchell, C. Gordon, & P. Miller (Eds.), *The Foucault effect: Studies in governmentality* (pp. 119–150). Chicago: University of Chicago Press.

Burden, Jack. (1995). The Conspiracy conspiracy. *Steamshovel Press*, *14*, 61–64.

Butler, Judith. (1997). *The psychic life of power: Theories in subjection*. Stanford: Stanford University Press.

Byrd, Scott. (2005). The Porto Alegre consensus: Theorizing the forum movement. *Globalizations*, 2(1).

Campbell, Glenn. (1996). Invasion of the pod people! Am I the only one left who sees the "Independence Day" conspiracy? *The Groom Lake Desert Rat, 36*. Retrieved March 27, 1999, from http://www.ufomind.com/area51/desert_rat/1996/dr36/pod_people.shtml

Campbell, K. K. (1997, December 26). Internet's success leads to its own destruction. *The Toronto Star*, p. F6.

Campbell, W. Joseph. (2001). *Yellow journalism: Puncturing the myths, defining the legacies*. Westport, CT: Praeger Publishers.

Canon, Scott. (1997, July 6). Look out: It's media overload. *Kansas City Star*, p. A1.

Cantwell, Alan, Jr. (1995). Paranoid/paranoia: Media buzzwords to silence the politically incorrect. *Steamshovel Press, 14*, 1.

Carey, James. (1988). *Communication as culture: Essays on media and society*. London and New York: Routledge.

Carlsen, William. (2001, January 14). Theories Point at Medical Origin of AIDS. *The San Francisco Chronicle*, p. 1.

Carpenter, John. (1964). *Extremism USA*. Phoenix: Associated Professional Services.

Castel, Robert. (1991). From dangerousness to risk. In G. Burchell, C. Gordon, & P. Miller (Eds.), *The Foucault effect: Studies in governmentality* (pp. 281–298). Chicago: University of Chicago Press.

Castillo, Celerino, III. (1994). *Powderburns; Cocaine, Contras and the drug war*. Sundial Mosaic Press.

Charney, Marc. (1995, July 23). Conspiracy theories; The unending search for demons in the American imagination. *The New York Times*, section 4, p. 7.

Chermak, Steven M. (2002). *Searching for a demon: The media construction of the militia movement*. Boston: Northeastern University Press/University Press of New England.

Chertoff, Ben (with the editors). (2005, March). 9/11: Debunking the myths. *Popular Mechanics*. http://www.popularmechanics.com/science/defense/1227842.html

Chomsky, Noam, & Herman, Edward S. (1988). *Manufacturing consent: The political economy of the mass media*. New York: Pantheon.

CIA director John Deutch in Los Angeles defending CIA from reports that it spread crack cocaine in America's inner cities. (1996, November 15). *CBS Evening News*. Newscast.

Claiborne, William. (1996, November 16). CIA chief faces angry crowd at Los Angeles meeting on drug allegations. *The Washington Post*, p. A6.

Clark, Cathy. (1995, November 13). Conspiracy theories about HIV puts individuals at risk. *Blood Weekly*, 19–20.

Clark, Cheryl. (1992, May 31). Many blacks see AIDS virus as white conspiracy. *The San Diego Union-Tribune*, p. B1.

Clark, George. (1997). Why do militias exist? *Skeptic*, 5(3).

Clinton rips hatemongers on airwaves: "Loud and angry voices" promote violent society. (1995, April 25). *The Toronto Star*, p. A10.

Cochran, Wendell. (1995). Searching for the right mixture. *Quill*, 83(4), 36–39.

Cockburn, Alexander. (1995, June 12). Who's Left? Who's Right? *The Nation*, 820.

Cockburn, Alexander. (2000), March 26. CNN and psyops. *CounterPunch*. http://www.counterpunch.org/cockburn09092006.html

Cockburn, Alexander. (2006a, September 9–10). The 9/11 conspiracy nuts: How they let the guilty parties of 9/11 slip off the hook. *CounterPunch*. http://www.counterpunch.org/cockburn09092006.html

Cockburn, Alexander. (2006b, September 25). Flying saucers and the decline of the Left. *CounterPunch*. http://counterpunch.org/cockburn09252006.html

Cockburn, Alexander, & St. Clair, Jeffrey. (1998). *Whiteout: The CIA, drugs and the press*. London: Verso.

Coffey, Mary. (2003). From nation to community: Museums and the reconfiguration of Mexican society under neoliberalism. In J. Bratich, J. Packer, & C. McCarthy (Eds.), *Foucault, cultural studies, and governmentality* (pp. 207–242) Albany: State University of New York Press.

Cohen, Richard. (1996, October 24). Crack and the CIA: Why the story lives. *The Washington Post*, p. A21.

Cohen, Richard. (2004a, May). Welcome to the conspiracy. *Vanity Fair*, 138–154.

Cohen, Richard. (2004b, July 1). Baloney, Moore or less. *The Washington Post*, p. A23.

Cohen, Richard. (1995, May 4). The salute that wasn't. *The Washington Post*, p. A21.

Cohen, Richard. (1996, October 27). A racist past and a wary present. *The Washington Post*, p. 2C.

Cohen, Stanley. (1972). *Folk devils and moral panics*. London: MacGibbon & Kee.

Colker, David. (1997, September 4). On Internet, conspiracy theorists take Diana's death and run with it. *The Los Angeles Times*, p. 13.

Cooper, Melinda. (2006). Pre-empting emergence: The biological turn in the war on terror. *Theory, Culture, and Society*, 23(4), 113–135.

Cooper, William. (1991). *Behold a pale horse*. Sedona, AZ: Light Technology Publishing.

Corn, David. (2002a, March 01). When 9/11 conspiracy theories go bad. *Alternet*. Retrieved December 13, 2005, from http://www.alternet.org/story/12536/

Corn, David. (2002b, May 30). The September 11 x-files. *The Nation* (Blog). Retrieved January 3, 2005, from http://www.thenation.com/blogs/capitalgames?bid=3&pid=66

Cosgrove, Ben. (1996, November 17). Cocaine import agency. Retrieved July 27, 1997, from http://www.netizen.com/netizen/96/37/special4a.html

Coulter, Ann. (2003, June 23). *Treason: Liberal treachery from the cold war to the war on terrorism*. Crown Forum.

Court TV, *Forensic files*. (2004, August).

Crandall, Jordan, & Armitage, John. (2005). Envisioning the homefront: Militarization, tracking and security culture. *Journal of Visual Culture*, 4(1), 17–38.

Crouse, Bill. (2005). Conspiracies, hidden agendas, secret societies, and world government. Retrieved January 3, 2005, from http://www.rapidresponsereport.com/briefingpapers/Conspiracies68.pd

Crowley, Christopher. (1996, June 30). Caught in the Web. *The Washington Post*, p. Y07.

Cruikshank, Barbara. (1999). *The will to empower*. Ithaca, NY: Cornell University Press.

Davis, Erik. (1995, May 2). Barbed wire net. *Village Voice*, 28.

Davis, Susan. (2004, July 28). Melt down. *Anderson Valley Advertiser*.

Dean, Jodi. (1998). *Aliens in America*. Ithaca, NY: Cornell University Press.

Dean, Jodi. (2000a). Declarations of independents. In *Cultural studies and political theory* (pp. 285–349). Ithaca, NY: Cornell University Press.

Dean, Jodi. (2000b). Webs of conspiracy. In T. Swiss & A. Herman (Eds.). *The World Wide Web and contemporary cultural theory: Magic, metaphor, power* (pp. 61–76). New York: Routledge.

Dean, Jodi. (2002). *Publicity's secret*. Ithaca, NY: Cornell University Press.

Dean, Mitchell. (1996). Foucault, government, and the enfolding of authority. In A. Barry, T. Osborne, & N. Rose (Eds.), *Foucault and political reason* (pp. 209–230). Chicago: University of Chicago Press.

Dean, Mitchell. (1999). *Governmentality: Power and rule in modern society*. Thousand Oaks, CA: Sage Publications.

Debord, Guy. (1983). *The Society of the spectacle*. Detroit: Black & Red.

Debord, Guy. (1998). *Comments on the society of the spectacle*. London: Verso.

De Certeau, Michel. (1986). In Brian Massumi (Trans.), *Heterologies: Discourses on the other*. Minneapolis: University of Minnesota Press.

Dees, Morris (with Corcoran, James). (1996). *Gathering storm: America's militia threat*. HarperCollins.

Deleuze, Gilles. (1973). Letter to a harsh critic. In Martin Joughin (Trans.), *Negotiations* (pp. 3–12). New York: Columbia University Press.

Deleuze, Gilles. (1977). Many politics. In H. Tomlinson & B. Habberjam (Trans.), *Dialogues* (pp. 124–147). New York: Columbia University Press.

Deleuze, Gilles. (1980). On *A thousand plateaus*. Rpt. in Martin Joughin (Trans.), *Negotiations* (pp. 25–35). New York: Columbia University Press.

Deleuze, Gilles. (1988). *Foucault*. Sean Hand (Trans.). Minneapolis: University of Minnesota Press.

Deleuze, Gilles. (1990a). Control and becoming. In Martin Joughin (Trans.), *Negotiations* (pp. 169–176). New York: Columbia University Press.

Deleuze, Gilles. (1990b). Postscript on control societies. In Martin Joughin (Trans.), *Negotiations* (pp. 177–182). New York: Columbia University Press.

Deleuze, Gilles. (1990c). The simulacrum and ancient philosophy. In Mark Lester (with Charles Stivale) (Trans.), *The logic of sense* (pp. 253–266). New York: Columbia University Press.

Deleuze, Gilles. (1993). Toward freedom. *Dialogues*. Rpt. in Constantin V. Boundas (Ed.), *The Deleuze reader* (pp. 253–256). New York: Columbia University Press.

Deleuze, Gilles. (1997). To have done with judgment. In Daniel W. Smith and Michael A. Greco (Trans.), *Deleuze: Essays critical and clinical* (pp. 126–135). Minneapolis: University of Minnesota Press.

Deleuze, Gilles, & Guattari, Felix. (1972). On *Anti-Oedipus*. In Martin Joughin (Trans.) *Negotiations* (pp. 13–34). New York: Columbia University Press.

Deleuze, Gilles, & Guattari, Felix. (1987). *A thousand plateaus* (B. Massumi, Trans.). Minneapolis: University of Minnesota Press.

Deleuze, Gilles, & Guattari, Felix. (1994). *What is philosophy?* New York: Columbia University Press.

Demac, Donna A., & Downing, John. (1995). The tug of war over the first amendment. In John Downing, Ali Mohammadi, & Annabelle Sreberny-Mohammadi (Eds.) *Questioning the media: A critical introduction* (pp. 122–137). Thousand Oaks, CA: Sage Publications.

Deparle, Jason. (1991, August 11). For some blacks, social ills seem to follow white plans. *The New York Times*, p. 5.

Desantis, Alan D., & Morgan, Susan E. (2004). Civil liberties, the Constitution, and cigars: Anti-smoking conspiracy logic in cigar aficionado, 1992–2001. *Communication Studies*, 55, 319–339.

De Tocqueville, Alexis. (1988). *Democracy in America*. HarperCollins.

Deuze, Mark. (2003). The web and its journalisms: Considering the consequences of different types of news media online. *New Media and Society*, 5(2), 203–230.

de Vries, Abe. U.S. Army "psyops" worked for CNN. Retrieved September 13, 2004, from http://www.emperorsclothes.com/articles/devries/psyops2.htm

Dickey, Christopher. (2003, October 24). Death of a princess. *Newsweek/MSNBC*. http://www.msnbc.msn.com/id/3339602/site/newsweek/

Doraemi, John. (2004, November 23). Open letter to Alexander Cockburn. *Crimes of the state*. http://crimesofthestate.blogspot.com/2004/11/open-letter-to-alexander-cockburn.html

Douglas, Mary. (1966; 1984). *Purity and danger: An analysis of concepts of pollution and taboo*. London & Boston: Ark Paperbacks.

Douglas, Mary. (1992). *Risk and blame: Essays in cultural theory*. New York: Routledge.

Douglas, Susan. (1987). *American broadcasting, 1899–1922*. Baltimore: Johns Hopkins University Press.

Douglas, Susan. (1995, June). The real barbarians. *The Progressive*, 17.

Down with crime, up with New York. (2005, December 28). *Daily News* (New York), p. 28.

Duke, Phillip S. (1999, Spring). The AIDS-ET connection. *Paranoia: The Conspiracy Reader*, 6(1), 51–54.

Dunbar, David, & Reagan, Brad. (2006). *Debunking 9/11 myths: Why conspiracy theories can't stand up to the facts*. New York: Hearst.

Dyer, Joel. (1997. *Harvest of rage: Why Oklahoma City is only the beginning*. Boulder, CO: Westview Press.

Dyer-Witheford, Nicholas. (1999). *Cyber-Marx: Cycles and struggles in high technology capitalism*. Urbana: University of Illinois Press.

Easton, Nina J. (1995, June 18). America the enemy; Their politics are light years apart, but the bombers of the '60s and '90s share volatile rhetoric, tangled paranoia and a belief that violence is a legitimate weapon. *Los Angeles Times*, p. 8.

Editorial. (1994, November 14). Crimes of the "Net." *Newsweek*, p. 46.

Editorial. (1995, June 26). Thinking about Net crime. *The Washington Post*, p. A20.

Editorial. (1996, October 15). Pushers of a racial conspiracy. *The Boston Globe*, p. A14.

Editorial. (1997, February 8). Online Pratfall. *The Washington Post*, p. A20.

Editorial. (2005, October 18). Dangerous gullibility. *The Post and Courier*, p. 12A.

Editors. (1995, March 11). Fanatics threaten the devout. *The Economist*, p. 85.

Egan, Timothy. (1995a, April 25). Terror in Oklahoma: Western violence; Federal uniforms become target of wave of threats and violence. *The New York Times*, p. A1.

Egan, Timothy. (1995b, April 30). Men at war: Inside the world of the paranoid. *The New York Times*, p. 1.

El-Tablawy, Tarek. (2005, October 10). Conspiracy theories underpin difficulty of achieving unity in Iraq. *Associated Press, Associated Press Worldstream*.

Elliott, Tom. (2005, September 14). The big lie. *The American Spectator Online*.

Elrich, David J. (1995, June 1). A road map to the information superhighway. *The New York Times*, p. C2.

Elsworth, Peter. (1996, December 23). Taking in the sites. *The New York Times*, p. D5.

Emory, Dave. Homepage. Retrieved August 23, 1997, from http://www.kfjc.org/emory/

Epperson, A. Ralph. (1985). *The unseen hand*. Tucson, AZ: Publius Press.

Epperson, A. Ralph. (1990). *New world order*. Tucson, AZ: Publius Press.

Ewen, Stewart. (1996). *PR! A social history of spin*. New York: Basic Books.

Fallows, James. (1999, November 23). But is it journalism? *The American Prospect*, p. 58.

Fears, Darryl. (2005, January 25). Study: Many blacks cite AIDS conspiracy; Prevention efforts hurt, activists say. *The Washington Post*, p. A2.

Fenster, Mark. (1999). *Conspiracy theories: Power and secrecy in America*. Minneapolis: University of Minnesota Press.

FinalCall.com. (2004, October 5). AIDS is man-made—Interview with Dr. Boyd Graves. http://www.finalcall.com/artman/publish/printer_1597.shtml

Fiske, John. (1994). *Media matters: Everyday culture and political change*. Minneapolis: University of Minnesota Press.

Fitzgerald, Mark. (1995a, February 31). AP chief: Beware of yellow journalism in cyberspace. *Editor and Publisher*, 128(6), 11.

Fitzgerald, Mark. (1995b, March 4). First job in cyberspace: Establish trust. *Editor and Publisher*, 128(9), 34–35.

Fletcher, Michael A. (1996, October 04). Conspiracy theories can often ring true; History feeds blacks' mistrust. *The Washington Post*, p. A01.

Ford, Catherine. (1997, November 25). Web of lies: Internet feeds paranoia of unwise and unwary. *The Gazette* (Montreal), p. B3.

Foster. (2003, December 8). Now this from Baghdad. *Milwaukee Journal Sentinel* (Wisconsin), p. 10A.

Foucault, Michel. (1977). Nietzsche, genealogy, history. In Donald F. Bouchard (Ed.), *Language, countermemory, practice* (pp. 139–164). Ithaca, NY: Cornell University Press.

Foucault, Michel. (1980a). Truth and power. In C. Gordon (Ed.), *Michel Foucault: Power/knowledge* (pp. 109–133). New York: Pantheon.

Foucault, Michel. (1980b). Two lectures. In C. Gordon (Ed.), *Michel Foucault: Power/knowledge* (pp. 78–108). New York: Pantheon.

Foucault, Michel. (1981). The order of discourse. In Robert Young (Ed.), Ian McLeod (Trans.) *Untying the text* (pp. 48–78). London: Routledge.

Foucault, Michel. (1982). The subject and power. In H. Dreyfus and Paul Rabinow, *Michel Foucault: Beyond structuralism and hermeneutics*. Chicago: University of Chicago Press.

Foucault, Michel. (1983). Preface. In Gilles Deleuze & Felix Guattari, *Anti-Oedipus*. Robert Hurley, Mark Seem, & Helen R. Lane (Trans.). Minneapolis, MN: University of Minnesota Press.

Foucault, Michel. (1985). *The use of pleasure: The history of sexuality*, Vol. 2. New York: Vintage.

Foucault, Michel. (1988a). Politics and reason. In L. D. Kritzman (Ed.), *Foucault, politics, philosophy, culture* (pp. 57–85). New York: Routledge.

Foucault, Michel. (1988b). Practicing criticism. In L. D. Kritzman (Ed.), *Foucault, politics, philosophy, culture* (pp. 152–156). New York: Routledge.

Foucault, Michel. (1988c). The concern for truth. In L. D. Kritzman (Ed.), *Foucault, politics, philosophy, culture* (pp. 255–267). New York: Routledge.

Foucault, Michel. (1989). Clarifications on the question of power. In Sylvere Lotringer (Ed.), *Foucault live* (pp.179–192). New York: Semiotexte.

Foucault, Michel. (1991a). Governmentality. In G. Burchell, C. Gordon, & P. Miller, *The Foucault effect: Studies in governmentality* (pp. 119–150). Chicago: University of Chicago Press.

Foucault, Michel. (1991b). Questions of method. In G. Burchell, C. Gordon, & P. Miller, *The Foucault effect: Studies in governmentality* (pp. 73–86). Chicago: University of Chicago Press.

Foucault, Michel. (1997a). The birth of biopolitics. In Paul Rabinow (Ed.), *Michel Foucault: Ethics: Subjectivity and truth* (pp. 73–79). New York: New Press.

Foucault, Michel. (1997b). Polemics, politics, and problematizations. In Paul Rabinow (Ed.), *Michel Foucault: Ethics: Subjectivity and truth* (pp. 111–120). New York: New Press.

Foucault, Michel. (1997c). Preface to *The history of sexuality*, Vol. 2. In Paul Rabinow (Ed.), *Michel Foucault: Ethics: Subjectivity and truth* (pp. 199–206). New York: New Press.

Foucault, Michel. (1997d). What is enlightenment? In Paul Rabinow (Ed.), *Michel Foucault: Ethics: Subjectivity and truth* (pp. 303–320). New York: New Press.

Foucault, Michel. (1997e). On the government of the living. In Paul Rabinow (Ed.), *Michel Foucault: Ethics: Subjectivity and truth* (pp. 81–86). New York: New Press.

Foucault, Michel. (1997f). The ethics of the concern for self as a practice of freedom. In Paul Rabinow (Ed.), *Michel Foucault: Ethics: Subjectivity and truth* (pp. 281–301). New York: New Press.

Fowler, Roger. (1991). *Language in the news: Discourse and ideology in the press.* London: Routledge.

Frank, Joshua. (2006, September 11). Proving nothing: How the 9/11 Truth Movement helps Bush & Cheney. *CounterPunch.* Retrieved October 17, 2007, from http://www.counterpunch.org/frank09112006.html

Fukuyama, Francis. (1995, August 24). Extreme paranoia in government abounds. *USA Today*, p. 17A.

Furedi, Frank. (2002). *Culture of fear: Risk taking and the morality of low expectation.* London: Continuum Press.

Furedi, Frank. (2005). *Politics of fear: Beyond Left and Right.* London: Continuum Press.

Frazer, James. (1922). *The golden bough.* New York: Macmillan.

Frewin, Anthony. (1993). *The assassination of John F. Kennedy: An annotated film, TV, and videography, 1963–1992.* Westport, CT: Greenwood Press.

Friedhoff, Paul. (1995, November 9). U.S. must get hate speech under control. *St. Petersburg Times* (Florida), p. 2.

Freilich, Joshua D. (2003). *American militias: State-level variations in militia activities.* New York: LFB Scholarly Publishing.

Fulton, Katherine. (1996, March/April). Tour of our uncertain future. *Columbia Journalism Review*, 34(6), 19.

Furuhashi, Yoshie. (2004, July 10). Why does *Fahrenheit 9/11* pursue conspiracy theory? Retrieved December 18, 2005, from http://www.indymedia.org.uk/en/2004/07/294646.html

García, Manuel, Jr. (2005, September 14). Why conspiracy theories help Bush: The power of water. *CounterPunch.*

García, Manuel, Jr. (2006, September 16–30). The physics of 9/11 (part two). *CounterPunch* 13(16): 1–6.

Gardner, James. (1997). *The age of extremism: The enemies of compromise in American politics, culture, and race relations.* New York: Birch Lane Press.

Gehorsam, Jan. (1991, November 14). Black fears of an AIDS conspiracy must be overcome, doctors warn. *The Atlanta Journal and Constitution*, p. 6.

George, John, & Wilcox, Laird. (1996). *American extremists: Militias, supremacists, klansmen, communists and others.* Amherst, NY: Prometheus Books.

Gilbert, David. (1996). Tracking the *real* genocide: AIDS—conspiracy or unnatural disaster? *Covert Action Quarterly*, 58, 55–64.

Gilliam, Dorothy. (1990, November 26). Despairing for the young. *The Washington Post*, p. E3.

Glass, Andrew. (1995, April 23). Paranoia about bombing thrives; Internet users swap conspiracy theories. *The Atlanta Journal and Constitution*, p. 11A.

Glasser, Theodore L., & Craft, Stephanie. (1998). Public journalism and the search for democratic ideals. In T. Liebes and J. Curran (Eds.), *Media ritual and identity* (p. 205). London: Routledge.

Glassner, Barry. (2000). *The culture of fear: The assault on optimism in America*. New York: Basic Books.

Goddard, Ian. The military industrial media versus the Internet: *60 Minutes*. Anticonspiracy slop job. http://users.erols.com/igoddard/rebuttal.htm

Godzich, Wlad. (1986). Foreword. In Brian Massumi (Trans.), *Heterologies: Discourses on the other* (pp. vii–xxi), Minneapolis: University of Minnesota Press.

Goldberg, Jonah. (2002, May 17). Still an idiot: No vindication for Cynthia McKinney. *National Review online*. Retrieved January 5, 2006, from http://www. nationalreview.com/goldberg/goldberg051702.asp

Goldberg, Robert Alan. (2001). *Enemies within: The culture of conspiracy in modern America*. New Haven, CT: Yale University Press.

Golden, Tim. (1996, October 21). Though evidence is thin, tale of C.I.A. and drugs has a life of its own. *The New York Times*, p. 14.

Goode, Erica. (2002, March 10). Finding answers in secret plots. *The New York Times*, p. 3.

Goodman, Ellen. (2004, July 1). Limbaughing to the Left? *The Boston Globe*, p. A17.

gop.com. *Nine lies of Fahrenheit 9/11, The*. (2004, July 12). Retrieved December 18, 2005, from http://www.gop.com/news/read.aspx?ID=4386

Gordon. Colin. (1980). Afterword. In C. Gordon (Ed.), *Power/knowledge* (pp. 109–133). New York: Pantheon.

Gordon, Colin. (1991). Governmental rationality: An introduction. In G. Burchell, C. Gordon, & P. Miller, *The Foucault effect: Studies in governmentality* (pp. 1–52). Chicago: University of Chicago Press.

Goshorn, Keith. (2000). Strategies of deterrence and frames of containment: On critical paranoia and anti-conspiracy discourse. *Theory & Event* (online), 4(3). Retrieved April 19, 2002, from http://muse.jhu.edu.proxy.libraries.rutgers.edu/ journals/theory_and_event/v004/4.3r_goshorn.html

Gosier, Elijah. (1995, January 5). Ranters of radio have a hold on the fringe. *St. Petersburg Times* (Florida), p. 1B.

Grabbe, J. Orlin. Retrieved April 29, 1997, from http://www.aci.net/kalliste/

Griffin, David Ray. (2004). *The new Pearl Harbor: Disturbing questions about the Bush Administration and 9/11*. Northampton, MA: Interlink Publications.

Grossberg, Lawrence. (1992). *We gotta get out of this place*. New York: Routledge.

Grossberg, Lawrence. (1995). Cultural studies: What's in a name? One more time. In L. Grossberg (1997).

Grossberg, Lawrence. (1997). *Bringing it all back home*. Durham & London: Duke University Press.

Grossberg, Lawrence. (2000). The figure of subalternity and the neoliberal future. *Nepantla: Views from South*, 1(1), 59–89.

Grossman, Lev. (2006, September 3). Why the 9/11 conspiracies won't go away. *Time*.

Guattari, Felix. (1996). Cinema Fou. In *Soft subversions*. New York: Semiotexte.

Haas, Tanni, & Steiner, Linda. (2002). Fears of corporate colonization in journalism reviews' critiques of public journalism. *Journalism Studies*, 3(3), 325–341.

Hall, Stuart; Critcher, Chas; Jefferson, Tony; Clarke, John; & Roberts, Brian. (1978). *Policing the crisis: Mugging, state, law and order*. London: MacMillan.

Hall, Stuart. (1986). On postmodernism and articulation: An interview with Lawrence Grossberg. *Journal of Communication Inquiry*, 10, 45–60.

Hallin, Daniel. (1985). The American news media: A critical theory perspective. In John Forester (Ed.), *Critical theory and public life* (pp. 121–146). Cambridge, MIT Press.

Hallin, Daniel C. (1986). *The "uncensored war": The media and Vietnam*. New York: Oxford University Press.

Halpern, Thomas, & Levin, Brian. (1996). *The limits of dissent: The constitutional status of armed civilian militias*. Amherst, MA: Aletheia Press. Hamilton, (Ontario, Canada). Retrieved January 5, 2006, from http://hamilton.indymedia.org/front.php3?article_id=972&group=webcast

Hanson, Christopher. (1997, May/June). The dark side of online scoops. *Columbia Journalism Review*. Retrieved November 17, 2007, from http://backissues.cjrarchives.org/year/97/3/scoops.asp

Hardt, Michael. (1995). The withering of civil society. *Social Text*, 14(4): 27–44.

Hardt, Michael, & Negri, Antonio. (2000). *Empire*. Cambridge, MA: Harvard University Press.

Hartley, John. (1996). *Popular reality: Journalism, modernity, popular culture*. London: Arnold.

Hay, James. (2003). Unaided virtues: The (neo)liberalization of the domestic sphere and the new architecture of community. In J. Bratich, J. Packer, & C. McCarthy (Eds.), *Foucault, cultural studies, and governmentality* (pp. 165–206). Albany: State University of New York Press.

Hay, James. (2005). The new techno-communitarianism and the residual logic of mediation. In Charles Acland (Ed.), *Residual media*. Minneapolis: University of Minnesota Press.

Hay, James. (2006). Designing homes to be the first line of defense. *Cultural Studies*, 20(4–5), 349–377.

Hay, James, & Andrejevic, Mark. (2006). Introduction. *Cultural Studies*, 20(4–5), 331–348.

Hay, James, & Ouellette, Laurie. (2007). *Better living through television*. Oxford: Blackwell.

Hayes, Christopher. (2006, December 25). 9/11: The roots of paranoia. *The Nation*. 283(22), 11–14.

Healthwatcher. Retrieved January 9, 2006, from http://www.healthwatcher.net/Quackerywatch/Horowitz/

Hecht, Jamey. (2004). Richard Clarke's orchestra: Maestro plays simple waltz; shackled media manage to dance along. *From the Wilderness Publications*. Retrieved

January 9, 2006, from http://www.fromthewilderness.com/free/ww3/ 040504_Clarke_orchestra.html

Herek, Gregory M., & Capitanio, John P. (1994). Conspiracies, contagion, and compassion: Trust and public reactions to AIDS. *AIDS Education and Prevention* 64, 365–375.

Heyboer, Kelly. (1996, November). A furor over the CIA and drugs. *Free Press, American Journalism Review.*

Hicks, Joe R. (2005, October 2). Levees let loose an ugly flood of black paranoia; Some leaders are spreading myths—as unfair as they are untrue—that are doing damage to us all. *Los Angeles Times*, p. 3.

Hicks, Sander. (2005). 9/11 truth movement: Vox pop reports from the red states. Retrieved January 5, 2006, from http://voxpopnet.net index.php?id=54&tx_ ttnews[tt_news]=69&tx_ttnews[backPid]=41&cHash=eb5925cbb8

Hidell, Al. (1997). TWA 800: No single missile theory. *Paranoia: The Conspiracy Reader* 5(2), 11–15.

Hier, Sean (2003). Risk and panic in late modernity: Implications of the converging sites of social anxiety. *British Journal of Sociology*, 54(1), 3–20.

Hill, Martin. (1995, November 10). AIDS as conspiracy theory taken seriously. *CNN.* Transcript # 24–28.

Hinckley, David. (1995, April 25). Talk radio and the extreme fright wing. *Daily News* (New York), p. 34.

Hindess, Barry. (1996). *Discourses of power: From Hobbes to Foucault.* Oxford: Blackwell.

Hitchens, Christopher. (2004, June 21). Unfairenheit 9/11: The lies of Michael Moore. *Slate.* Retrieved December 18, 2005, from http://www.slate.com/id/2102723/

Hitchens, Christopher. (2005, June 21). Conspiracy theories: If you liked *The Da Vinci Code*, you'll love the Downing Street memo. *Slate.* http://www.slate.com/ id/2121212/

Hoagland, Jim. (1995, April 30). Demonizing talk. *The Washington Post*, p. C7.

Hoffman, David. (1998). *The Oklahoma City bombing and the politics of terror.* Venice, CA: Feral House Publishing.

Hofstadter, Richard. (1967). The paranoid style in American politics. In R. Hofstadter, *The paranoid style in American politics and other essays.* New York: Vintage.

Holland, Catherine. (2001). *The body politic; Foundings, citizenship, and difference in the American political imagination.* New York: Routledge.

Honig, Bonnie. (1993). *Political theory and the displacement of politics.* Ithaca, NY: Cornell University Press.

Hornung, Mark N. (1994, November 16). We have met the enemy: It is us. *Chicago Sun-Times*, p. 45.

Horowitz, Leonard. (1996). *Emerging viruses: AIDS and Ebola.* Rockport, MA: Tetrahedron.

Horowitz, Leonard. (1997, December 6). Press kit letter from *Tetrahedron.*

Horrie, Chris. (2002, April 4). Paranoia paradise. *BBC News Online.* Retrieved January 13, 2006, from http://news.bbc.co.uk/1/hi/uk/1909378.stm

House Committee on Appropriations. (1969). *Hearings on Department of Defense appropriations for 1970*, 91st Congress, 1st Session, H.B. 15090, Part 5, Research, Development, Test and Evaluation, Dept. of the Army.

Hoyt, Mike. (1995, October). Are you now, or will you ever be, a civic journalist? *Columbia Journalism Review, 34*(3), 27.

Humphrey, Hubert. (November 1996). Virtual casinos, real stakes. The *New York Times*, A25.

Hutchinson, Earl Ofari. (2005, January 31). Chasing AIDS conspiracies. *AlterNet*. Retrieved January 13, 2006, from http://www.alternet.org/story/21127/

Impoco, Jim. (1996, January 15). Laying off bets on the Internet. *U.S. News & World Report 120*(2), 60.

Isikoff, Michael. (2004, June 28). Under the Hot Lights. *Newsweek*. Retrieved December 18, 2005, from http://www.msnbc.msn.com/id/5251769/site/newsweek?cb

Jacobsen, Mark. (2006, March 27). The ground zero grassy knoll. *New York Magazine*. Retrieved October 13, 2006, from http://nymag.com/news/features/16464/

James, John S. (1986, September 12). AIDS conspiracy—Just a theory? *San Francisco Sentinel*. http://www.immunet.org/atn/ZQX01301.html

Jameson, Frederic. (1988). Cognitive mapping. In C. Nelson and L. Grossberg (Eds.), *Marxism and the interpretation of culture* (pp. 347–357). Chicago: University of Chicago Press.

Jamieson, Les. (2005, September 7). What action looks like: Going viral with 9/11 truth. Retrieved January 4, 2006, from http://www.ny911truth.org/articles/what_action_looks_like.htm

Jarach, Lawrence. (2005–2006). Democracy and conspiracy: Overlaps, parallels, and standard operating procedures. *Anarchy: A journal of desire armed. 23*(2), 33–37.

Jaschik, Scott. (2006, August 29). Another scholar under fire for 9/11 views. *Insidehighered.com*

Jenkins, Philip. (1998). *Moral panic: Changing conceptions of the child molester in modern America*. New Haven, CT: Yale University Press.

Jenkins, Philip. (1999). *Synthetic panics: The symbolic politics of designer drugs*. New York: New York University Press.

Jensen, Robert. (2004, July 5). Stupid white movie: What Michael Moore misses about the empire. Retrieved December 18, 2005, from http://counterpunch.org/jensen07052004.html

Johnson, George. (1995, April 30). The conspiracy that never ends. The *New York Times*, p. 5.

Johnson, Peter. (2001, October 9). Al-Jazeera's stature is rising. *USA Today*, p. 4D.

Johnstone, Diana. (2006, September 15). In defense of conspiracy. *CounterPunch*. http://www.counterpunch.org/johnstone09152006.html

Judge, John. (1995). The only honest judge? An interview by Kenn Thomas. *Steamshovel Press, 14*, 3–12.

Judge, John. (1998). Letter. Caries, cabals, and correspondence. *Steamshovel Press, 16*, 49–54.

Juris, Jeffrey S. (2005). The new digital media and activist networking within anticorporate globalization movements. *The ANNALS of the American Academy of Political and Social Science, 597,* 189–208.

Kahn, Richard, & Kellner, Douglas. (2004). New media and Internet activism: From the "Battle of Seattle" to blogging. *New Media & Society,* 6(1), 87–95.

Kane, Michael. (2006, October 9). 9/11 and the new Pearl Harbor: A response to Bill Weinberg. *From the Wilderness.* http://www.fromthewilderness.com/free/ww3/100906_new_harbor.shtml

Katsiaficas, George, Yuen, Eddie, & Burton-Rose, Daniel. (2003). *Confronting capitalism: Dispatches from a global movement.* New York: Soft Skull Press.

Katz, Jon. (1992, March 5). Rock, rap and movies bring you the news. *Rolling Stone,* 33–40.

Katz, Jon. (1996, October 10). *Mercury Rising.* http://www.netizen.com/netizen/96/41/katz4a.html.

Kelly, Michael. (1995, June 19). The road to paranoia. *The New Yorker.*

Kelly, Michael. (1997, December). *CIA psyops on the Internet.* http://www.copi.com/deepbook.html

Kellner, Douglas. (2002) The *X-Files* and conspiracy: A diagnostic critique. In P. Knight (Ed.), *Conspiracy nation: The politics of paranoia in postwar America* (pp. 205–232). New York: New York University Press.

Kemper, Bob. (2005, July 22). McKinney revisits 9/11. Cox News Service.

Kempton, Murray. (1996, November 28). Drugs and the CIA. *NY Review of Books,* 43(19), 65.

Kerry, John. 1989. Drugs, law enforcement and foreign policy: A report prepared by the Subcommittee on Terrorism, Narcotics and International Operations of The Committee on Foreign Relations, United States Senate. 100th Congress, 2d session. S.Prt. 100–165.

Key, Keith K. (1995a, November 13). Conspiracy theories about HIV puts individuals at risk. *AIDS Weekly Plus,* 23–25.

King, Samantha. (2006). *Pink Ribbons, Inc.: Breast cancer and the politics of philanthropy.* Minneapolis: University of Minnesota Press.

Knight, Peter. (2001). *Conspiracy culture.* London: Routledge.

Knight, Peter (Ed.). (2002). *Conspiracy nation.* New York: New York University Press.

Kopel, Dave. (2004) Fifty-nine deceits in Fahrenheit 9/11. Retrieved December 18, 2005, from http://i2i.org/

Kornbluh, Peter. (1997). Crack, Contras and the CIA: The storm over "Dark Alliance." *Columbia Journalism Review,* 35(5), 33–39.

Kovaleski, Serge F. (1995, July 9). Oklahoma bombing conspiracy theories ripple across the nation. *The Washington Post,* p. A3.

Krupey, G. W. (1993). AIDS: Act of God or the Pentagon? In Jim Keith (Ed.), *Secret and suppressed: Banned ideas and hidden history* (pp. 240–255). Portland, OR: Feral House.

Kurtz, Howard. (1996). *Hot air: All talk, all the time.* Times Books.

Laclau, Ernesto. (2005). Populism: What's in a name? In Lukas and Sternberg (Eds.), *The populism reader* (pp. 101–112). The Nordic Institute for Contemporary Art. New York: Lukas & Sternberg.

Laclau, Ernesto, & Mouffe, Chantal. (1985). *Hegemony and socialist strategy: Toward a radical democratic politics*. London: Verso.

Lakely, James. (2003, December 18). Albright's joke joins growing list of Bush theories. *Washington Times*. http://www.washtimes.com/national/20031217-115113-2173r.htm

Lane, Charles. (1996, November 25). Just say no. *New Republic, 215*(22), 4.

Lardner, George. (1991). Outlook: Or just a sloppy mess? Reprinted in O. Stone, Z. Sklar (Eds.). (1992) *JFK: The book of the film* (pp. 202–205). New York: Warner Brothers.

Larsen, Ivind, & Olsen, Bent Olav (Eds.). (1996). *The shaping of a profession: Physicians in Norway, past and present*. Canton, MA: Science History Publications.

Lasica, J. D. (1996). Net gain. *American Journalism Review* (November), 20.

Lasica, J. D. (1997, December). Preserving old ethics in a new medium. *American Journalism Review, 19*(10), 52.

Lasica, J. D. (2003). What is participatory journalism? *Online Journalism Review*. Retrieved May 1, 2004, from http://www.ojr.org/ojr/workplace/1060217106.php

Lasswell, Harold. (1927). *Propaganda technique in the world war*. New York: Knopf.

Lasswell, Harold. (1930). *Psychopathology and politics*. New York: Viking Press.

Lasswell, Harold. (1948). *Power and personality*. New York: Viking Press.

Lee. Martin A. (1997). *The beast reawakens*. Boston: Little Brown.

Lee, Martin A., & Shlain, Bruce. (1986). *Acid dreams: The CIA, LSD, and the sixties rebellion*. New York: Grove Press.

Lee, Martin A., & Solomon, Norman. (1990). *Unreliable sources: A guide to detecting bias in news media*, New York: Carol Publishing Group.

Leiby, Richard. (1995, May 8). Paranoia: Fear on the Left. Fear on the Right. Whoever they are, THEY'RE CLOSING IN. *The Washington Post*, p. D1.

Lemann, Nicholas. (2006, October 16). Paranoid style. *The New Yorker, 82*(33), 96.

Leo, John. (1995, March 20). Life among the cyberfolk. *US News & World Report, 118*(11), 26.

Leo, John. (2000, December 18). The Selma mind-set. *US News & World Report, 129*(24), 18.

Lieber, Robert. (2003, May 2). The neoconservative conspiracy theory: Pure myth. *Chronicle of Higher Education*. Retrieved January 5, 2006, from http://chronicle.com/free/v49/i34/34b01401.htm

Lippman, Walter. (1914/1986). *Drift and mastery*. Madison, WI: University of Wisconsin Press.

Lippman, Walter. (1955). *The public philosophy*. New York: Mentor Books.

Lipset, Seymour M., & Raab, Earl. (1970). *The politics of unreason: Right-wing extremism in America, 1790–1970*. New York: Harper.

Lovink, Geert. (2003). *Uncanny networks: Dialogues with the virtual intelligentsia*. Cambridge, MA: MIT Press.

Lubinger, Bill. (2004, December 5). Conspiracy theories on Ohio vote refuse to die. *Plain Dealer* (Cleveland), p. A1.

Luke, Timothy W. (2001). Globalization, popular resistance and postmodernity. *Democracy and Nature: The International Journal of Inclusive Democracy, 7*(2), 317–329.

Lynch, Dianne. (1998, January). Without a rulebook. *American Journalism Review, 20*(1), 40–45.

MacGregor, Karen. (2000, September 4). Conspiracy theories fuel row over AIDS crisis in South Africa. *The Independent* (London), p. 12.

Madhubuti, Haki R. (1990). *Black men: Obsolete, single, dangerous? The Afrikan-American family in transition.* Chicago: Third World Press.

MalcontentX. (2002). What's "LEFT" to talk about? A discussion on why many of the leading voices on the "Left" have avoided asking questions about the "official story" surrounding the events of Sept. 11, 2001. Retrieved January 4, 2006, from http://www.questionsquestions.net/documents2/whats_left.html

Mankeiwicz, Frank. (1992). About the Debate. In O. Stone, & Z. Sklar (Eds.), *JFK: The book of the film* (pp. 187–188). New York: Warner Brothers.

Marcus, George. (1999). Introduction: The paranoia style now. In *Paranoia within reason: A casebook of conspiracy as explanation* (pp. 1–12). Chicago: University of Chicago Press.

Margolis, Jon. (1991). JFK movie and book attempt to rewrite history. Reprinted in O. Stone, & Z. Sklar (Eds.), *JFK: The book of the film* (pp. 189–91). New York: Warner Brothers.

Markoff, John. (1994, January 30). The executive computer. *The New York Times*, 10.

Marin, Rick, & Gegax, T. Trent. (1996/1997, December 30/January 6). The sum of all our fears: Conspiracy mania feeds our growing national paranoia. *Newsweek*, 64.

Mashberg, Tom. (1995, May 7). U.S. culture conspiracy thrives. *The Boston Herald*, p. 1.

Massing, Michael. (1999, January 24). Dead end. Book review of *Dark Alliance* and *Whiteout. Los Angeles Times*, p. 4.

Mason, Fran. (2002). A poor person's cognitive mapping. In Knight (Ed.), *Conspiracy nation: The politics of paranoia in postwar America.* New York: New York University Press.

Massumi, Brian. (1987). Translator's foreword. In Gilles Deleuze & Felix Guattari, *A thousand plateaus.* Minneapolis: University of Minnesota Press.

Massumi, Brian. (1992). *A user's guide to capitalism and schizophrenia: Deviations from Deleuze and Guattari.* Cambridge: MIT Press.

Massumi, Brian. (2005). Fear (the spectrum said). *Positions, 13*(1), 31–48.

Mattelart, Armand. (1994). *Mapping world communication: War progress culture.* Susan Emanuel & James Cohen (Trans.). Minneapolis: University of Minnesota Press.

Maxwell, Bill. (1996, October 21). Believing in conspiracies can be self-destructive trap. *Denver Rocky Mountain News*, p. 32A.

May, Todd. (1994). *The political philosophy of poststructuralist anarchism.* University Park: Pennsylvania State University Press.

McCaughey, Martha, & Ayers, Michael D. (Eds.) (2003). *Cyberactivism: Online activism in theory and practice*. New York: Routledge.

McChesney, John. (1997). The Net as media savior (an interview with James Fallows). Retrieved March 15, 2000 from http://hotwired.lycos.com/synapse/hotseat/97/36/transcript2a.html

McClellan, Jim. (1995, May 28). Cyberspace web of conspiracy. *The Observer*, 63.

McCoy, Adrian. (1996, July 17). On-air threat shows dark side of talk radio. *Pittsburgh Post-Gazette* (Pennsylvania), p. D8.

McCoy, Alfred W. (1972). *The politics of heroin in Southeast Asia*. New York: Harper & Row.

McCoy, Mary E. (2001). Dark alliance: News repair and institutional authority in the age of the Internet. *Journal of Communication 51*(1), 164–193.

McFeatters, Ann. (2001, January 7). 1600 Pennsylvania Ave. looks awfully white. *Chicago Sun-Times*, p. 47.

McGiffert, Michael (Ed.). (1964). *The character of Americans*. Homewood, IL: Dorsey Press.

McMurtry, John. The shadow subject of history: Understanding 9–11 and the 9–11 wars. Retrieved January 8, 2006, from scienceforpeace.sa.utoronto.ca/Essays_Briefs/McMurtry/McMurty-9-11.rtf

McNally, David. (2002). *Another world is possible: Globalization and anticapitalism*. Winnipeg, Canada: Arbeiter Ring.

McQuinn, Jason. (1996, Winter). Conspiracy theory vs. alternative journalism? *Alternative Press Review*, 2.

McRobbie, Angela. (1994). *Postmodernism and popular culture*. London: Routledge.

McRobbie, Angela, & Thornton, Sarah. (1995). Rethinking "moral panic" for multimediated social worlds. *British Journal of Sociology, 46*, 559–74.

Melley, Timothy. (2000). *Empire of conspiracy: The culture of paranoia in postwar America*. New York: Cornell University Press.

Melley, Timothy. (2002). Agency panic and the culture of conspiracy. In Peter Knight (Ed.), *Conspiracy nation: The politics of paranoia in postwar America*. New York: New York University Press.

Meyer, Philip. (1995). Public journalism and the problem of objectivity. Talk given to the IRE conference on computer-assisted reporting in Cleveland in September 1995. Retrieved May 1, 2004, from http://www.unc.edu/%7Epmeyer/ire95pj.htm

Miklaucic, Shawn. (2003). God games and governmentality. In J. Bratich, J. Packer, & C. McCarthy (Eds.), *Foucault, cultural studies, and governmentality*. (pp. 317–335). Albany: State University of New York Press.

Militia groups use TV and Internet to spread their message. (1995, April 24). Newscast on CBS *Evening News*.

Miller, Greg. (1996, March 15). O.C. company 1 of 9 charged with new fraud. *Los Angeles Times*, D1.

Miller, Laura (1995). Women and children first: Gender and the settling of the electronic frontier. In James Brook and Iain A. Boal (Eds.), *Resisting the Virtual Life: The Culture and Politics of Information* (pp. 49–57). San Francisco: City Lights.

Miller, Mark Crispin. (2000). Interview. Joining forces. Retrieved January 10, 2006, from http://www.pbs.org/newshour/bb/media/jan-june00/media_alliance_1–19.html

Miller, Mark Crispin. (2003). Mark Crispin Miller on conspiracies, media, and mad scientists. Interview by Carrie McLaren. *Stay Free! 19*. Retrieved March 29, 2004, from http://www.stayfreemagazine.org/archives/19/mcm.html

Miller, Melinda. (1997, January 3). "I'm from the government, and I'm out to get you"; Of the 10 top money-making films of 1996, at least seven depicted some branch of the government as being at least intolerant and hypocritical, and at worst downright murderous. *The Buffalo News*, p. 14G.

Miller, Toby. (1993). *The well-tempered self: Citizenship, culture, and the postmodern subject*. Baltimore: Johns Hopkins University Press.

Miller, Toby. (1998). *Technologies of truth: Cultural citizenship and the popular media*. Minneapolis: University of Minnesota Press.

Miraldi, Robert. (1990). *Muckraking and objectivity: Journalism's colliding traditions*. Westport, CT: Greenwood Press.

Mishra, Raja. (1995, June 9). Paranoia a little-misunderstood mental disorder. *Detroit Free Press*.

Mitchell, John, & Fulwood, Sam. (1996, October 22). History fuels outrage over crack allegations: Many blacks are more likely than whites to believe CIA had role In L.A.'s drug epidemic. *Los Angeles Times*, p. A1, A14.

Mobilization against hatred. (1996, July 7). *The Boston Globe*, p. 72.

Moench, Doug. (1995). *The big book of conspiracies*. New York: Paradox Press.

Monbiot, George. (2007, February 20). 9/11 fantasists pose a mortal danger to popular oppositional campaigns. *The Guardian* (London), p. 29.

Moore, John P. (1999). Up the river without a paddle? *Nature*. 40: 325–326.

Morison, John. (2000). Government-voluntary sector compacts: Governance, governmentality, and civil society. *Journal of Law and Society, 27*(1), 98–132.

Morris, Phillip. (1996, October 22). Killer stoplights were bound to be discovered. *The Plain Dealer*, p. 9B.

Murphy, Jarrett. (2005). Open and shut. *Village Voice*. Posted December 5.

Murphy, Jarrett. (2006a). The seekers. *Village Voice*. Posted February 21.

Murphy, Jarrett. (2006b). Conspiracy 101. *Village Voice*. Posted February 21.

Murphy, Jarrett. (2006c). The usual suspects. *Village Voice*. Posted February 21.

Muwakkil, Salim. (2002, May 24). Nightmares of reason: Sorting fact from fiction in 9/11 conspiracy theories. *In These Times*. http://www.inthesetimes.com/issue/26/15/feature1.shtml

Myer, Michael. (1995, February 6). Stop! cyberthief! *Newsweek*, p. 36.

The National Insecurity Council. (1992). *It's a conspiracy!* Berkeley: EarthWorks Press.

Naureckas, Jim. (1997, January/February). Sidebar: That delusional mindset. *Extra! 10*, 14.

Negri, Antonio. (1999). *Insurgencies: Constituent power and the modern state*. Minneapolis: University of Minnesota Press.

Nerone, John (Ed). (1995). *Last rights: Revisiting four theories of the press*. Urbana: University of Illinois Press.

Neuwirth, Robert. (1997, October 6). Property rights. *In These Times*, p. 18.

New York Post staff. (1997). *Heaven's Gate: Cult suicide in San Diego*. New York: Harper Paperbacks.

Nightline. ABC Newscast. (1996, November 15).

Nimmo, Kurt. (2006, September 8). Gatekeeper Cockburn attacks 9/11 "conspiracy nuts." http://kurtnimmo.com/?p=556

9/11 Debate: *Loose Change* filmmakers vs. *Popular Mechanics* editors of "Debunking 9/11 Myths." (2006, Sept 11). *Democracy Now!* Amy Goodman (producer/host). http://www.democracynow.org/article.pl?sid=06/09/11/1345203

911review.com. Retrieved November 13, 2006, from http://www.911review.com/disinfo/press/index.html

9/11Truth. Retrieved December 15, 2005, from http://www.911truth.org/links.php

Oil Empire.us. Retrieved December 15, 2005, from http://www.oilempire.us/

OilEmpire.us. Retrieved November 9, 2006, from http://www.oilempire.us/popular-mechanics.html

Olasky, Marvin. (1991). *Central ideas in the development of American journalism*. Hillsdale, NJ: Lawrence Erlbaum Associates.

O'Leary, Stephen. (2001, October 5). Rumors of grace and terror. *Online Journalism Review*. Retrieved November 22, 2001, from www.ojr.usc.edu/content/story.cfm?request=648

Olivers, Doris. (2004). Counterhegemonic dispersions: The world social forum model. *Antipode, 36*(2), 175–188.

O'Malley, Pat. (2004). The uncertain promise of risk. *Australian and New Zealand Journal of Criminology, 37*(3), 323–343.

Ouellette, Laurie. (2004). "Take responsibility for yourself": Judge Judy and the neoliberal citizen. In Susan Murray & Laurie Ouellette (Eds.), *Reality television: Remaking television culture* (pp. 231–50). New York: New York University Press.

Overstreet, Harry, & Overstreet, Bonaro. (1964). *The strange tactics of extremism*. New York: Norton.

Oxford English Dictionary, compact ed. (1971). New York: Oxford University Press.

Packer, Jeremy. (2002). Mobile communications and governing the mobile: CBs and truckers. *The Communication Review, 5*(1), 39–57.

Packer, Jeremy. (2003). Disciplining mobility: Governing and safety. In J. Bratich, J. Packer, & C. McCarthy (Eds.), *Foucault, cultural studies, and governmentality* (pp. 135–161). Albany: State University of New York Press.

Packer, Jeremy. (2008). *Mobility without mayhem: Safety, cars, and citizenship*. Durham, NC: Duke University Press.

Palmer, Gareth. (2003). *Discipline and liberty: Television and governance*. Manchester, UK: Manchester University Press.

Parenti, Michael. (1993). *Inventing reality: The politics of news media*. 2nd ed. New York: St. Martin's Press.

Parenti, Michael. (1995). Conspiracy phobia. *Steamshovel Press, 12*, 1–2.

Parenti, Michael. (1996). *Dirty truths: Reflections on politics, media, ideology, conspiracy, ethnic life, and class power*. San Francisco: City Lights.

Parfrey, Adam. (1995). Finding our way out of Oklahoma. In *Cult Rapture* (pp. 322–347). Portland, OR: Feral House.

Parry, Robert. (1997a, June 2). CIA, Contras and cocaine: Big media celebrates. *Consortium*. Retrieved February 26, 1999, from http://www.consortiumnews.com/archive/crack8.html

Parry, Robert. (1997b, December 23). CIA, drugs and the national press. *Consortium*. Retrieved February 26, 1999, from http://www.consortiumnews.com/archive/crack5.html

Parry, Robert. (1998a, July 23). *The New York Times's* Contra-cocaine dilemma. *Consortium*. Retrieved February 26, 1999, from http://www.consortiumnews.com/consor12.html

Parry, Robert. (1998b, October 1). *The New York Times's* new Contra lies. *Consortium*. Retrieved February 26, 1999, from http://www.consortiumnews.com/consor26.html

Parry, Robert. (1998c, October 25). Editorial: A media disgrace. *Consortium*. Retrieved February 26, 1999, from http://www.consortiumnews.com/consor31.html

Parsons, Charlotte. (2001, September 24). Why we need conspiracy theories. Retrieved October 3, 2003, from http://news.bbc.co.uk/1/hi/world/americas/1561199.stm

Patton, Paul. (1985). Conceptual politics and the war machine in *mille plateaux*. *SubStance, 13*(3/4), 61–80.

Patton, Paul. (1988). Marxism and beyond: Strategies of reterritorialization. In C. Nelson & L. Grossberg (Eds.), *Marxism and the interpretation of culture* (pp. 123–137). Urbana: University of Illinois Press.

Patton, Paul. (1996). Introduction. In Paul Patton (Ed.), *Deleuze: A critical reader*. Cambridge, MA: Blackwell.

Patton, Paul. (1998). Foucault's subject of power. In J. Moss (Ed.), *The later Foucault: Politics and philosophy* (pp. 64–77). London: Sage Publications.

Pavlik, John. (2001). *Journalism and new media*. New York: Columbia University Press.

Pegoraro, Rob. (1997, October 31). The FFWD directory of internet service providers. *Washington Post*, p. N34.

Peoples Lenses Collective. (2003). *Under the lens of the people: Our account of the peoples' resistance to the FTAA, Quebec City*. April 2001. Peoples Lenses Collective Press.

Perlman, David. (1996, March 17). The professor who claims HIV doesn't cause AIDS. *The San Francisco Chronicle*, p. 3.

Pierre, Robert E., & Morello, Carol. (2000, December 12). Irregularities cited in Florida voting; Blacks say faulty machines, poll mistakes cost them their ballots. *The Washington Post*, p. A38.

Pipes, Daniel. (1996). *The hidden hand: Middle East fears of conspiracy*. New York: St. Martin's Press.

Pipes, Daniel. (1997). *Conspiracy! The paranoid style and why it flourishes*. New York: Free Press.

Pipes, Daniel, & Khashan, Hilal. (1997, November 10). Diana and Arab conspiracy. *Weekly Standard*. http://www.danielpipes.org/article/290

Plante, David J., & Niemi, William L. (2004). Antecedents of resistance: Populism and the possibilities for democratic globalization. Conference Paper. American Political Science Association, 2004. Annual Meeting, Chicago, IL, pp. 1–34.

Playing politics with the bombing. (1995, May 8). *The Washington Post*, p. A20.

Pogrebin, Robin. (1996, January 28). The angriest man in talk radio. In this city, call-in shows crackle with controversy. But when is enough enough? *The New York Times*, section 13, p. 1.

Pogrebin, Robin. (1997, January 9). Controversial gay magazine shuts down. *The New York Times*, p. 2.

Popp, Richard K. (2006). History in discursive limbo: Ritual and conspiracy narratives on the History Channel. *Popular Communication*, 4(4), 253–272.

Portland, OR, Independent Media Center. (n.d.). http://portland.indymedia.org/front.php3?article_id=8824&group=webcast

Posner, Gerald. 1993. *Case closed*. New York: Random House.

Powell, Michael. (2006, September 8). The disbelievers: 9/11 conspiracy theorists are building their case against the government from ground zero. *The Washington Post*, p. C1.

President Bush speaks to United Nations. (2001, November 10). Retrieved September 15, 2005, from http://www.whitehouse.gov/news/releases/2001/11/20011110-3.html

Purnick, Joyce. (1995, May 8). An unlikely matchmaker for Shabazz and Farrakhan. *The New York Times*, p. B1.

Putnam, Robert D. (2000). *Bowling alone*. New York: Simon and Schuster.

Quinby, Lee. (1991). *Freedom, Foucault, and the subject of America*. Boston: Northeastern University Press.

Rabinow, Paul. (1997). Introduction. In *Michel Foucault: Ethics: Subjectivity and truth* (pp. xi–xlv). New York: New Press.

Randolph, Eleanor. (1996, June 4). Kinsley in cyberspace: A lot is on the line. *Los Angeles Times*, p. A1.

Randolph, Eleanor, & John M. Broder. (1996, October 22). Cyberspace contributes to volatility of allegations. *Los Angeles Times*, p. 14A.

Raskin, Marcus S. (1992). JFK and the culture of violence. *American Historical Review*, 97(2), 486–499.

Raspberry, William. (1995, April 26). Bomb throwers and broadcasters, *The Washington Post*, p. A23.

Raymond, Neville. (2004/2005). No outrageous conspiracy theories, please. *Global Outlook*, 9(85).

Read, Jason. (2003). *The micro-politics of capital*. Albany: State University of New York Press.

Reed, Terry, & Cummings, John. (1995). *Compromised: Clinton, Bush and the CIA*. Roseville, CA: Penmarin Books.

Rehm, Diane. (1996, February 18). Hot mouths, hot buttons and the danger to public dialogue. *The Washington Post*, p. C03.

Remnick, David. (2005, October 3). High water: How presidents and citizens react to disaster. *The New Yorker*, 48.

Reuters dispatch (1995, March 12). Brokerages become first to let investors buy, sell stocks through Internet. *Los Angeles Times*, p. D8.

Reynolds, Barbara. (1990, December 12). Our violent society: U.S. culture teaches violence as a solution. *USA Today*, p. 13A.

Rich, Frank. (1995a, April 27). New world terror. *The New York Times*, p. 25.

Rich, Frank. (1995b, May 11). The "Rambo" culture, *The New York Times*, p. A29.

Richtel, Matt. (1997, June 9). Legal situation is confused on Web content protections. *The New York Times*, p. D5.

Riding, Alan. (2002, June 21). Sept. 11 as right-wing U.S. plot: Conspiracy theory sells in France. *The New York Times*, p. A1.

Rieder, Rem. (1997a, April). A breakthrough in cyberspace. *American Journalism Review*, p. 6.

Rieder, Rem. (1997b, June). The lessons of "Dark Alliance." *American Journalism Review*, p. 6.

Rimer, Sarah. (1995, April 27). Terror in Oklahoma: The far Right; New medium for the far Right. *The New York Times*, p. A1.

Robins, Robert S., & Post, Jerrold M. (1997). *Political paranoia: The psychopolitics of hatred*. New Haven, CT: Yale University Press.

Roeper, Richard. (1997, April 6). Just the facts, please. *Chicago Sun-Times*, p. 2.

Roeper, Richard. (2004, November 30). Some conspiracy theorists elect to ignore the truth. *Chicago Sun-Times*, p. 11.

Rogin, Michael. (1987). *Ronald Reagan: The movie*. Berkeley: University of California Press.

Rogin, Michael. (1992). JFK: The movie. *American Historical Review*, 97(2), 500–505.

Roig-Franzia, Manuel, & Keating, Dan. (2004, November 11). Latest conspiracy theory—Kerry won—hits the ether. *The Washington Post*, p. A2.

Rose, Nikolas. (1996). Governing advanced liberal democracies. In A. Barry, T. Osborne, & N. Rose (Eds.), *Foucault and political reason* (pp. 37–64). Chicago: University of Chicago Press.

Rose, Nikolas. (1999). *Powers of freedom: Reframing political thought*. New York: Cambridge University Press.

Rosen, Jay. (1995, May/June). Public journalism: A case for public scholarship. *Change*, 27(3), 34–38.

Rosenberg, Tina. (1996, December 31). Editorial notebook; crazy for conspiracies. *The New York Times*, p. A12.

Ross, Dennis. (2005, January 30). Battle Station. *The Washington Post*, p. T4.

Rothschild, Matthew. (2006, September 18). Enough of the conspiracy theories, already. *Alternet*. Retrieved January 17, 2007, from http://www.alternet.org/story/41601/

Rothschild, Matthew. (2006). Enough of the 9/11 conspiracy theories, already. *The Progressive*. Posted September 18, 2006, http://www.alternet.org/story/41601/

Roush, Matt. (1996, April 11). The heartland's ache: Two very different looks at Oklahoma bombing. *USA Today*, p. 3D.

Russakoff, Dale. (1995, August 20). Fax networks link outposts of anger; Discontented citizens find their voice. *The Washington Post*, p. A1.

Russell, Gordon, & Donze, Frank. (2006, January 8). Officials tiptoe around footprint issue, but buyouts, flood maps may decide matter. *Times-Picayune* (New Orleans), p. 1.

Sanders, James. 1997. *The downing of TWA flight 800*. New York: Zebra Books.

Sargent, Lyman. (1995). Introduction. In L. T. Sargent (Ed.), *Extremism in America: A reader*. New York: New York University Press.

Sauer, Mark, & Okerblom, Jim. (1995, May 4). Patriotism or paranoia? Videos, radio, Internet all used to spread fears of the far Right that government poses danger. *The San Diego Union-Tribune*, p. E1.

Saunders, Frances Stonor. (2000). *The cultural cold war: The CIA and the world of arts and letters*. New York: New Press.

Scanlon, Bill. (1998, November 24). Black teens groomed for healthy life; Microbiologist tackles conspiracy theory. *Rocky Mountain News* (Denver, CO), p. 19A.

Schechter, Danny. (2005, July 24). Conspiracy theories and the fight for truth. *Common Dreams News Center*. Retrieved December 11, 2005, from http://www.commondreams.org/views05/0724–26.htm

Schiffler, Carol. (2002, March 25). Piercing the media veil: 9-11, in context. Retrieved December 15, 2005, from http://makethemaccountable.com/schiffler/020325_9-11InContext.htm

Schlesinger, Arthur. (1962). *The vital center: Our purposes and perils on the tightrope of American liberalism*. Cambridge, MA: Riverside Press.

Schlesinger, Arthur M. (1997). Has democracy a future? *Foreign Affairs 76*, 2–12.

Schudson, Michael. (1978). *Discovering the news: A social history of American newspapers*. New York: Basic Books.

Scott, Peter Dale. (2000, June 19). What will Congress do about new CIA-drug revelations? *San Francisco Chronicle*, p. A19.

Scott, Peter Dale, & Marshall, Jonathan. (1991). *Cocaine politics: Drugs, armies, and the CIA in Central America*. Berkeley: University of California Press.

Seitz, Matt Zoller. (1997, May 4). Evil president as pop culture cliche; Recent White House thrillers play to public distrust of government. *Star Tribune* (Minneapolis, MN), p. 9F.

Seoane, Jose, & Taddei, Emilio. (2002). From Seattle to Porto Alegre: The antineoliberal globalization movement. *Current Sociology, 50* (1), 99, 24.

Shalom, Stephen, & Albert, Michael. (2002). Conspiracies or institutions: 9-11 and beyond. *Zmag*. http://www.zmag.org/content/Instructionals/shalalbcon.cfm

Shaw, Charles. (2005a, April 26). Regulated resistance: Is it possible to change the system when you are the system? *Newtopia Magazine*. http://www.911truth.org/article.php?story=20050430002758978

Shaw, Charles. (2005b, May 03). Gatekeepers of the so-called Left, part 2: Regulated resistance. *Newtopia Magazine*. http://www.newtopiamagazine.net/articles/40

Shaw, David. (1997, June 17). MercuryCenter.com. *Los Angeles Times*, p. 14.

Shelton, Deborah L. (1997, April 15). Mistrust of doctors lingers after Tuskegee; Many blacks remain wary—and underserved—a quarter-century after infamous syphilis study. *The Washington Post*, p. Z08.

Sheppard, Judith. (1995, May). Climbing down from the ivory tower. *American Journalism Review*, 18.

Showalter, Elaine. (1997). *Hystories: Hysterical epidemics and modern culture*. New York: Columbia University Press.

Simon, Art. (1996). *Dangerous knowledges: The JFK assassination in art and film*. Philadelphia: Temple University Press.

Simons, Jon. (2002). Governing the public: Technologies of mediation and popular culture. *Cultural Values*, 6(1–2), 167–181.

Smart, Barry. (1986). The politics of truth and the problem of hegemony. In D. C. Hoy (Ed.), *Foucault: A critical reader* (pp. 157–173). Oxford, UK: Blackwell.

Smith, Daniel W. (1997). A life of pure immanence: Deleuze's *critique et clinique* project. In Daniel W. Smith & Michael A. Greco (Trans.), *Deleuze: Essays critical and clinical* (pp. xi–lii). Minneapolis: University of Minnesota Press.

Smith, Daniel W. (1998). The place of ethics in Deleuze's philosophy: Three questions of immanence. In E. Kaufman and K. J. Heller (Eds.), *Deleuze and Guattari: New mappings in politics, philosophy, and culture* (pp. 251–269). Minneapolis: University of Minnesota Press.

Smith, Sam. (1995, July). America's extremist center. *The Progressive Review*.

Snider, Brandon J. (2004, July 18). Yet another *Fahrenheit 9/11* review. Retrieved December 18, 2005, from http://www.antiwar.com/blog/comments.php?id= 1168_0_1_0_C.

Soderlund, Gretchen. (2002). Covering urban vice: *The New York Times*, white slavery, and the construction of journalistic knowledge. *Critical Studies in Media Communication*, 19(4), 438–460.

Soderlund, Gretchen. (2005). Rethinking a curricular icon: The institutional and ideological foundations of Walter Lippmann. *The Communication Review*, 8(3), 1071–4421.

Solomon, Norman. (1997, January/February). Snow job: The establishment papers do damage control for the CIA. *EXTRA!*

Solomon, Norman. (2002, April 28). Media and the hazards of political faith. *Znet*. http://www.zmag.org/Sustainers/content/2002-04/28solomon.cfm

Spark, Alisdair. (1998). Conspiracy thinking and conspiracy studying. Unpublished manuscript. http://www.2.winchester.ac.uk/ccc/resources/essays/thinkstudy.htm

Starr, Paul. (1982). *Social transformation of American medicine*. New York: Basic Books.

Staudenmaier, Peter. (2004). The anarchism of fools: Conspiracy theory as a substitute for social critique. Paper delivered at Renewing the Anarchist Tradition Conference, September.

Stein, M. L. (1994a). A catalyst for public awareness? *Editor and Publisher*, 127(42), 11–12.

Stein, M. L. (1994b). In praise of public journalism. *Editor and Publisher*, 127(46), 15–16.

Stern, Kenneth S. (1996). *A force upon the plain: The American militia movement and the politics of hate*. New York: Simon & Schuster.

Sterne, Jonathan. (1999). Thinking the Internet: Cultural studies and the Internet. In Steve Jones (Ed.), *Doing Internet Research: Critical issues and methods for examining the Net*. Thousand Oaks, CA: Sage.

Stone, Oliver, & Sklar, Zachary (Eds). (1992), *JFK: The book of the film* (pp. 205–207). New York: Warner Brothers.

Suber, Bruce, Sr. (1997, December 3). Talk radio can fuel racism. *St. Louis Post-Dispatch* (Missouri), p. B7.

Sullivan, Will. (2006, September 11). BYU takes on a 9/11 conspiracy professor. *USNews Online*. http://www.usnews.com/usnews/news/articles/060911/11conspiracy_2.htm

Sutton, Antony. (1986). *America's secret establishment*. Billings: Liberty House.

Tagg, John. (1988). *The burden of representation: Essays on photographies and histories*. Minneapolis: University of Minnesota Press.

Tarpley, Webster Griffin. (2006). *9/11 synthetic terror: Made in USA*. Joshua Tree, CA: Progressive Press.

Taussig, Michael. (2002). *Defacement*. Stanford: Stanford University Press.

Taylor, Eric. (1994/1995, Winter). PWAs vs. the USA. *Paranoia: The conspiracy reader* 2(4), 52–54.

Taylor, Paul A. (1999). *Hackers: Crime and the digital sublime*. New York: Routledge.

Teepen, Tom. (1996, November 13). Salinger, TWA Flight 800 and the price of paranoia. *Minneapolis Star Tribune*, p. 17A.

Terrorism over the Internet. (1995, November 2). News segment on *ABC World News Tonight*. Transcript # 5219-3.

Terry, Don. (1994, July 10). Waters are roiled in the civil rights mainstream. *The New York Times*, p. 6.

Terzian, Philip. (1996a, February 27). *Denver Rocky Mountain News*, p. 31A.

Terzian, Philip. (1996b, November 26). Mr. CIA man meets the people. *The Tampa Tribune*, p. 11.

Thomas, Cal. (2005, October 19). Black "leaders" on wrong path. *The Baltimore Sun*, p. 17A.

Thomas, Evan, (with Bill Turque, Andrew Murr, John McCormick, Mark Hosenball, Martha Brant, Gregory Beals, Leslie Jorgensen, Peter Annin, Sherry Keene Osborn, Melinda Liu, & Michael Isikoff). (1995, May 8). The plot. *Newsweek*, 28.

Thomas, Evan, & Campo-Flores, Arian (with Sarah Childress, T. Trent Gegax, & Daren Briscoe). (2005, October 3). The battle to rebuild. *Newsweek*, 36.

Thomas, Stephen, & Crouse Quinn, Sandra. (1991). The Tuskegee syphilis study, 1932 to 1972: Implications for HIV education and risk education programs in the black community. *American Journal of Public Health*, 81(11), 1498–1505.

Thompson, Kenneth. (1998). *Moral panics*. London and New York: Routledge.

Thompson, Paul. (2004/2005). The complete 9/11 terror timeline. *Global Outlook*, 9, 27–30.

Tierney, John. (1995, April 30). How talk radio gets at what's real. *The New York Times*, p. 1.

Timko, Steve. (1995, April 24). Theorists abound on global Internet. *USA Today*, p. 4A.

Treichler, Paula A. (1988). AIDS, gender, and biomedical discourse: Current contests for meaning. In Elizabeth Fee & Daniel M. Fox (Eds.), *AIDS: The burdens of history*. Berkeley: University of California Press.

Treichler, Paula A. (1999). *How to have theory in an epidemic*. Durham & London: Duke University Press.

Tucker, Cynthia. (1995, May 1). Economic insecurity breeds contempt. *The San Francisco Chronicle*, p. A21.

Tumber, Howard. (2001). Democracy in the information age: The role of the fourth estate in cyberspace. *Information, Communication, and Society*, 4(1), 95–112.

Turner, Patricia, (1993). *I heard it through the grapevine: Rumor in African American culture*. Berkeley: University of California Press.

Tyrangiel, Josh. (2001, September 30). Did you hear about . . . *Time.com*. Retrieved January 17, 2002, from http://www.time.com/time/magazine/article/0,9171,1101011008–176941,00.html

Ungar, Sheldon. (2001). Moral panic versus the risk society: The implications of the changing sites of social anxiety. *British Journal of Sociology*, 52(2), 271–292.

U.S. Department of State. National strategy for combating terrorism. http://www.state.gov/s/ct/rls/wh/71803.htm

U.S. Department of State. (2005). How to identify misinformation. Retrieved December 15, 2005, from http://usinfo.state.gov/media/Archive/2005/Jul/27-595713.html

U.S. Department of State. (2006). The top September 11 conspiracy theories. Retrieved November 7, 2006, from http://usinfo.state.gov/xarchives/display.html?p=pubs-

Vankin, Jonathan. (1995). Q: What's crazier than a roomful of conspiracy nuts? A: The journalists who psychoanalyze them. http://www.conspire.com/curren11.html

Vankin, Jonathan. (1996). *Conspiracies, cover-ups, and crimes: From Dallas to Waco*. Lilburn, GA: Illuminet Press.

Vankin, Jonathan, & Whalen, John. (2001). *The 80 greatest conspiracies of all time*. New York: Barnes & Noble Books.

Varoga, Craig. (2004/2005, December/January). Stolen election conspiracy theories, campaigns and elections. *Campaign Doctor*, 93.

Verity, John. (1994, November 14). The Internet. *Business Week*, 80.

Verniere, James. (2004, June 11). "Room" with a view not popular. *The Boston Herald*, p. E18.

Vincent, Jean-Marie. (1993). Les automatisms sociaux et le "general intellect." *Futur Anterieur*. 16, 121–30. Translated and cited in Nicholas Dyer-Witheford (1999). *Cyber-Marx: Cycles and struggles in high technology capitalism* (p. 223). Urbana: University of Illinois Press.

Virilio, Paul. (1990). *Popular defense and ecological struggles*. New York: Semiotexte.

Voboril, Mary. (2005, November 6). Conspiracy theories: The truth is out there—maybe. *Newsday* (New York), p. A16.

WACO: the Big Lie. Video. Director: Linda Thompson.

Walsh, David. (2004, July 9). Liberal philistinism and Michael Moore's *Fahrenheit 9/11.* Retrieved December 18, 2005, from http://www.wsws.org/articles/2004/jul2004/cohe-j09.shtml

Ward, Mike. (2004, May 18). Top 10 conspiracy theories of 2003–2004. *Alternet.* Retrieved November 13, 2004, from http://www.alternet.org/story/18735/

Warner, Michael. (1990). *The letters of the republic: Publication and the public sphere in eighteenth-century America.* Cambridge, MA: Harvard University Press.

Watney, Simon. (1994). *Practices of freedom.* Durham & London: Duke University Press.

Watson, Steve. (2005, August 31). Pot, kettle, black: State Department tells us how to identify misinformation. Retrieved December 15, 2005, from http://www.infowars.net/Pages/Aug05/300805potkettleblack.htm

Webb, Gary. (1996, August 18–20). Dark Alliance. *San Jose Mercury News.* Retrieved April 24, 1997, from http://cgi.sjmercury.com/drugs

Webb, Gary. (1998). *Dark Alliance: The CIA, the Contras, and the crack cocaine explosion.* New York: Seven Stories Press.

Weeks, Jeffrey. (1981). *Sex, politics, and society: The regulation of sexuality since 1800.* New York: Longman.

Weinberg, Bill. (2006, September 8). 9/11 and the new Pearl Harbor: Aw shut up already, will ya? *World War 4 Report.* http://ww4report.com/node/2413

Weinberg, Steve. (1996). Can "content-providers" be investigative journalists? *Columbia Journalism Review, 35*(4), 34.

Weiner, Eric. (2005, August 18). U.S. conspiracy theories abound in Arab world. *NPR.* http://www.npr.org/templates/story/story.php?storyId=4805337

Weiss, Robin. (1999). Is AIDS man-made? *Science 286,* 1305–1306.

Westley, David. (1995, August 27). Guinea pigs staring at you too intently? Little green men giving you grief? Cyberspace can be a paranoid place. *The (London) Independent,* p. 12.

What Really Happened. Retrieved December 15, 2005, from http://www.whatreallyhappened.com/

White, Jack E. (1996, September 30). Crack, Contras, and cyberspace. *Time.* v148n16, p. 59.

Wiese, Elizabeth. (1996, December 18). CIA-crack story brings many blacks to the World Wide Web. *Los Angeles Sentinel,* p. A13.

Willman, Skip. (2002). Spinning paranoia: The ideologies of conspiracy and contingency in postmodern culture. In P. Knight (Ed.), *Conspiracy Nation: The Politics of Paranoia in Postwar America* (pp. 21–39). New York: New York University Press.

Wilson, Robert Anton. (1995). *Cosmic Trigger III: My life after death.* Tempe, AZ: New Falcon Publications.

Witkin, Gordon. (1997, June 2). Conspiracy's twisted appeal. *US News & World Report,* p. 9.

Wood, Daniel B. (1996, November 15). California's newspaper war confuses readers—and facts. *The Christian Science Monitor*, p. 1.

Woods, Ian. (2004/2005). We REJECT the official 9/11 report. *Global Outlook*, 9, 3.

Wright, Michael (2000, May 24). A dissenting view on AIDS policy. Retrieved June 8, 2003, from http://www.sfgate.com/cgibin/article.cgi?file=/chronicle/archive/2000/05/24/ED82697.DTL

Wypijewski, JoAnn. (2006, September 22). How far we have fallen: Conversations at ground zero. *CounterPunch*. http://counterpunch.org/jw09222006.html

Yardley, Jonathan. (1995, May 1). Drive-time drivel. *The Washington Post*, p. D02.

Yardley, Jonathan. (1996, November 3). Ideology and the politics of emotion. *The Washington Post*, p. X3.

Yoder, Edwin. (1991, December 3). Black genocide plot is latest conspiracy. *St. Louis Post-Dispatch*, p. 3B.

Yoder, Edwin. (1996, October 6). The CIA-crack scandal myth. *The Denver Post*, p. D-05.

Young, Cathy. (1997, March 25). Media need to clean up act, stop worrying about Internet. *Detroit News*, p. A7.

Young, Jock. (1971). *The drugtakers: The social meaning of drug use*. London: Paladin.

Zelizer, Barbie. (1992). *Covering the body: The Kennedy assassination, the media, and the shaping of collective memory*. Chicago: University of Chicago Press.

Zeller, Tom, Jr. (2004, November 12). Vote fraud theories, spread by blogs, are quickly buried. *The New York Times*, p. A1.

Zinn, Howard. (2003, Spring). War is the health of the state. Interview by Paul Glavin & Chuck Morse. *Perspectives on Anarchist Theory*, 7(1).

Zogby's (2004, August). Poll: 50% of NYC says U.S. government knew. Publishers of *Zogby's Real America Newsletter*. Retrieved December 15, 2005, from http://www.911truth.org/article.php?story=20040830120349841

Zoglin, Richard. (1991). More shots in Dealey Plaza. Reprinted in O. Stone & Z. Sklar (Eds.). (1992). *JFK: The Book of the Film* (pp. 205–207). New York: Warner Brothers.

Zuckerman, Mortimer B. (1995, June 12). Beware the adversary culture. *U.S. News & World Report*, 118(23), 94.

Zurawik, David. (1996, August 4). Prime-time paranoia; Television: Fall shows troll for fans of the dark side with tales of aliens, lying governments and cynicism. *The Sun Baltimore*, p. 1J.

Zwicker, Barrie. (2004). The great conspiracy: The 9/11 news special you never saw. Transcript reprinted in *Global Outlook*, 9, 2004/2005.

Zwicker, Barrie. (2006). *Towers of deception: The media cover-up of 9/11*. Gabriola Island, British Columbia, Canada: New Society Publishers.

INDEX